THE KEEPER'S BOOK

A GUIDE TO
THE DUTIES OF A GAMEKEEPER

Yours faithfully
P. Jeffrey Mackie.

Dedicated

TO ALL GOOD KEEPERS

WHO KNOW THEIR WORK

AND TO

ALL INDIFFERENT ONES

WHO DO NOT

The latter have sent us various effusions, generally anonymous. A few choice extracts will prove instructive—

" I am a keeper's son, and my grandfather was a keeper. I have not read your book, but I know it is full of d——d rubbish." " The gun is the proper instrument for the keeper. Gentlemen who write books are not supposed to know a keeper's work; they were not brought up to it." " Keepers have neither time nor inclination for books." " No man likes to work more than he can." " Nature rules all; you can't help nature or improve it." " Books do a deal of harm," " I don't like yours," and so on. All of which rather indicate that there are certain raw places in the hides of keepers of the indifferent and inefficient classes which have been touched.

In this thoroughly revised edition will be found many corrections, some omissions, and numerous additions. One point not touched upon in the body of the book may be noted. Since we first went to press, there has appeared an extensive correspondence on the subject of Heather-burning, Mr. Christopher Wilson advocating burning in autumn, instead of early spring. It is hardly necessary at this point to recall the fact that the law, as far as it affects Scotland, forbids burning before 1st November. The present writers have tried autumn burning, and after a spell of dry weather, they confess to find it a great improvement. The burning seems to be more effective. There appears to be an oil in the green heather which prevents the fire from spreading as rapidly as in spring. In the autumn it burns evenly and against the wind, and the work can, on the whole, be carried out much more thoroughly than in the spring. We certainly advise Scottish keepers to start burning in small patches on the first possible day after 1st November, and continue to do so on every opportunity until sufficient is burnt.

It has been the fashion for many landed proprietors to affect a total ignorance of business methods, with results that are so apparent, that the fashion is likely to change; only in Britain does this exist.

Upon one point all sportsmen must congratulate themselves,—that is, the present tendency of shooting proprietors to take a really intelligent interest in developing the sporting capacities of their estates. Lochs once neglected are being restocked and en-

sulting the material that has already appeared in the works of experienced authorities, would be acting contrary to all the accepted traditions of scientific literature, and while one may, in reading *The Keeper's Book*, recognise much that is already well known, yet facts have an awkward trick of deserting the memory just at the moment we require them most, and in this way the present volume may not only add to our storehouse of knowledge, but refresh the memory with ideas long forgotten, as well as assist the intelligent keeper to investigate the many problems waiting solution, instead of accepting as gospel old women's stories of fifty years ago.

Keepers are too prone to think they know everything. There is no standing still, except in stupidity; it alone refuses to advance. If they would only remember, there must be a reason for everything, and a cure for everything, if such can only be found.

The reception of the book at the hands of the keeper is exactly as expected; it has been welcomed by the men who take their profession seriously, and avoided by the lazy, who are suspicious of anything that may multiply their duties.

PREFACE TO FOURTH EDITION.

———•◆•———

The call for another edition has proved the necessity for *The Keeper's Book*.

The reception of the first edition at the hands of the press, led off by an enthusiastic notice in the *Times*—" We have seldom read a better, more succinct, or more practical treatise. . . . It is an acquisition to the keeper's bookshelf which should be in every gun-room "—has, on the whole, coincided with the response given by the public to the book.

Of course, there were a few reviewers who were disappointed because the book was not perfect. This disappointment can only be regarded as an indirect compliment. One critic hinted that the book was a compilation rather than an original work. It is neither, but it is both. Any man who would attempt to write an entirely new book on sport, without con-

past, and thus bring their shooting and fishings up to the highest and most efficient capacity.

From an economic standpoint, our present fiscal policy is unnatural and unbusinesslike,—excluding aliens (a protective movement), yet admitting free the product of aliens' work, is inconsistent and unjust to the nation as a whole. Such tinkering will never restore the economic equilibrium, and is at best a quack palliative to certain classes.

The cry of "back to the land" seems to be no cure for rural depopulation, so long as home prices are kept at an unpayable figure, by our providing the foreigner with a free market for his grain and beef, and paying all the rates, taxes, and upkeep for him. The return on land is smaller than that from any other kind of investment, including Consols, yet a man can never live on a small holding without extraneous work.

In large towns the trade unionists, who are the strongest protectionists of their own interests, uphold Free Trade, and want cheap food at the expense of the agricultural districts. If the country districts are to supply this, they should be freed of taxation by the populous centres, and not made to

riched with food and plant life ; moors are being
more carefully drained, burnt, and freed from vermin ;
with the result of largely increased bags.   The
slackness of many keepers is owing to the want of
interest and supervision by the master, who should
have a monthly return of all vermin killed, and see
the heads regularly, and otherwise supervise the work
of game preserving.

We have been accused of being rather hard on
the West Country keepers.   With every wish to be
just, and after careful observation, we see no reason
to alter our estimation of his character.   We know
many who for eight months in the year do
nothing for the good of the shoot under their
charge.

A commission of inquiry into the grouse disease
is sitting, but as yet has discovered nothing new ;
it is to be hoped its efforts will be crowned with
success.

Socialistic legislation in the shape of Land Tenure,
Crofters and Small Holdings Bills, together with
increased taxation on land, make it necessary for
proprietors to manage their properties on business-
like principles, which have been so absent in the

provide there a free market for the foreigner. In fact, the rural districts are sacrificed to provide cheap food for the large manufacturing centres.

There is no earthly reason why landed property, where the margin of profit is so small, should not be managed with ordinary intelligence like any other commodity.

P. JEFFREY MACKIE.

GLENREASDELL, *July* 1906.

CONTENTS

CONTENTS

THE KEEPER'S BOOK

———◆———

CHAPTER I

INTRODUCTION

SOME years ago one of the present writers visited a
school in the West Highlands, and having listened for
some time to a cross-examination of one of the senior
classes in History, he expressed a desire to present
a prize to the boy whose powers of observation and
definition were the best, apart from mere book learning.
Amongst the questions addressed to the class was
the one, "What is a gamekeeper?" and an answer
he received from a bright-eyed, sandy-haired Celt of
about ten years of age was, "A big man who goes
about in a braw suit of tweeds, wi' a dog and a gun,
and does naethin'." Now, though out of the mouths
of babes and sucklings we are apt to perfect wisdom,
we must not, of course, attempt to justify humour
at the expense of justice. The little Highlander's
answer was very much on the line of the street boy's

I

definition of a Club as " A house where gentlemen read newspapers on Sunday," although there is more of real truth in the latter than in the former reply. Both, however, indicate a real impression that had been made upon two fairly observant youngsters, and both replies are not to be despised as suitable texts for reflection.

It must be admitted that there are many keepers whose chief occupation up till the 12th of August, or even till the 1st of September or the 1st of October, seems to consist in going about with a dog and a gun and in virtually doing nothing—that is, nothing of real value to the shooting under their control. In no other class of men do we find such extremes, on the one hand of skill, energy, and efficiency, and on the other of stupidity, laziness, and incapability. Taking the profession as a whole, and regarding it as a department of skilled labour, we must admit, though in doing so the admission gives offence, that it does not in the main come up to the uniform efficiency of other skilled labour.

The fact that an outstanding minority of keepers are more than efficient, and combine the qualities of patient and intelligent keepers of ground and stock with all the instincts and capacities of thorough sportsmen, does not get rid of the truth of the general criticism. Of course no one would insult the profession of gamekeeping by placing it in the same category with any branch of unskilled labour in the industrial community. It is because we believe the duties of a keeper demand a high standard of observation, skill, patience, and energy that we have to admit the failure, in the common run of the profession, to reach that standard. Viewing them on the moral side alone, we are only too willing to recognise that for probity and general temperance gamekeepers compare more than favourably with any other section of society. In 50 per cent. of cases they are sober, honest, good tempered, and generous natured, and to all these qualities they add, as a rule, an exceptionally keen sense of humour. But considering the responsibilities of their profession, the percentage of efficient and trustworthy workmen is infinitely smaller than the figure quoted above.

This book is written for "all good keepers who know their work, and for the indifferent ones who do not." How competent a person, as a rule, is the good keeper who knows! He is not only a grand sportsman, but a splendid servant—a man who knows nearly everything that is to be known of game, their habits and habitats, and of the necessary methods to manage and improve the ground, stock, and shootings under his care, and yet is always on the outlook to learn more. The really first-class keeper is a precious jewel in the crown of sport—a man who often puts to shame the knowledge and skill of a well-read and keenly observant master, and this capable servant is the man of all others who deplores the fact that the status of his profession is lowered by men with the sporting knowledge of farm labourers, the energy of vagabond hucksters, and the initiative of village loons—who are thoroughly convinced that they know everything.

It has been said that the ideal keeper combines skill with energy, but even in good keepers the combination is rare. An ideal keeper, in our view, would combine the sporting capacities of the Highlander with the energy and perseverance of the Southerner. The first has probably more insight and general intelligence, the latter more initiative and energy. As Mr. Stuart Wortley has so aptly said, "Highlanders are, as all the world knows, a very fine race of men, courageous and loyal, courteous and amiable—they make the best sportsmen and the best soldiers in the world ; but they are neither so practical nor so energetic under ordinary conditions as the northern Englishman, and laziness is their great failing." The fact of the matter is that the Highlander is a born hunter, and the descendant of a long line of hunters. His ancestors having been brought up under the clan system, "blue" blood runs in his veins, and his instincts are still strong for fighting and hunting, not for butt-building and draining. He is a lineal descendant of men of the

type of Maclean of Ardgour, "strong Donald the
hunter, Macgillean Mohr."

> "Low down by yon burn that's half hidden with heather,
>   He lurked like a lion, in the lair he knew well ;
> 'Twas there sobbed the red-deer to feel his keen dagger,
>   There pierced by his arrow, the cailzie cock fell.
> How oft when at e'en he would watch for the wild-fowl,
>   Like lightning his coracle sped from the shore ;
> But still, and for aye, as we cross the lone Lochan,
>   Is Donald the hunter Macgillean Mohr."

Time and circumstances of civilisation have done
much to modify the Highland spirits and instincts,
but the independence, pride and tradition, which
make a Highlander naturally antagonistic to that
manual labour which is a necessary accompaniment
of a gamekeeper's duties, still remain to a marked
extent, especially amongst the keepers of the
Western Highlands and Islands. Let one of the
latter have a gun or rod in his hand, or let him
be spying out your deer in the forest or tracking
your birds on the moor, and there is no man in
the world to compare with him ; but put him to
drain your water-soaked ground, repair or rebuild
your butts, or to do any of the innumerable prosaic
duties inseparable from a gamekeeper's responsibilities, and he is not to be compared either with
the Yorkshire or Norfolk keeper, or with the man
from the Lothians.

The pride and exigencies of race which have confined the Highlander's instincts to hunting and fighting also assert themselves in a marked way in his relations to his master. If the latter is "the laird," one of a line of fifty Campbells, a hundred Mackintoshes, or a thousand Grants, then the Highlander is a much more satisfactory workman than if his master is a "Sassenach," or comes of a branch of what he still virtually regards as an alien people. In the former case he is one of a family, in the latter he has an instinctive feeling of resentment in being reduced to a position of mere servitude. He is slow to come into touch with modern social conditions.

But though these reflections may be allowable, it is dangerous to generalise more, and while admitting the marked distinctions between Highlander and Lowlander, it would be idle to shoot their characters into separate pigeonholes. We have in our mind many Highland keepers who combined keen sporting instincts and capacities with indomitable energy and perseverance in the pursuit of their more irksome duties ; and we also recall many Lowlanders and English shire keepers who were preternaturally lazy.

It is to be regretted that the qualities of charm and laziness so often go together. Some of the most interesting keepers we have known have been the most indolent. We have in our mind at this moment one particular keeper in Perthshire whose knowledge of sport and whose facility for narrative made of him a fascinating companion in the chase, yet who invariably neglected such duties as the killing of vermin, the digging out of springs, the proper burning of heather, and the hundred little duties for which he was paid. Of course, he knew all about the rights and wrongs of these matters, but in dealing with these questions he spoke in the vaguest generalities, and rapidly turned the conversation to some famous day on the hill when late in the season " the Captain," his master, killed forty brace to his own gun, or to a story of some record stalk in the forests of Ross-shire or Aberdeenshire. There was not an experience of our own that he could not cap with a story of brilliant shooting on his old master's part, and equally skilful manœuvring on his own, and his exploits were all told with such a power of picturesque description as to disarm in the hearer any criticism of his constant disregard of the prose of moor and stock improvement. The net result of this keeper's inequalities has been a sad deterioration of the shooting capacities of the moor which was under his control—a deterioration which it will take many years for a new and probably more reticent keeper to correct. The particular moor in question is loaded with vermin, the heather

is long and rank, the springs are clogged with undergrowth, and a thousand-acred shooting now realises
about ten brace of grouse a year. In our younger
days, before we began to understand the science of
maintaining a moor as breeding ground for grouse,
we considered this old keeper infallible. He could
cast a better line than any man we had met, he
seemed to know the actual capacity of every fly
in the fly-book. We can vouch as to the brilliance
of his shooting, as to his knowledge of the habits
and habitats of birds, and as to his skill in leading
his master through the intricacies of the most
difficult stalk, and it is sad that we have now to
dethrone him from the pedestal on which we had
placed him, as we view in cold blood the inefficiencies
of his character as a responsible workman.

Let it be frankly admitted that the responsibility
for the prevalence of inefficient keepers lies, to a great
extent, at the door of the owners or occupiers of the
shootings. There has been and there is too little
recognition of the services of good keepers. There
is not sufficient sliding in the scale of wages to
urge on the keeper in general to improve his
knowledge and his capacity for work. Remunera-
tion for labour is conducted in too stereotyped a
fashion. The efficient keeper is in general paid
the same wage as the inefficient one. There is
too little recognition of superiority and too little

condemnation of the reverse. This being the case, the result is obvious. The keeper has little stimulus to improvement, outside his own personal self-respect, and the standard of general efficiency is kept lower than it should be.

Much of the inefficiency of the keeper is also due to the ignorance or indifference of the master. Want of supervision from either of these causes is sure to lead to slackness, and this is bound to lead to deterioration of sport. But it must be pointed out that the ignorance or carelessness of a master may account for a keeper's slackness and inefficiency, it does not excuse it. Even taking the master on the highest plane, he can seldom be more than a very good amateur. *The keeper is, or ought to be, a specialist.* Within the limits of his duties, a keeper should know all that is to be known, and in the majority of cases should know infinitely more than his master. Not only should he be independent of any chance instruction from his employer, but he should be in the position to give advice and convey information at all points, when called upon to do so. In fact, the ideal can only be reached if a keeper bases his knowledge and his work on the possibility of his master being an absolute ignoramus on all matters, not even excepting the handling of a gun.

The relationship between master and keeper varies largely on all shootings. In some cases the former

takes little or no concern with the details connected
with the improvement and management of his
ground and stock, and is only concerned with the
sport on the days on which he or his friends shoot.
In other cases the master assumes the direction of,
and dictation on, all matters affecting his sport,
and requires that his keeper should make him conversant with every step he takes in the pursuit of
his calling.

Between these two extremes are found masters
whose interest and attention are keen on some points
and indifferent on others. It is chiefly in dealing with
the latter cases that the keeper will have to use any
discretion and tact he possesses, discerning when
and where he is expected to seek or give advice
and when and where he is not. In those cases
where the masters virtually assume the whole control
of the details connected with their shootings, it is
often found that, with a desire to please—especially
common amongst the courteous Highlanders—keepers
often hold back any definite knowledge they possess
and definite views they hold which ought to be of
infinite value to the master. The intelligent and
responsible keeper can always give information or
make suggestions without being dogmatic, and he is
but a poor gamekeeper who hides his knowledge
and his opinions in order to be obsequious or from
fear of contradiction. Civilly, quietly, yet firmly he

should state his facts and express his views, and he will find that he is seldom misunderstood and always respected. The man who prevaricates for the sake of pleasing, who pretends to know when he is ignorant, or pretends to be ignorant when he knows, is a bad servant, and is sure in the long run to get into difficulties.

It will be gathered from what we have already said that we are dealing with the keeper as a skilled specialist. We have not much to say as to that anachronism—the occasional keeper. We mean the man who is really not a gamekeeper at all, but a farm hand who goes out with the guns, and who is the only person in charge of the shooting. To attempt to instruct such a person would be a waste of energy and a dissipation of sense. Such a man may learn a little, but he has neither the time nor the instincts for sport. And yet how many of our so-called keepers are but mere labourers? They might possibly know the difference between a grouse and a grey hen, but as to the habits and habitats of game, as to the destructive capacity of vermin, as to the tempers and temperament of dogs, they are as ignorant as the sedentary Cockney, whose only knowledge of game has been obtained at the "jungle" at Earl's Court.

CHAPTER II

THE IDEAL KEEPER

WHAT we have already written will enable the reader to picture the main lines upon which the good keeper is constructed. There are so many tantalising curbs on human endeavour that it is difficult to reach perfection on this earth. However, it is good for us to have practical ideals—signposts which point to success, even although we find in the long run that our reach far exceeds our grasp. One thing is certain, that the good keeper never stands still, he never stagnates; his knowledge and his capacity ripen as the years go on. How many keepers there are who never seem to improve, who gradually forget all they have learned, and become impervious to new ideas, and add to this mental deterioration the slow disease of indolence. The average gamekeeper is the most conservative man on earth. Not only does he conserve the long-practised methods of the shooting on which he is trained, but he is impatient of any suggestion that might interfere with his own settled convictions. Even the best of keepers is apt to be solid, stable,

to shun them accordingly. It would be as well for
them to understand that this is an error of the
first magnitude. Nothing is more fortunate for sport
than that its literature emanates from some of its
greatest disciples, and it was this very fact that
deterred the present writers, for a time, from going to
press with the present volume, for up till now there
has been no valuable work on sport that has not
been written by a great sportsman. An analogous
remark cannot be made of other branches of literature,
and this fact should upset the prejudice amongst
keepers against that which they regard as mere
book learning. It will be found that most masters
are only too delighted to lend to their keepers such
volumes as the Fur, Feather, and Fin series, the
volumes of the Badminton Library dealing with
shooting, the *Encyclopædia of Sport*, and the contri-
butions of Mr. Speedy, Mr. John Colquhoun, Mr.
Hutchinson, Mr. Bromley Davenport, Sir E. Grey,
Mr. Innes Shand, Mr. Lloyd Price, Mr. Harting,
Mr. Carnegie, and others. In fact, it is the
master's duty to see that his keeper is put in
possession—temporarily, it may be—of some of
the more practical of these volumes, and to insist
that advantage be taken of the advice there put
forward.

Not that all the knowledge is on the side of the
writers of books. There are skilful arts practised

by some of our best keepers that have never yet
been put down in black and white. There are many
" tricks of the trade" that are still sacred to particular shootings. For sport, in its widest sense, as
embracing the preservation of game, is, like shooting,
not only a science—it is an art. A man may know
everything about law without being a great lawyer ;
a man may be conversant with most of the facts of
medical science, and yet be a poor physician. An
analogous remark applies to the profession of gamekeeping to such an extent that a keeper, like a
poacher, is supposed to be " born," not " made." But
a belief in this fact often leads to the most disastrous
results. The man who is thoroughly convinced *in his
own mind* that he is a born keeper, is apt to be conceited, opinionative, dogmatic, despotic, and imperious,
and to regard with disdain the suggestions of the man
who has learned his business by mere patient plod-
ding. Let even the keeper who is a sportsman by
instinct and a keeper by nature not hesitate to learn
of men who are his inferiors in everything except,
perhaps, a little knowledge.

Enthusiasm, although it is not everything, is an
invaluable quality in the good keeper. It inspires
enthusiasm not only in his underlings, but in the
sportsmen themselves. Nothing is more depressing
to a day's shooting than to have a keeper who seems
bored by his work. Such a day's shooting is bound

to be a failure, or, at best, an imperfect success. The joy of sport, the keenness for a good bag, the evident just pride in knowledge which he is only too willing to impart, the calm, firm, and deliberate manner in carrying out a plan, skilfully and patiently constructed,—these are the conditions that inspire confidence in and respect from the sportsman. But seeming indifference, evident ignorance, a noisy, changeful, aimless plan of campaign, these are the conditions that make for the irritation of the guns and for a general feeling of dissatisfaction. When the latter condition exists, it will in all likelihood be found that the courtesy of the keeper is in proportion to the size of his tips and his geniality to the number of his "nips." Such a keeper is a disgrace to a great and responsible profession. He can be of no satisfaction to himself, and is a nuisance to everybody else. He quarrels with the farm servants; he indiscriminately shoots every suspicious dog that he meets; he is outwitted by poachers, and is hated by his assistants. Knowledge, skill, perseverance, discrimination, firmness, order, courtesy, and enthusiasm, —these are the eight primary necessities for a good keeper. Knowledge of the technicalities of his craft, skill to carry them out, perseverance in face of difficulty and failure, discrimination in dealing with superiors, equals, neighbours, and inferiors, firmness in all he does, order in all his methods—in his

2

books, his kennels, and his sporting arrangements,
—and enthusiasm to carry out what he has carefully planned, modified by a gracious civility, will
all tend to his own, his master's, and his servants'
satisfaction.

CHAPTER III

Relations with Farmers, etc.

However skilful and energetic a keeper may be, however brilliant are his capacities for sport, he will find himself and his master considerably handicapped unless he is able to keep at peace with his neighbours. And, as far as he is concerned in the position of keeper, his principal neighbours are the shepherd, the farmer, the farm labourers, the neighbouring keepers, and the villagers. A little tact is worth a world of bullying, a little give and take more powerful than endless argument. In all his relations the main point to be remembered is that consideration for a neighbour's interest is the first step to the security of one's own. It should be admitted to start with that as a rule farmers and their servants have had too much their own way, and are difficult to pull with. If relations do get strained, let the keeper report the matter to his employer, and let him take up the quarrel; it is better the keeper keep on friendly terms, for many obvious reasons unnecessary to mention.

Let us take for instance the case of a shepherd or his master, the sheep farmer, who may have the grazing on a moor on which the keeper is in charge of the game. Enmity or tactlessness can only result in more damage to the latter's interests than to the former's. A resentful shepherd has a tantalising habit of destroying nests and of making friends with poachers, and, by a curious coincidence, it may somehow happen that he collects his sheep on the very days when we wish the hill to be kept quiet. During the breeding and nesting season his dog has a habit of ranging the moor, with the result that many eggs are destroyed, many young birds perish, and the moor is generally disturbed. Heather is badly burned, oftentimes butts and springs are tampered with. All of which unsatisfactory state of affairs might have been different if a little tact had been used, and a friend made of the shepherd, and this friendship shown in many little acts of consideration, as helping an occasional sheep or lamb in distress, or giving information to the shepherd as to their possible danger, or as to the whereabouts of a sheep that has gone astray. The occasional present of rabbits —given, of course, with the consent of the master— is also to be recommended.

The majority of farmers are inveterate, greedy grumblers, and difficult to satisfy, and have been spoiled by rich shooting tenants giving them all they ask. Farmers should be treated justly, yet firmly— in many cases the harm they do is overrated, and used as a threat to blackmail wealthy Sassenachs innocent of anywhere except Piccadilly or the Park. Yet good relationships with the farmers are more important in low ground than on moor shootings. Here antagonism between keeper and farmer or master and farmer is possibly disastrous to good sport. Of course, farmers have no right to enter coverts, which should always be strictly reserved in the lease to the landlord. As for the farm labourers, they possess opportunities of poaching which render them particularly dangerous. They can with ease set traps, nets, and snares without being observed. Their presence in the fields seldom arouses suspicion, and they may take the opportunity of following the principle of every man for himself, unless friendship for the master and the keeper has stimulated their interest in sport and in justice. Far too little is attempted by the average keeper to conciliate the farm labourer, either by common human sympathy and kindness or by an occasional present of rabbits. The keeper is far too apt to be oppressed by the idea of his own dignity, and to despise the mere clod of the fields. Let him remember that dignity does not necessarily mean austerity. A keeper can be firm and even suspicious without being "a pompous

ass." We remember once, at a big covert shoot in
the North of England, taking particular note of
the relationship that existed between the head-
keeper and his corps of beaters—which was chiefly
made up of farm labourers—hired at 2s. 6d. a day
plus a scratch lunch of bread and cheese. The month
was December, it may be added, and the temperature
stood just above zero. At a glance we discovered that
not only was the keeper feared—not a bad condition of
affairs—but that he was actively hated. One or two
stray remarks dropped by the beaters in highly
flavoured Yorkshire dialect soon convinced us of
this. As for the keeper, he ordered his rank and
file about as if they all combined roguery with
stupidity and laziness. No doubt many of his beaters
were brainless, lumbering loons, but it is not always
wise to call a man a fool in this sensitive world,
especially when numerous adjectives of a sanguinary
and condemnatory nature are prefixed. Let us not be
charged with desiring the keeper to proceed, say,
on these lines : "Would you mind, Mr. Clodhopper,
kindly accompanying the rest of the men in beating
out this cover ?" But there is a medium between this
and the not uncommon, "Nah, then, ye ——, stir yer
—— legs and look sharp, you —— —— ——." Not
only does such want of common consideration, such
absolute ignorance of human nature—which in all
its manifestations has some form of pride and self-

respect, however small—tend to the ill-being of a particular shooting, it has in the long run a damaging effect on sport in general. We do not suggest that the keeper's attitude should be one of obsequious fawning for favour, but he should remember that there are elements in society which are daily becoming more antagonistic to the game laws, and that there is no need for him to further emphasise the antagonism of class to class.

Let it be said, not for the first time, that on all occasions when the help of farm hands is called in for the purposes of sport, the keeper should, where such is needed, give the master a gentle hint as to the advisability of ministering well to the stomachs of these temporary employees. Irish stew or hot-pot with a little "fat ale" does not cost much, and at most would be but a drop in the bucket of shooting expenses.

Even in shootings where farm hands are not engaged, much valuable information may be at the disposal of the farm servant, and this is likely to be given or withheld in proportion to the popularity of the master, but more particularly of the keeper. Where an amicable feeling exists on all sides, sport is robbed of many of its handicaps. Good relations with the farmer may lead to the latter acquiescing in the desire that he should cut his corn *towards* the cover, so as to keep the birds on to the sports-man's ground. On the other hand, enmity will in all likelihood deter him from assisting the keeper, for example, by leaving a strip of uncut corn in the middle of a field so that he may drive out the game that remain in it before the reaping is finished.

A good understanding with the farmer may also checkmate the poaching facilities of his underlings. Despite his powers under the Ground Game Act, hares and rabbits will not be overshot, and orders may be given that the driver of the mowing machine keep a good lookout for nests, so that any possible danger may be reported. Informa-tion as to the movements and whereabouts of poachers will be placed at the keeper's disposal, and an altogether intelligent interest taken in, and considerable assistance given to, the sporting capacities of the land. Surely such a satisfactory outlook is worthy of more than condescension or mere indifference.

Let there be, at all costs, some considerable respect for the pets of the neighbourhood. The keeper should not treat all dogs and cats as vermin. If he does he will not only break the law, but also cause offence. In the fifth chapter he will get some hints as to the law of the matter. It is only necessary to add here, that while as a rule the collie and the pet tabby should be respected, no mercy should be shown to the lurcher, or that king of poachers, Tom the vagabond. An intelligent keeper will soon discover the ownership of every living creature on his ground, and be able to judge fairly well as to the way they should be treated. There are many other points at which the relationship of keeper and farmer meet which may suggest themselves to the thoughtful keeper. Those we have indicated may assist him in endeavouring to meet any other possible clashing of interests in a spirit which combines tact with firmness and justice with not too sacrificing yet not too niggling a form of generosity.

Friendship with neighbouring keepers is an absolute necessity where there is much interchange of shooting. In average cases, where an owner or tenant finds a difficulty in getting assistance for his drives or beats in a not over thinly populated country, he may safely set it down either to the indolence or the unpopularity of his keeper.

Every keeper who is worth his salt will, of course, soon have a good general knowledge of the character of every man and woman, dog and cat, that comes within the radius of his shootings. He will have fairly well gauged the potential poacher and know whom to appease, whom to seek favour of, and whom to control.   And of all general rules let him keep this one foremost in his mind.   Let him not make a habit of drinking with his neighbours.   There is a curious notion abroad in the earth that a man's courtesy is judged by his acquiescence in an expressed desire that he should have a drink.   Except amongst the wisest and the most far-seeing of men, very few friendships are sealed and very little respect is born in the presence of the bottle.   To drink habitually with any man diminishes authority, and no keeper can ever afford to lose that most valuable of assets. No person who counts will value a man less because he is temperate or because he refuses to give way to the silly habit of promiscuous drinking.   And the keeper is to be warned even of the very occasional glass with the suspicious stranger.   If a man must have his glass, let him have it at home, or with men with whom he is thoroughly acquainted—men whom he respects and by whom he is respected—men who will neither misunderstand him nor inveigle him into slackness of duty or other mischief.   The man who to-day seems a friend, who is laughing with us, may turn out to-morrow to be a poacher who is laughing at us.   There is no law in the country outside the laws of physiology and the law of any religion he may profess, that prevents a man from taking a fairly good "skinful of liquor," but the general rule must be emphasised that no drunkard, or even habitual "nipper," can retain respect, and without that priceless jewel in the chaplet of authority, a keeper had better change his profession and take to breaking stones.

CHAPTER IV

THE APPRENTICE KEEPER

WHAT we have already said will give the young man who aspires to be a gamekeeper some idea of the qualities of character and temperament, and of the knowledge and skill, that go to make a successful servant. There are one or two other points we may indicate that may be of use to the uninitiated at the threshold of his career.

First, let it be stated that the sooner he starts his work the easier it will be for him to learn.

It goes without saying that no man deficient in power of observation or in ordinary intelligence should ever think of giving his life up to the care and the pursuit of game. The 'prentice hand must not only have a good groundwork of the common rudiments of reading, writing, and arithmetic, but must be keenly interested in natural history; for, unless he is careful in reading up and noting the haunts, habits, and peculiarities of the various beasts and birds which people his district, he will never be a success in the sphere he has selected for his life's work. And having noted such facts, he will never attain to any great height of trustworthiness and dependence unless he is able to put facts together in his mind and make the necessary deductions. How often do we find a keeper whose brain is well stored with facts and experiences, and yet so stored that each item seems to be pigeon-holed in a separate department in his brain and not to be on speaking terms with one another? Let, therefore, the wise apprentice start in life with the belief that everything is done for a purpose, and that there is some connecting link between cause and effect. Let him always be asking in his own mind the question—Why? At first he may have great difficulty in finding an answer, and then the question must be repeated aloud to those who know, whose duty it will be to explain, and to direct the eyes and the brain of the 'prentice to observe facts and reasons which have eluded him. Let him remember this law,—that everything is done either from reason or from experience, and that the rule-of-thumb gospel is only for the inefficient and incapable workman. There are very few things in this world that should be done merely from routine and habit. The 'prentice must therefore get into the practice of using his eyes, his memory, and his power of reasoning in all he does. In saying so much, let us recall what we expressed in our first chapter. On no account should he pretend to know when he is ignorant, or pretend to be ignorant when he knows. The man who is too conceited to admit his ignorance will never learn anything, and the man who is so good-natured as to hide his knowledge for the sake of being pleasant, may be a good courtier, but he is a dishonest servant.

Generally speaking, the first duty of the apprentice gamekeeper is to be kennel boy. Simple as it may appear, the keeping of a kennel requires a good deal of attention and intelligence. It is sad to see how often a valuable kennel of dogs is subjected to neglect. Unless the head-keeper has a knowledge and a keen love of dogs, it is impossible that the kennel boy can be properly trained. It will add to his store of knowledge if he can borrow or acquire books written on the subject, provided he has sufficient intelligence to discriminate what is practical. There are two or three points which may be briefly noted—(1) The kennels should be kept scrupulously clean, and periodically disinfected with weak carbolic and water ; (2) the bed, which should consist of clean straw, should be shaken up every day and any dust swept out of the benches. Let the 'prentice keeper note the appearance of a dog that sleeps in a stable among clean straw, and he will at once understand the necessity for cleanliness in the bedding of dogs. There is nothing a dog seems to revel in more than a roll among clean

straw when it is put into his bed. (3) After the
kennel has been washed, or during very hot sunshine,
dogs should not be allowed to lie upon the pavement,
as their bodies are apt to draw damp from it and
cause rheumatism. Many dogs are rendered unfit
for work by neglecting this important precaution.
(4) The dogs should get plenty of fresh water,
and be fed regularly.

The 'prentice keeper should always be out with
the head-keeper when he is training his dogs. As
to the management of dogs in the field, the experience must be gradually acquired, but the perusal
of books on dog-breaking by such authorities as
General Hutchison, Sir Henry Smith, and others,
may be useful in giving him hints. But without
observation, common sense, patience, and perseverance, he will never become a practical dog-breaker.
However pure the breed, and however satisfactory
the condition in which dogs may be kept, perfection in breaking is neither to be secured nor
expected except with very considerable experience
amongst game.

The 'prentice keeper must also, as soon as possible,
be put in contact with ferrets. He must be instructed
as to the cleaning of their sleeping and feeding
quarters, and learn in detail the whole question
affecting their breeding, their feeding, and their
working. Next to these, the management of hill

ponies and other horses used in sport must come
under his observation.

Of other matters for early observation mention
must be made of the burning of heather, the improvement of soil, and questions of draining, fencing,
planting. In all these matters the 'prentice keeper
should be compelled to use his hands as well as his
brains. His early days must be partly those of a
labourer, a joiner, and a forester. He will find that
having dealt with these matters in a practical way,
he has laid a better foundation for his position as
keeper than if his knowledge were only based on
observation and theory. Let him have an accurate
knowledge of the use of the spade, the saw, the
hammer, long before he knows the use of a gun.

The third part of his training should be concerned
with the "engines" of sport, with the construction
and use of snares, traps, and nets, and, finally, of
guns. He must not only see the former set by
others, but he must be allowed to set them himself,
great care being taken that he understands the why
and wherefore of his procedure, and to see that he
proceeds, not from theory or imitation merely, but
from his knowledge of the habits and habitats of
game.

While he is learning these branches of his craft,
he will, of course, be out with the guns, acting as
beater, driver, stop, flank, or marker, and thus slowly

accumulating valuable knowledge as to the questions of finding birds and bringing them to the guns.

At this stage the present book, it is hoped, will be intelligible to him, and he will be well on the road to become a qualified keeper.

CHAPTER V

POINTS IN LAW A GAMEKEEPER SHOULD KNOW

By JOHN LAMB, Advocate

THE whole subject of game, in regard alike to its preservation and its destruction or capture, is so fenced about by law that no keeper can properly do his work without knowing at least the main restrictions which the law places on himself and others. Space forbids that more than an outline be given here, but for the sake of those wishing more detailed information a list is given at the close of the chapter of the leading books on the subject.

"Game," in its general sense, means all birds and beasts which are both used as food for man and are usually shot or hunted by man for sport. But the word is also used in the narrow sense of the birds and beasts mentioned in the leading Game Act of each of the three kingdoms. These are hare, pheasant, partridge, grouse, heath or moor game, black game, and bustards. For Ireland add deer,

landrails, and quail. Many Acts of Parliament use
the word game in this sense when they state that
the provisions of the Act apply to "game and
rabbits, teal, widgeon, deer," etc. By various Acts
it has been made illegal to kill birds during the
nesting season. A table of the close times for each
species of game is given at the end of this chapter.

There is no property in game or other wild
animals in their natural state. In Scotland they
become the property of whoever captures them
(in the legal phrase, "reduces them into possession"),
even if the captor breaks the law in taking them,
unless forfeiture of the game is made a part of
the penalty for the offence. In England and
Ireland the law is more complicated. There, if
game is flushed and killed on the ground of one
proprietor, it becomes his property. If it is flushed
on the ground of one man and killed or captured
on another's ground, it becomes the property of
its captor. Young game unable to leave the nest,
or, at least, the soil of its home, is the property of
the owner of the soil. In all three countries tame
animals (or those which have been tamed) are the
property of the person who keeps them. Young
pheasants, hatched from a setting of eggs by a
barn-door hen, are considered to be tame so long
as they follow their foster-mother. To steal them
is therefore punishable as theft or larceny, and they

do not require the protection of the game laws. Dead game also does not fall under the provisions of the game laws. It has therefore been decided in Scotland that if a man, passing along a public road while pheasants were being shot on the adjoining land, picked up a dead bird which fell at his feet and walked off with it, he was not guilty of either theft or contravention of the game laws. There is no decision quite so clear in England or Ireland, but the law is understood to be the same.

In England and Ireland the property in game is sometimes affected by the peculiar privileges belonging to royal forests, chases, purlieus, parks, free warrens, and manors. The keepers on such estates have also exceptional powers, but such privileged places are not so numerous as to require notice here.

The right of hunting and shooting game (which is a different thing from the property in the game) belongs naturally to the owner of the ground. In Scotland this right remains with the proprietor, though he lets the land on an agricultural lease, unless the lease contains an express stipulation that the tenant should have the game rights. In England and Ireland the agricultural tenant has the game rights unless the lease contains a contrary stipulation. This, however, is subject to what must afterwards be said about the Ground Game Act, 1880, which applies

to all three countries. Of course, the owner of the
land may let the game rights to a sporting tenant,
and the farming rights to an agricultural tenant. In
such a case disputes may easily arise between the
two tenants if either exercises his rights in such a
way as to interfere with the rights of the other. The
law is, that each is fully entitled to exercise his rights,
provided he does so in such a manner as not to
interfere unduly with the rights of the other. For
example, the sporting tenant must not tramp through
a field of standing corn, but he is quite entitled to
walk through turnips after partridges, provided he
does not unnecessarily trample down the turnips or
go so frequently through them as to seriously damage
the crop. The rights of the game tenant (or the
landlord when the shooting is in his own hands)
include a right to enter on the land during the close
time for game for the purpose of killing vermin and
otherwise protecting the game, provided he does not
unnecessarily or unduly interfere with the agricultural
tenant. Of course, each case must be judged by
itself, but the rule for the keeper to remember is that
the Courts will only protect him in his duty if he
acts with reasonable consideration for the farmer's
rights.

When a landowner lets a farm to an agricultural
tenant, reserving to himself the game rights, he
becomes liable for damage to the farmer's crops by

game, unless he shoots the game regularly so as to prevent the stock becoming excessive. In the case of hares and rabbits, this obligation has now been removed by the provisions of the Ground Game Act, 1880, which, as previously stated, applies to all three kingdoms. This Act gives to every occupier of land the right (of which he cannot divest himself) to kill the hares and rabbits on his holding. The right may be exercised by the occupier or persons authorised by him in writing. The occupier and one other person so authorised are the only persons who may use firearms. No person shall be authorised by the occupier to kill ground game except—(1) members of his household resident on the land ; (2) persons in his ordinary employment on the land ; and (3) one other person *bonâ fide* employed by him for reward to kill ground game. The keeper, if authorised in writing by the landlord or game tenant (who has a concurrent right to kill ground game), may demand any person killing game for the occupier to produce his written authority. If he has none he may be prosecuted as a poacher. This Act also forbids the use of firearms at night (*i.e.* from end of first hour after sunset to beginning of last hour before sunrise), and the use of spring traps except inside rabbit holes. The right of killing ground game under this Act must not be exercised on moors or unenclosed lands which are not arable except from the 11th day of December in one year till the 31st day of March in the following year—a provision probably designed to favour the grouse.

In Scotland and Ireland, but not in England, farmers are accustomed to burn the heather and old grass or bent on the moorland pastures periodically. This operation, known as "muirburn," is also beneficial to the grouse, as they feed on the young shoots of the heather or ling which come up afterwards. Obviously a moor cannot be burned without risk of damage to growing woods, etc., by the fire spreading, and the certainty of some damage to wild birds' nests on the ground burned. Most leases of such ground in Scotland regulate the amount which can be burned in any one year ; and by Act of Parliament such burning may not be done between 11th April and 1st November in any year, except in the case of high, wet muirlands, which, by leave of the proprietor in writing, may be burned between 11th and 25th April.[1] In Ireland the burning is permitted only between 14th June and 2nd February. In both countries a penalty is incurred if the Act is broken.

These being the leading conditions as regards the persons legitimately on the lands which the sportsman must observe, the conditions in regard to the Government are chiefly contained in the provisions as to licences. The second table at the end of the chapter shows all the licences required in the

[1] See page 131.

three kingdoms, and the times during which they
run. In the remarks following it is assumed that the
reader has that table before him. A licence as a
male servant is not required for a servant who is
bonâ fide employed in a capacity not requiring such a
licence (as, *e.g.*, a farm labourer), though he should be
taken for an odd day to beat a covert or to kill
vermin, or to do any duty for a gamekeeper. Similarly a gun licence is not required by a person sent
out with a gun to kill vermin—*i.e.* animals of a purely
noxious kind, such as weasels, stoats, etc. At one
time it was thought that rabbits were vermin, but it has
now been settled that no one can shoot rabbits, even
under the Ground Game Act, without a gun licence.
The only exceptions from the need of a game licence
which require notice here are—(1) the taking or
destroying of conies (rabbits) in Great Britain ; (2)
the killing of hares—(*a*) in England, by one person
authorised in writing by the occupier of the land ;
(*b*) in Scotland, by the owner or lessee of any land, or
any person authorised by him in writing ; (3) the
killing or taking of ground game under the Ground
Game Act ; (4) coursing or hunting hares or deer
with hounds; and (5) the taking of woodcock or
snipe with nets or springs in Great Britain. A
keeper's game licence can only be taken out by his
employer, who has himself a full licence to kill game.
Such a licence is not available except on the land on

which his employer has the right to kill game. Such
a licence may be transferred to a new keeper, if the
keeper for whom it was taken out dies or leaves his
employment while the licence is current. The officer
of excise who issued the licence must indorse the
name of the new keeper on the licence before the
transference can take effect.

Only persons who hold the licence to deal in game
may sell it retail or buy it wholesale. The only
persons entitled to sell to such licensed dealers are
those who have taken out the full £3 licence to kill
game; but a gamekeeper holding a £2 licence may
sell game to a dealer on the account and with the
written authority of his master, who, it will be
remembered, must have the full £3 licence. As this
exception in favour of gamekeepers is ignored or
misstated in some well-known books, it seems
necessary to add that the exception is made in
section 17 of the Game Act, 1831 (1 and 2 William
IV., c. 32), expressly referred to in the Game
Licences Act, 1860 (23 and 24 Vict., c. 90, section
13). See also Highmore's *Excise Laws*, 2nd Ed.
Part II., p. 181. Another exception is introduced
by the Ground Game Act, 1880, in favour of persons
killing hares or rabbits under that Act, who may sell
such game killed by them to a licensed dealer
though they have not a licence to kill game.

Any person doing any act in Great Britain for

which a licence to kill game is necessary, must show his licence to, and allow a copy of it to be taken by, any officer of Inland Revenue, or any person duly licensed to kill game, or the owner, occupier, or gamekeeper of the land on which he then is, who demands to see his licence. If the licence is not produced, the person must give his true name and address and state the place where he took out the licence, under a penalty of £20 in case of refusal, or of the information proving false.

The laws of Ireland in regard to this part of the subject are too complex to be adequately treated in the space at our disposal, nor is it necessary in a book expressly for keepers. No reference, therefore, is made to such questions as property qualification, manorial privileges, and those of "persons not under the degree of an esquire," and, in short, all matters with which an ordinary keeper is not concerned. No licences as male servants are required in Ireland. Licences for dogs must be got on 31st March in each year, from the Petty Sessions Clerk of the district. Duty, 2s. for each dog, and a 6d. stamp on the certificate of registration. A gamekeeper in Ireland, instead of taking out a *licence* to kill game, registers his deputation or appointment (which is chargeable with a 10s. stamp duty) with the supervisor of excise within whose district the lands are situated, and the officers of excise thereupon, on payment of the duty (*i.e.* £3), grant a *certificate* to such gamekeeper to kill game. Such certificate may be transferred to a new keeper if the keeper to whom it is granted dies or quits the service, just as in the case of a keeper's licence in England and Scotland. There is a provision in Ireland about showing a certificate to kill game on demand similar to that in England and Scotland, with two differences, viz. (1) the person making the demand must show his certificate, which is not necessary in England or Scotland, and (2) the penalty for refusing to show is £50, not £20.

The keeper's legal powers and duties in regard to persons who come on the ground with no legitimate title to be there (whom we may call generally "poachers") cannot be stated intelligibly without first giving a short outline of the legislation for the protection of game against such persons. For all practical purposes the law is contained in a very few Acts of Parliament, the first of which was passed in 1828 and the last in 1862. The subject is divided into three parts—(1) Trespassing in pursuit of game in the nighttime; (2) trespassing in pursuit of game in the daytime; and (3) the prevention of poaching.

Night poaching is forbidden by two Acts, which both apply to the whole United Kingdom, viz. the Night Poaching Acts, 1828 and 1844.

For the purpose of both Acts night is defined as the

period between the expiration of the first hour after sunset and the commencement of the last hour before sunrise, and " game " is defined as including hares, pheasants, partridges, grouse, heath or moor game, black game, and bustards.

An offence under these Acts is committed by any person who, during the night, (1) unlawfully takes or kills any game or rabbits on any land, or on any public road or path or the sides thereof, or at the openings or gates from any such land into such road or path ; or (2) unlawfully enters, or is on such *land* (no mention of *roads*, etc.), with any instruments for the purpose of taking or destroying *game*.   In the section creating the second offence there is no mention of rabbits, so it is incompetent to charge a person under the statute with unlawfully entering or being upon the lands in pursuit of rabbits.   But this does not make it lawful for a person to trespass by night in pursuit of rabbits.   A person caught on the ground with poaching instruments, such as nets, and charged with being there in pursuit of game, could hardly defend himself by saying he only meant to take rabbits.   In Ireland, under a separate Act (Night Poaching Act, 1826), the penalty is incurred by entering the land with intent to illegally take or kill game or rabbits.

Any person committing the offence first mentioned may be arrested and given into custody by the owner

or occupier, or by his gamekeeper or servant, or anyone assisting such gamekeeper or servant, wherever
he may be seized, provided the pursuit started on
the land. Anyone committing the offence second
mentioned may be similarly arrested and given into
custody provided the seizure be made, or the pursuit
begun, on the land on which the offence is committed.
In either of these cases an assault by the offender
on any person authorised to arrest him is a serious
aggravation of the offence. A person authorised to
make such arrest may, without being guilty of assault,
use sufficient violence to effect this arrest, whereas in
Scotland a person not so authorised would commit
an assault by the attempt to arrest and be liable in
damages to the poacher if he used violence; while
the poacher who violently resisted the unauthorised
attempt to arrest him would be justifiably acting in
self-defence. In England and Ireland the Prevention
of Offences Act, 1851, section 11, authorises any
person whatsoever to apprehend any person found
committing an indictable offence in the night; and
this has been held to authorise anyone to arrest
a person found committing an aggravated offence
against the Night Poaching Acts. It is an aggravation
of these offences if they are committed by three or
more persons acting in concert, provided any of them
be armed with gun, bludgeon, or other offensive
weapon.

Trespassing in pursuit of game by day, *i.e.* between
the commencement of the last hour before sunrise
and the expiry of the first hour after sunset, is a less
serious offence than night poaching, and the law
is different in each of the three kingdoms.

In Ireland trespassing in pursuit of game in daylight is prohibited by the Game Trespass Act, 1864.
It needs no further mention here, as it confers no
special power on anyone to enforce it or turn trespassers off the ground, but merely provides a penalty
for such trespass. The keeper there must rely on
his common law right to turn trespassers off the
land on his master's orders.

In Scotland the Act is the Day Trespass Act,
officially called the Game (Scotland) Act, 1832.
This Act imposes a penalty on anyone who trespasses on any land in the daytime (as defined above)
in pursuit of game or of deer, roe, woodcocks, snipes,
quails, landrails, wild ducks, or conies (*i.e.* rabbits).
The penalty is larger if the offender have his face
blackened or is otherwise disguised. A man who
remains on the highroad may commit the trespass
by sending his dog into a field to chase rabbits or
by acting in concert with others who are in the fields
in pursuit of game, etc.

A man who has a perfect right to be on the lands
for another purpose may be convicted under this
Act of " unlawfully entering " if he takes game when

on the lands. For example, a farm servant whose employment requires him to be on a particular field to plough, becomes a trespasser if he takes game on that field.

Any such trespasser may be required, by the person having the right to kill game on the land, or the occupier, or the gamekeeper, or other person authorised by either of them, to quit the land and give his full name and address. If he refuses to do either of these things, the gamekeeper or other such person may apprehend the offender and take him before the Sheriff. If the offender cannot be brought before the Sheriff within twelve hours of his arrest, he must be discharged, but may be proceeded against for his offence by summons or warrant. The gamekeeper (or other) may also require the offender to give up any game he has with him, and, if he refuses, may take it from him.

The gamekeeper cannot be sued for anything wrong he has done in carrying out the Act after six months have elapsed since the act complained of.

A trespass to pick up dead game is not an offence under this Act.

In England the law as to day poaching is contained in the Game Act, 1831. By that Act a penalty is imposed on anyone who trespasses in the daytime (defined above) on any land in pursuit of game or woodcocks, snipes, quails, landrails, or conies. The penalty is increased if five or more persons so trespass together. As in Scotland, the offender or offenders may be ordered to quit the land and to give their names and addresses, and, on refusal, may be arrested and taken before a Justice of the Peace. If they cannot be brought before a Justice within twelve hours, they must be discharged, but may be proceeded against for the offence by summons or warrant. They may also be required to give up any game in their possession. The persons authorised in England to make and enforce these demands are the persons having the right of killing game on the land, the occupier of the land, any gamekeeper or servant of either of them, or any person authorised by either of them, or, where the offence takes place in a royal forest, park, chase, or warren, the warden, ranger, verderer, forester, master-keeper, under-keeper, or other officer thereof. Armed resistance aggravates the offence.

The Poaching Prevention Act, 1862 (25 and 26 Vict. c. 114), applies to the United Kingdom. For the purposes of the Act, "game" includes any one or more hares, pheasants, partridges, woodcocks, snipes, rabbits, grouse, black or moor game, and eggs of pheasants, partridges, grouse, and black or moor game. The Act empowers any constable or peace officer in any highway, street, or public place to search any person whom he may have good cause to suspect of coming from any land where he was unlawfully in pursuit of game, or any person aiding or abetting him, and having in his possession any game unlawfully obtained, or any gun, part of a gun, or nets or engines used for killing or taking game, and also to stop and search any cart or conveyance in which such constable shall have good cause to suspect that any such game or such articles are being carried by any such person, and if he (the constable) finds such game or articles, to seize and detain them. It must be noted that the powers of search and seizure conferred by this Act are conferred on constables and peace officers only. Consequently all that the keeper can do to carry out this Act is to give information to the constable, if his covers have been disturbed by poachers, or if he has other reasons for supposing that poaching is going on.

What the gamekeeper must not do may be stated more shortly.

In all three countries it is absolutely forbidden to put poison in any shape or form upon any land, enclosed or unenclosed. This prohibition is not only contained in many Acts relating to game, but is extended by Special Acts to the use of poison for any purpose—with the sole exception of the use of poison, under very strict precautions, about a house or steading for the destruction of rats,

4

mice, and such small vermin. In connection with
this exception, the gamekeeper must see that means
are taken to prevent any dog from getting at
such poison.

In England and Ireland it is illegal to kill game
on Sunday or Christmas Day. There is no such
direct prohibition in Scotland, but the Act 1661,
cap. 18, which has been held to be still in force,
prohibits salmon-fishing and *all other profanation*
of the Sabbath day. Under this Act a conviction
for shooting on Sunday might be obtained.

The use of firearms by night to kill ground game
is forbidden in all three countries, but the Acts
forbidding this in regard to other game do not
extend to Ireland.

One of the ordinary duties of the keeper is the
destruction of vermin which might destroy the game
which it is his duty to preserve.

By a series of Acts (extending to the whole United
Kingdom) for the preservation of wild birds, it is
provided that a schedule be prepared for each county
of all the wild birds which are supposed to be quite
harmless; that the owner or occupier of the land,
or anyone authorised by him, may at any time kill
the birds not included in the schedule; but that no
one may kill the scheduled birds between 1st March
and 1st August in each year; and that no one
except such owner or occupier or person author-

ised by either may kill any bird between these dates.

The keeper will do well, before killing any birds between these dates in order to protect his game, to make sure that such birds are not included in the schedule for his county, by application to the county clerk.

The ordinary gamekeeper has no right to kill a dog or cat which is poaching on the land under his charge. If the dog or the cat is in the act of killing a valuable bird or animal, the keeper might be held entitled to kill such dog or cat, provided this were the only means of saving such valuable animal or bird. The cases in which this defence has been upheld are so rare that it would be safer for the ordinary keeper to refrain from such killing. Special powers, however, are given to the gamekeepers of any lord of the manor, lordship, or royalty, duly appointed under the hand and seal of the lord on a ten-shilling stamp, and registered with the clerk of the peace for the county. A keeper so appointed may seize and take for his master's use any dogs, nets, and other instruments for taking game as shall be used within such manor by any person not authorised to kill game.

Similar privilege is conferred upon the gamekeepers duly appointed in the same manner upon any lands in Wales of the clear annual value of £500.

A keeper must not set any spring-gun or any trap

which might be destructive either to men or dogs, but it is quite lawful to set a spring-gun with a detonating cartridge, which can only act as an alarm signal.

It is hardly necessary to say that a gamekeeper who fires a gun at a poacher may be tried for assault or murder, as the case turns out.

The question sometimes arises how far a person shooting may follow his wounded game on to the land of a neighbouring proprietor. The rule is that he may follow game which is dead or on the point of death. In this connection it may be noted that to enter land for the purpose of taking dead game is not a breach of the Day Trespass Act. In England no one may use firearms within fifty feet of the centre of a public roadway. In Scotland no one may use firearms on or in any exposed situation near a public roadway so as to cause annoyance to any passenger thereon.

In regard to fishing, the law lays no special duties on the gamekeeper and confers on him no special privileges, so nothing need be said on that subject in this chapter.

Leading books on the game laws in the different countries :—

Scotland—*The Law of Scotland on the Game Laws, Trout and Salmon Fishing.* J. H. Tait. 15s. Edinburgh: William Green & Sons. 1901.

England—Oke's *Game Laws.* J. W. Bund. 14s. London: Butterworth & Co. 1897.

Ireland—*The Irish Game Laws.* M'Carthy Conner. 6s. Dublin: Hodges & Figgins. 1891. Supplement. 1s. 1903.

No. 1.—TABLE OF CLOSE TIMES.

CREATURE PROTECTED.	ENGLAND.	SCOTLAND.	IRELAND.
Grouse. Ptarmigan.	10th December to 12th August.	10th December to 12th August.	10th December to 12th August.
Bustard or wild turkey.	1st March to 1st September.	1st March to 1st August.	10th January to 1st September.
Partridge.	1st February to 1st September.	1st February to 1st September.	1st February to 1st September.
Pheasant.	1st February to 1st October.	1st February to 1st October.	1st February to 1st October.
Black game.	10th December to 20th August. In Somerset, Devon, and New Forest, 10th December to 1st September.	10th December to 20th August.	10th December to 20th August.
All other wild birds.	1st March to 1st August.	1st March to 1st August.	1st March to 1st August.
Deer, red (male). ,, fallow (male).	... ...	... ...	10th June to 28th October. 29th September to 10th June.
Hare.	1st March to 1st August. (The prohibition here is only against selling or exposing for sale.)	1st March to 1st August. (The prohibition here is only against selling or exposing for sale.)	20th April to 12th August.

No. II.—Table of Excise Licences.

Licences Required.	Duties to be Paid for Them. (£ s. d.)	Dates on which they Terminate.	Penalties which may be incurred in respect of them.
1. For each gamekeeper or under gamekeeper a licence for a "male servant"	0 15 0	31st December following issue.	For not taking out sufficient licences . £20 For making a false declaration, or no declaration . . . £20
2. For each dog above six months old	0 7 6	31st December following issue.	For keeping a dog without a licence, or for refusing to produce licence on demand of excise officer or police constable . . . £5 and costs.
3. Gun licence (only required by persons who have not a game licence)	0 10 0	31st July following issue.	For using or carrying gun outside house, or for refusing to produce licence on demand of excise officer or police constable . . . £10
4. Licence to kill game— (a) Full period of a year	3 0 0	31st July following issue.	For taking or pursuing game without licence, or for failing to produce licence on demand of excise officer, gamekeeper, person with proper licence to kill game, owner, lessee, or occupier of
(b) To expire on 31st October, if taken out before that date	2 0 0	31st October following issue.	

	£	s.	d.		
(c) To expire on 31st July following, if taken out after 31st October	2	0	0	31st July following issue.	the land, or for giving false answer to such demand . . . £20
(d) For a continuous period of fourteen days	1	0	0	Fourteen days after issue.	
(e) For a gamekeeper for whom the "male servant" licence is paid	2	0	0	31st July following issue.	
5. Licence to deal in game	2	0	0	1st July following issue.	For dealing in game without excise licence, whether he shall have a justices' licence or not . . . £20

For every head of game sold or offered for sale without the licence of the justices being granted to the seller . . . £2 and costs.

For every head of game bought by a person not licensed to deal in game from anyone except a licensed dealer . . . £5 and costs.

For a licensed dealer buying, from other than a person licensed to kill game, or selling without the sign up, or putting the sign at more than shop, or selling game at any other place than the shop where his sign is up . . . £10 and costs. |

Note.—The special licensing provisions applicable to Ireland are dealt with in the text. See page 42.

CHAPTER VI

THE POACHER

WE have dwelt on many points affecting poaching in the last chapter, dealing with the laws of sport, and in our study of the various game which it is the object of the poacher to illegitimately secure, more will be said. The days are long past when a halo of sentiment hung round this law-breaker. He no longer inspires the song-writer or the writer of romance. "The Lincolnshire poacher" and his contemporaries were no doubt men with a glamour about them, instinctive hunters, impatient of the trammels of game legislation, and lineal descendants of a breed of sportsmen that knew not Acts of Parliament, and had no fear of the power of the constable and the police court. But the glamour has passed, like many a halo of simpler and freer days. The twentieth century poacher is an ill-conditioned, lazy, drunken, and slinking scoundrel, an enemy to law and order, without a particle of true sportsmanlike feeling in his veins. Taken as a class, poachers are a set of hardened criminals, careless of everything but their own besotted lives. The occasional poacher is a much rarer bird and is the uncurbed expression of the natural poaching tendency which exists in human nature. He may be a farm hand, a village loon, or even a medical student home for the vacation, but whatever he may be, he is in the majority of cases an amateur and not so dangerous as his professional brother, who is a cast-off from honest trades—a grain in the sediment of society. Drink has him, as a rule, in its grip. He has a shifty and congested eye and a tremulous tongue. He is the friend of no man and an enemy to most, and is in the majority of cases an arrant coward. Remarkably ignorant on most questions, he is terribly acute on all matters affecting the poaching of game, and although a coward, he is prepared at a pinch to get rid of another life to keep the security of his own.

There used to be a popular impression that the best man to secure as a keeper was one who had been a poacher. If we limit the word "poacher" to the occasional, and not the habitual, criminal, there may have been some truth in the belief, but, for our purposes, there is much more wisdom in the reverse statement that the best poacher is the man who has been a keeper. A gamekeeper discharged for drunkenness or dishonesty is a dangerous man to deal with, especially if he continues to hang about the district in which he formerly had respectable employment. He is thoroughly conversant with every preserve in the county and knows to a nicety the habits and habitats of the game in the district. The inference is obvious. He is the very man to lead a gang of poachers. It is therefore unwise to allow a discharged keeper to remain on the property.

We have indicated, in a previous chapter, the line of conduct which it is advisable for keepers to pursue in dealing with men who are potential poachers—farm servants and the like — and it will not be necessary for us to say more on the subject. In dealing with the professional poachers, individually or in gangs, in addition to such usual procedure as the bushing of fields to prevent partridge-poaching, the construction of wire and bells in pheasant coverts and by pheasant coops, and other forms of special protection, it will be necessary that the keeper should institute a regular system of watching, and a system which is flexible enough to stand modification in time and season. The nesting season, and the days when birds are young, must be periods for particular alertness. A cloudy, windy night must at once suggest to the keeper the idea of special vigilance, for this condition of weather offers an especial chance to the plans of the poacher. The artful keeper also should not get into the habit of making regular rounds—he should vary them daily.

When a district is habitually invaded by gangs of poachers, the keepers of neighbouring estates should work in unison, and should lay their heads together to carry out a joint plan of campaign to frustrate the villainy of the trespassers in pursuit of game. The use of rockets as signals is an excellent practice and should be more generally carried out. Not only do rockets give warning to keepers at a distance, but they put fear into the heart of the cowardly poacher, who, as a rule, takes to his heels on the faintest suspicion of danger. It is advisable not to give too long notice to beaters as to the locale of a shoot, as poachers are apt to mature their plans for another part of the ground. Late the night before, or, better still, early the morning of the day on which the shooting is to take place, is soon enough.

Finally, let gamekeepers be feared. There is nothing like a reputation for strength to keep off the intruder. There is much to be gained when the keeper is held in awe. To illustrate the truth of this remark, we may quote an experience of our younger and more irresponsible days. One of the present writers had a lease of a shooting in the upper ward of Lanarkshire, an estate with excellent covers, in which were preserved a large stock of pheasants. He had been much troubled by the inroads of poachers, and had a suspicion that they were, in fact, stimulated by the " softness " of the

head-keeper.   Mr.   Gaiters was a mild - speaking,
humorous, yet patient and godly man, and despite
his honest endeavours to get the better of his unscrupulous enemies, the victories were generally
on their side.   Things went from bad to worse till
one eventful night.   The tenant had retired to his
smoking-room for the evening, when a servant came
running in to inform him that a big tussle was
going on at the end of one of the coverts, owing
to the fact that a gang of poachers had been surprised in their work by the head and under-keeper.
From the account he received, he imagined it to
be an encounter of the first magnitude.   He was
about to set out for the field of action when an
eccentric idea came into his brain.   He rushed to
the gunroom, took down his gun, put some cartridges into his pocket, and "rushed into the night."
As soon as he got within fifty yards of the cover
in which the "fun" was proceeding, he loaded his
gun and began to empty cartridge after cartridge
on to the tops of the trees.   He could hear the
tramp of feet in the distance and the evident sound
of struggle.   When he ceased firing, this sound
ceased also.   Another servant at this moment came
running up, and then the second part of the *coup*
was carried out.   A sheep had been killed that
very day, and he immediately gave orders that
some of the blood should be brought to him.   This

he mixed with water in a bucket. He then secured an old pair of tweed trousers, which he roughly tore into pieces. Accompanied by his servant, he now set out for the cross-roads near to the point where the encounter had taken place. In a few moments the watered blood and the tattered garment had been scattered indiscrimately here and there about the road, and two pairs of feet began to trample them into the mud and dust. The night was so dark that the immediate effect was not discernible. Having completed this piece of work, he returned to the house, and warning his servant to keep a quiet tongue in his head, retired to bed. Next morning there was "the devil to pay." An early visitor in the shape of a constable found an unusually early riser in the shape of the shooting tenant, who listened with keen attention to a story of the strange doings of the night before. The constable suspected manslaughter, though no body had been found. His hearer, evidently much impressed with the seriousness of the situation, accompanied him to the cross-roads, where already a small crowd had collected, peering into hedges and over dykes to find a mutilated corpse. For the roadside presented a gruesome spectacle. Even the innocent humorist was impressed by the ghastliness of the experiment. As for the head-keeper, he was quite nonplussed. The fight had been a severe one, but

he could not account for the roadside shambles.
The constable was, of course, sceptical at his mild
protestations, and the crowd voted him a new
quality of humour. However, to cut a long story
short, there was a private interview between tenant
and constable, and " the smile on the face of
bobby " was modified by the fact that he
discerned a new way of keeping the law. The
moral of which tale is, that a reputation as
a fighting man, and one whose blows do not
merely go skin deep, is not an objectionable
adjunct of the character of a keeper.

Correlative Matter.

CHAPTER VII

VERMIN

By TOM SPEEDY

THE first essential condition in order to increase a stock of game on an estate is the destruction of vermin. As soon as game begin to increase, vermin will arrive upon the scene, although how and from what quarter they have introduced themselves are among those mysteries in natural history which are as yet unexplained. As bearing somewhat on the subject, it may be mentioned that in a recent visitation of a plague of voles, when these rodents threatened to devastate the pasture-lands in the Border counties, a foreign owl, the short-eared species, which, though an occasional winter visitant to this country, has only on rare occasions been previously known to breed with us in any numbers, congregated in hundreds in the vole-infested districts and nested in the heather. Whence they came in such numbers must ever remain a mystery, but there they suddenly appeared. I have noted a similar coincidence with regard to game. I have introduced hares to an island, where they at first rapidly increased. The eagle and the buzzard soon made their appearance, and nested on the island, when the hares vanished at an alarming rate. It must therefore be manifest that a fundamental principle in game-preserving is, that a sharp eye be kept on the destruction of vermin.

There are few things more interesting than the trapping of vermin, and no keeper will prove very successful in this task unless he makes a careful study of the object of his pursuit. By keeping a diary in which to note carefully the kinds of vermin got, and by duly recording the contents of their stomach, or crop and gizzard, the young keeper will, with a few years' experience, possess an amount of knowledge which will give him power among his fellows. So much nonsense is written on this subject, that, without practical acquaintance with the habits of the various kinds of vermin, he may be very easily led astray by non-practical writers promulgating their fanciful theories. When man first appeared on the scene there was, presumably, what some are pleased to call the "balance of nature." Man, however, was given dominion over the beasts of the field and over the fowls of the air; and by gradually destroying those which were useless and those which preyed on others which were useful to him, a somewhat different state of things was by-and-by arrived at. A few hundred years ago wolves, foxes, and other vermin were so plentiful in this country that sheep-farming was out of the question. By killing down the wolves and other large beasts of prey, sheep-farming became so far a success. It was found, however, that a similar crusade had to be waged against birds as well as against beasts of prey. Sir William Jardine, in his " Naturalists' Library," tells us regarding eagles: " Such was the depredation committed among the flocks during the season of lambing that every device was employed and expense incurred by rewards for their destruction. From March 1831 to March 1834, in the county of Sutherland alone, 171 old birds with 53 young and eggs were destroyed."

Now that sheep-farming hardly pays and grouse have become so valuable, it is necessary to cultivate the latter by destroying their natural enemies, in the same manner as it was necessary to destroy the wolves, etc., for the sake of the sheep. Of ground vermin we have the badger, otter, fox, pole-cat, stoat, weasel, hedgehog, and rat. Among winged vermin we have the hawk species, from the eagle down to the merlin. The game-preserver has chiefly to guard against the peregrine falcon, the sparrow-hawk, and the merlin; also the corvidæ—ravens, carrion-crows, and magpies. There are others which do very considerable destruction to game, but not invariably

5

so. Amongst these may be mentioned rooks, jays, jackdaws, kestrels, and owls.

It is with a feeling of regret that I classify the badger with vermin. Being brought up in the historic Border land, and inheriting the hunting spirit of my ancestors, I in my boyhood regarded badger, fox, and otter hunting as the chief end of man. Badger hunts on the banks of the lower reaches of the Tweed are still to me a pleasing remembrance. Of late years the badger has in many places disappeared, in consequence of the common use of the steel trap. Many gentlemen, however, and notably the Earl of Rosebery, are preserving them, and have reintroduced them on their estates, so that it is to be hoped the day is yet far distant when the extermination of this, the largest, strongest, and fiercest of our British wild beasts, will have to be deplored.

The ravages of the badger among game are generally confined to the devouring of eggs and the digging out of rabbits' nests. Their scenting power is remarkable, as they dig down perpendicularly to a depth of three feet straight into the nest. I was recently interested in an illustration of their scenting powers by poison being inserted in a dead hind calf, and placed on an island in the centre of a deer forest for the purpose of destroying carrion-crows. The water round the island was deep and twenty yards across, yet the

badger had scented the carrion, and swam over
to its certain doom. This is the only illustration
of badgers swimming that has come under my
observation. They are very destructive among eggs,
and as a consequence their presence cannot be
tolerated in a game-preserve. I have frequently
trapped them with eggs as a bait, though they are
practically omnivorous, wheat in harvest-time being
found in their excrements, but they are likewise
attracted by any sort of carrion.

The otter may also be classified as a poacher.
It is generally believed that he preys only upon
fish, but instances have come under my observation of his killing rabbits and grouse, especially
the former, which fact can be corroborated by an
examination of the excrements.

But a much more dreaded enemy of the game-
preserver than either the badger or the otter is the
fox, — though here one must speak with bated
breath, fox-hunting being regarded as the national
sport. In hunting districts the fox lives the life
of a licensed freebooter, feasted on the best, from
the farmer's geese and turkeys and all kinds of
winged and ground game down to the smallest of
birds, and protected even by the "ruthless" gamekeeper. It is vastly otherwise where no foxhounds
are kept; yet even there, despite the co-operation
of farmers, gamekeepers, and shepherds, he holds

his own against his numerous enemies, among the barren waste lands of our Scottish mountains. Notwithstanding every device employed, the fox is still to be found in great numbers in the Highlands of Scotland, many cubs being dug out and sent to hunting districts every year. When a den is found containing cubs the usual method employed is to bolt them with terriers and then shoot them down like rabbits. Frequently, however, cubs find their way into crevices in the rocks where they cannot be followed by terriers. Keepers conceal themselves in different places and wait till the old ones approach with food for their progeny. As it is the invariable habit of the fox to approach from leeward, and as his scenting powers are so keen, it is difficult to take up a position. The love of foxes for their offspring, however, is so great that they run great risk to reach them, and in avoiding one keeper when approaching the den, they frequently go within range of another, and are shot. I have, when watching a cairn, known the vixen steal in unobserved and remove the cubs under cloud of night, when she must have passed within a few yards of where I lay. On one occasion she appeared on an eminence above me, and seeing her outline distinctly against the sky, I fired with fatal effect, though she ran a considerable distance before dropping dead. The piteous howling of the dog fox all through that night is still fresh in my mind, and indicates a love of offspring which might be an example to higher animals.

In such circumstances, and where the nature of the den or cairn admits, the cubs can be caught in traps. It is a common method to do this, and as fox cubs are in many cases a considerable source of income to the keeper, I would recommend that Cruickshank's patent rubber-jawed trap be used, in order to prevent the legs being broken. Any lady can put her hand on the plate and spring the trap without injury. Of course, the keepers have to watch all night in the vicinity to take the cubs out as they are caught.

Trapping is a common method of destroying foxes in mountainous districts. The usual way is to utilise a pool of water, and making a road into the centre of it, place a bait with the trap skilfully covered on the road. It is necessary that the pool of water be near a spring, in order that a summer's drought may not interfere with it. Any carrion will do for a bait, and, so far as my experience goes, nothing is better than the carcase of a fox or cat, as Reynard is almost certain to be attracted by the smell, and so venture on to the treacherous trap. It may be well to mention here that the traps should only be set for foxes in places where they can be seen by the telescope from a distance, so that the keeper need never go near them except when he sees the trap

has been sprung. The cunning of the fox is pro-
verbial, and he quickly associates the smell of the
keeper with the trap, and thus suspects danger.
When, however, the scent of man evaporates, he
becomes bolder, and ventures to the bait which
attracts him.

A successful way of trapping old foxes in early
spring is, if one is caught, to take out the bladder,
bury the carcase,—if possible among peat hags, or
in such places likely to be frequented by foxes,—
make a mound like a large mole-heap for a grave,
set a few traps round the base, and sprinkle the
contents of the bladder on it. So soon as human
scent has disappeared, foxes are certain to pay
this mound a visit.

Sometimes a couple of foxhounds are got to
scour the valleys in the early morning in order to
take up the scent and follow Reynard to his
mountain fastnesses. On such occasions, the co-
operation of a large number of keepers is secured,
and all the principal passes in the mountains
guarded by guns. Many foxes are killed in this
way.

Another animal most destructive to game is the
cat. The wild cat is now so rare that it is almost
superfluous to refer to it as an enemy of game.
Still, it is true that on one estate last year about
a dozen wild cats were trapped. As they were

sent on to me, I had them stuffed and exhibited at a meeting of the Field Naturalists' Society in Edinburgh, when I read a paper on Wild Cats to the members. This paper found its way into the newspapers, and endless discussion ensued, when it was asserted by no mean authority that the genuine wild cat was long since extinct, having crossed with the domestic cat, and was not now the original *Felis catus* of Scotland. Sir Herbert Maxwell, in his *Memories of the Months*, states, however, that he had some specimens sent from Argyllshire to Dr. Oldfield Thomas, of the British Museum, who pronounced them indistinguishable from the pure *Felis catus*. As cats have not the sagacity and cunning of foxes, they are easily trapped, and quickly fall a victim to the game-keeper. The same remark applies to the domestic cat : having no suspicion, it is easily trapped. The destruction of cats by gamekeepers is a continual source of discord between him and his neighbours. Once they begin to hunt for game, their presence cannot be tolerated, and it is desirable that they be kept down. Great judiciousness, however, should be exercised by the gamekeeper, and when a domestic cat is trapped it ought quickly to be put out of sight and its fate kept secret.

The stoat or ermine weasel is a species of vermin that the gamekeeper has good reason to be afraid of. He is a merciless tyrant, a meaningless murderer, shedding blood from mere wantonness. Both ground and winged game fall victims to his blood-thirstiness. Even wood-pigeons are not exempt from his rapacity, as I have seen one in a pigeon's nest ten feet from the ground, and watched him throw the young birds over the nest and carry them off. The climbing capacity of the stoat can scarcely be credited: in a pole-trap seven or eight feet from the ground, on the moor at Castle Menzies, in Perthshire, I witnessed a number of stoats captured. Whether they had scented the blood of birds that had been caught, or by what motive they were impelled to climb the pole, I cannot say, but the fact remains that the stoats climbed that pole and were secured in the trap at the top of it.

It is no use a keeper thinking that he has vermin trapped down on his estate, as the stoat is ubiquitous. Some years ago I collected five hundred stoats and weasels to transport to New Zealand, in order to cope with the rabbit plague. There were no rabbits and no stoats there till man introduced some rabbits, and with the most ruinous results. It was therefore found necessary to introduce the natural enemy of the rabbit, hence the transportation of stoats and weasels. Before they had been long in the colony, it was discovered that stoats had travelled a distance of ninety miles. Their scenting power enables them to track their prey like a beagle, and I have seen both rabbits and young hares lie down and squeal through sheer terror before a stoat was within many yards of them, when in an instant the stoat would spring on to the back of its victim, and, with that unerring instinct peculiar to the weasel tribe, seize it behind the ear, when, I am disposed to think, in many cases it sinks its tusks into the spinal cord. Fortunately the stoat is easily trapped, and nothing makes a better bait than one of their own species, their cannibalistic tendencies being a gruesome trait in their character. In the rabbit warren, in the covers, on the grouse moor, or by the hedgerows, the stoat demands the vigilance of the keeper. Some years ago a brood of magpies made their appearance in a strip of plantation, where a couple of broods of young pheasants had been frequently seen. Drilling holes in the side of three eggs and inserting a small quantity of strychnine, I had them placed in the strip late at night, in the hope that they would be seen by the magpies in the early morning. On going round, however, the eggs were gone, but there was no trace of the magpies. After a diligent search, I saw something white under some spruce branches, and on lifting them, found the eggs, two of them intact and one broken, while a large stoat, stiff dead, lay beside them. How it had removed the three eggs a distance of sixty-two yards, I cannot explain.

The weasel, though smaller in size, very much resembles the stoat. It is also very destructive among young game, and, like the stoat, bloodthirsty in its habits. Recently, while travelling over the moor of Tullimet, in Perthshire, in company with the keeper, we had our attention attracted by the peculiar action of a hen grouse jumping in the air. Approaching the place, we observed a weasel looking out of a hole among the heather. With the aid of our sticks we dug out the hole, and discovered five young grouse, about a week old, which had been killed and dragged in.

Another illustration in point. A neighbour's boy had a pair of rabbits confined in a house, with a brood of eight young ones nearly half grown, and a second litter, seven in number, about ten days old. Hearing a noise about seven o'clock one evening in the rabbit-house, the boy went to ascertain the cause. On opening the door, a weasel made its exit by a small hole, and effected its escape. It was soon found that the entire fifteen young rabbits had been cruelly slaughtered, the speck of blood behind the ear revealing the spot where the weasel tribe, with unerring accuracy, seize their prey and quickly extinguish the lives of their victims. The noise which attracted attention was caused by the old pair of rabbits defending themselves as they best could; but there can be no doubt that had attention not been attracted, they would have shared the same fate as their progeny.

Most keepers who have had experience in rearing pheasants are aware of the bloodthirsty habits of the weasel should it find its way into the rearing-field. As an invariable rule, however, precautionary means should be adopted by having traps set in every likely spot around the rearing-field. Care must be taken when the pheasant chicks extend their rambles that small conduits are made with stones, in which the traps should be placed, in order to secure immunity from the danger of the birds getting into them. Weasels are easily trapped, and nothing keeps them down better than rabbit - trapping, they being frequently caught in running in and out of rabbit-holes. Where stoats and weasels abound, it is most desirable to have a few flat stones or flags in suitable places, propped up by pieces of stick set with the old figure-of-four trap. The slightest disturbance fetches the flag down, and the victim is at once crushed to death.

The hedgehog is another species of vermin destructive to game. Its depredations are chiefly confined to nest-harrying. The amount of mischief done in a game-preserve by hedgehogs is great. Again and again I have trapped them, using eggs as a bait, and have seen one in a pheasant's nest devouring the eggs. This was on the Ladykirk estate, in Berwick-shire. The hen was sitting by the roadside, where she was seen daily by passers-by "in the know." On nearing the spot one evening, my attention was attracted by seeing the pheasant flying, or rather jumping up, flapping her wings, and making a chirring noise. On going forward, I found the eggs scattered in all directions, and some of them smashed in the scuffle, while a hedgehog was regaling him-self in the nest. Discovering my presence, he gradually curled himself into a bristly ball; but, needless to say, he got short shrift.

The hedgehog has been known to kill very young hares and rabbits, and even half-grown pheasants. Not only so, but it has frequently been found enter-ing coops and killing barn-door hens while acting as foster-mothers to young pheasants. The hedgehog's staple foods are snails, slugs, and beetles, but, as already mentioned, it is fond of flesh and eggs. Many people assert that it devours fruit, but, so far as my experience goes,—and I have dissected the stomachs of a large number,—it does not eat any-thing of a vegetable nature except small quantities of grass, which, I presume, are swallowed when it is grubbing for beetles among the roots.

Another enemy to game is the rat. After the rat is full-grown it acquires an appetite for flesh, and kills any young game it may come across, whether it be winged or four-footed. Rats are becoming a much more formidable enemy of the game-preserver than they used to be, as now they are burrowing more in hedgerows, so that it is difficult for partridges to nest and successfully hatch their young. The reason for this is obvious: the modern use of cement has quite baffled them in trying to undermine granary and stable floors; while sewer-pipes have displaced old-fashioned conduits, so that they no longer find farm-steadings a congenial home. They therefore take possession of rabbit-holes, where, in many cases, they are allowed to harbour and breed without restraint. Prior to the passing of the Ground Game Act, rabbits were in most cases killed by the use of traps, with the result that many rats were secured. Nowadays, rabbits on a farm are generally let to professional rabbit-catchers, who kill them in a simpler way, namely, by snares, with the result that rats get off scot free. A large East Lothian farmer who had the shooting on his farm informed me that he would not allow a snare to be set. In trapping the rabbits the previous year, the man he employed caught 114 large rats. What the result would have been had these rats been allowed to remain and breed, it is not difficult to imagine. No effort should therefore be spared in order to kill down this species of vermin.

Game also suffers, though not to a large extent, from

adders. I have seen one kill very young grouse and
black game, and on dissection found that another
had swallowed three nearly fledged larks. As the
hand of everyone is against adders, nobody misses a
chance of killing them whenever an opportunity presents itself. A reward of 6d. or 1s. a tail will stimulate
the attention of shepherds and keepers to them.

At the head of the list of birds of prey stands
the golden eagle. As already said, this bird has
suffered much persecution on account of its depredations among lambs, and is now so scarce that many
of our largest proprietors are preserving it. It is
gratifying to all lovers of natural history that this
should be so. At the same time, a pair of eagles
do incalculable damage to a grouse-moor, and more
especially a driving moor. I have frequently seen
drives destroyed by an eagle crossing the moor in
aërial circles in the distance. The circumstance of
their flying about drives the grouse from that
locality, as they shrewdly regard the presence of
the eagle to be incompatible with their security.
Some years ago I introduced seventeen mountain
hares, from Dalnaspidal and Castle Menzies moors,
in Perthshire, to Hoy, the most southerly isle of the
Orcadian archipelago. Being very prolific, the hares
soon increased to considerable numbers, when a pair
of eagles made their appearance and nested in the

Kame rock, on the north end of the island. They had long since deserted Hoy as a nesting-place, but the introduction and increase of hares again attracted them to this rock-bound island. The hares were quickly decimated, and the proprietor is most anxious that the eagles should there find a congenial home. This is certain, however — one cannot have both eagles and hares, and it is for the proprietor to say which he prefers. I am no advocate for the destruction of the eagle, but, being gluttonous birds, they are frequently captured in traps set for foxes.

The peregrine falcon is a very difficult bird to deal with, nesting generally in inaccessible precipices out of reach of the keeper. As he scorns to be attracted by any bait unless killed by himself, it is exceedingly difficult to get rid of this most dreaded enemy of grouse. I know of places where peregrines breed, and even if one is shot off her eggs, the male immediately starts in search of another mate. I have known five hen birds killed out of the same nest in succession, so mates must be plentiful somewhere. When they are allowed to rear their young, a heavy toll is taken from the number of grouse on the surrounding moor. The fastest cock grouse that ever flew has no more chance before the peregrine than a rat has before a terrier in an open field. Only those who have concealed themselves near the eyrie of this bird, and with a telescope watched the number of

victims brought to the nestlings, have any conception
of the havoc they commit among winged game.   I
once sat for hours with a glass and watched what was
carried to the eyrie by the peregrine.   In five hours
I saw five grouse brought, and it was interesting
to note how dexterously he transferred them to his
mate, which flew out of the eyrie and met him in
mid-air.   When the young are able to use their
wings, they fly out and snatch the prey from their
parents in the same manner.   Notwithstanding the
depredations among grouse, when in coveys, by the
peregrine when providing for its nestlings, it is in
the spring months that most damage is done, as he
then breaks up the pairs, it being almost certain that
either the cock or the hen will fall a victim.

How, then, are peregrines to be got rid of ?   This
is the question pressing for solution, on a moor where
they take up their abode.   Preparatory to nesting,
these birds are sometimes seen flying about the top of
a cliff.   I would therefore recommend a number of
cairns to be built with stones to a height of from four
to five feet, so as to be out of the way of sheep.
These cairns should taper to the top, and be capped
with a turf or divot, in which a hole should be cut
out.   A trap should be placed in this hole and
covered as carefully as possible, when it will be found
that the peregrine will frequently be caught.   I have
known many peregrines killed in this manner.   As

these traps are generally set in high altitudes, exposed
to the sweeping blasts, there is a difficulty in keeping
them covered with earth or other suitable material.
The peregrine is a 'cute bird, hence the necessity
for careful covering.

The sparrow-hawk, the merlin, and the kestrel are
the only other birds of prey which it is necessary
to refer to here, other species being now regarded as
raræ aves. The two first mentioned are both very
destructive among young game, and it is most
essential that they should be kept down. Sparrow-
hawks are exceptionally destructive, and whenever
they make their appearance in the "warbling grove
it is only for the purpose of depredation, and they
are gloomy intruders on the general joy of the land-
scape." I have found the remains of over twenty
young pheasants at the nest of a sparrow-hawk, and
have frequently seen him carrying off blackbirds
and thrushes, it being painful to hear the piteous
screams of the victims as they were borne off in the
cruel talons of the hawk. It will thus be seen that
the successful rearing of game is impossible when
this bird is allowed to exist. The vigilance of the
keeper is therefore necessary to find out the nesting-
place, and when this is accomplished the destruction
of the pair of birds is a simple matter. To put the
hen bird off the nest, then conceal oneself within
range and shoot her as she returns, is the general

6

mode of procedure. If this can be done at night, so much the better, as by being in concealment before daylight the following morning the cock bird will make his appearance, generally affording an easy shot. Many prefer to trap the cock bird on the nest, which is easily done. On dissecting the last sparrow-hawk I shot, the crop was found to contain the entire wing and other parts of a young grouse, while in the gizzard were the remains of small birds and other matter partly assimilated.

The merlin—the smallest British bird of prey—is a handsome bird. He is, however, a merciless tyrant among small birds and young game, and his presence cannot be permitted by the game-preserver. This bird, as far as my experience goes, breeds on the ground, generally in the bank of a gully in the open. It is asserted that merlins occasionally breed in rocks and trees, but this has never come under my observation.

The kestrel is the most common of our British hawks. He is a pretty object, for who does not love to see him hover? I am unwilling to shoot kestrels, as in the crop and gizzard of those I have killed I have found that mice, beetles, and caterpillars were usually present. It cannot be denied, however, that when catering for their hungry nestlings, young game are carried off in large numbers. That distinguished naturalist, the late Duke of Argyll, instructed his keepers not to kill kestrels, as they were harmless to game. His Grace, however, changed his mind on the head-keeper showing him the remains of many grouse at a kestrel's nest. When the kestrel makes a practice of visiting a field where pheasants are being reared, he is even worse than the sparrow - hawk. The latter comes at pretty regular intervals, and the keeper can depend upon him coming. Unless he be fired at, he will return to the same part of the field, frequently to the same coop, so that, as a rule, he is easily shot. The kestrel, however, is quite different in his habits. He may come twice within an hour, and perhaps not for a day or two. He is much more wary, perches on a tree and surveys the scene, or hovers to mark his prey, darts upon it with unerring aim, and is then off like an arrow. The least movement alarms him, and he suspects any unusual object. If fired at and missed, it takes some ingenuity to get him. Fortunately, he does not take young pheasants after they are about a fortnight old, in this being unlike the sparrow-hawk, which takes them till they are as large as he is fit to carry. Still, I do not advocate the destruction of this beautiful bird. Let the keeper find the nest, watch what is brought to it, and use his judgment as to whether or not the death warrant should be pronounced.

The buzzard is not very destructive to winged game; and the kite and hen-harrier are now so rare that I do not urge their extermination.

The raven is the largest of the corvidæ, and well known for its cruel rapacity on sheep-farms. It is not uncommon to find the eyes of sheep and lambs pecked out on the hills where these birds are allowed to exist. They are by no means so scarce as people believe, being still found in large numbers in the mountainous districts of Scotland. I have a couple of them as pets, and dirtier or more cruel ones I never possessed. Strange to say, some of our County Councils are protecting ravens, which act savours of ignorance on their part as to the habits of these birds. The raven nests very early, and with their young broods may be seen flying about from daylight till dark. Indeed, it is surprising how anything escapes them. I have seen a brood of ptarmigan, while enjoying themselves on the mountain tops, suddenly attacked by these sable butchers. The peculiar cry of the old birds, as they tried to lure the ravens away, was of no effect. The young brood squatted out of sight as they best could, but the keen eyes of the ravens soon discovered them, and the helpless ptarmigan were duly gobbled up. I managed to shoot one as they circled near my place of concealment, and in the gizzard I found a brace of young ptarmigan which had been swallowed

whole. The same tactics are followed with a covey
of grouse, and it is easy to see that a heavy toll must
be taken off by ravens in those districts where they
abound.

The hoodie-crow and the carrion-crow may be
bracketed with the raven as enemies of game. The
destruction to grouse eggs by these birds is incalculable. Sometimes a hoodie's nest will escape the
vigilance of the keeper. In such a case I have seen
the shells of hundreds of grouse eggs at a spring a
short distance from the nest. It will thus be evident
how impossible it is for game to be reared with
carrion-crows in the district. Young grouse are
picked up by these birds, even after they
are half - grown. I have seen a pair of hoodies
endeavouring to get at young grouse which were
pretty well grown, and had got their tail feathers.
So resolute were the savage birds in their purpose
that they never observed me, though I was concealed
within forty yards. The old grouse succeeded in
driving the crows off before they got a young
one. The siege continued for fully twenty minutes,
when one of the crows, in circling round, at last
got his eye on me, and uttered that peculiar call to
his mate, when they both quickly winged their way
up the glen. On going to the spot, I found a lot of
feathers lying about, and certainly but for my presence
they would have succeeded in their merciless work.

Setting the game-preserver aside, the destruction of these birds is necessary in the interest of the stock-farmer. Recently, on the farm of Cardon, in Peeblesshire, shortly before lambing, a blackfaced ewe had both her eyes pecked out by a hoodie-crow. Fortunately she was discovered alive, and with careful nursing the animal recovered and gave birth to a lamb, which she successfully reared. When the shepherd called for her, it was interesting to see her run and eat porridge out of a basin. Writing on the 5th October last, the owner of the ewe says : " This spring, on my return from the curling tour in Canada, a blackfaced ewe hogg had been treated in the same barbarous way, and had to be destroyed."

The magpie feeds much in the same manner as the hoodie, though it searches amongst underwood more, in order to get at the nests of small birds. The nests of the pheasant and partridge are very frequently discovered by the magpie's sharp, piercing eyes, after which shells will be found minus the contents. The vigilance of the keeper should never relax so long as his ground is infested by any of the corvidæ species. Though he should manage to shoot the hen bird off her nest, he must not imagine that he has destroyed the brood for that year. Another mate will soon be found, and hatching will go on. I have repeatedly shot a magpie off her eggs, and in a few days a second one shared the same fate. There appears to be a registry for unmarried magpies somewhere, as no sooner is one shot than another one is secured, and domestic arrangements go on as before. A pair of magpies recently nested in a tree close to my home. When the process of hatching was commenced, I had the bird disturbed and shot as she flew from the nest. Early the following morning a number of magpies appeared, and a great deal of hilarious chattering around the nest indicated to my mind that, in "pyet" language, a wedding was going on. The hilarity was brought to a sudden termination by a shot from the centre of a holly bush, when they quickly dispersed, minus one which fell to the ground. This continued in the early morning for a week, during which no fewer than six magpies were secured. Though I have all my life trapped crows and magpies with bits of rabbit and other flesh, eggs have an irresistible attraction for these birds.

With regard to owls, much diversity of opinion exists as to the damage they do to game. Many naturalists assert that they are perfectly harmless, but, as the result of practical observation, I fearlessly assert that they are wrong. I would not shoot an owl on any consideration, and they are in great numbers at my home, where they breed in holes in the old trees. (The tawny species is here referred to.)   At the same time, were pheasants or partridges being reared, or a large head of game expected, owls would not receive the same generous treatment. In Sir Herbert Maxwell's book already alluded to, the *Memories of the Months*, when writing on owls the author dwells at considerable length on the habits of these birds.   Much as I respect this distinguished writer, I regret that, as a Scotsman, he does not give us the result of practical observation in his native country.   Instead of this, he prefers to quote from a German author, Dr. Altum.   He states that this German doctor examined 210 pellets of the tawny owl and 706 pellets of the barn-owl, and goes on to enumerate the number of mice, amounting to thousands, found in these pellets.   Why such a recognised authority should go to the Continent, where birds of the singing class are conspicuous by their absence, in order to find the pellets of owls, requires some explanation.   Surely this Scottish naturalist could have found owls and made his observations on his own extensive estates, instead of having them "made in Germany."   I have all my life picked up the pellets of owls to examine them, and have found the remains of all song-birds.   One picked up the other day contained the feet and feathers of a thrush.   One sentence in the book above quoted would seem to indicate that the author had been nodding.   He says that he does not doubt

that if any young chick or pheasant "comes in the
way, the owl will pounce on it and enjoy it mightily.
But," adds Sir Herbert, "young chicks are not, or ought
not to be, abroad in the night, which is the only time
that most kinds of owls can hunt." It is exceedingly
unfortunate that distinguished authors should record
their opinions instead of their observations. I have
no desire to dogmatise on this subject, but have
again and again watched tawny owls at the nest, as
well as taken them from the nest and placed them
in a box, when from a window I could observe
what the parent birds brought to them for food.
They usually commenced to carry food to the
young between three and four in the afternoon. I
therefore exhort all young keepers to do the same—
to watch and carefully note the victims of the owl,
and so explode the theories of mere litterateurs. It
will be no use the young keeper doing this for one
season only, as the abundance or scarcity of mice
depends largely on climatic influences, and when
mice are plentiful there is no doubt that large
numbers are devoured by owls. The results of my
observations as to the food of owls compel me to
include the following: young hares, young rabbits,
bats, young pigeons both wild and tame, ducklings,
thrushes, blackbirds, sparrows, and all the smaller
birds, moths and beetles. It is right also to mention
that in some seasons a very large number of mice—

both the vole and the long-tailed field-mouse—are included in the owl's bill of fare.

The tawny owl has also been known to kill full-grown pheasants. In a large open pheasantry at Inveraray, Mr. Cameron, the head-keeper to His Grace the Duke of Argyll, and an observant naturalist, discovered that hen pheasants were being killed and eaten by some animal, though he could not at first make out which. He suspected rats, and had traps set to try to secure the depredator, but without success. One morning, however, after a fall of snow, he found another dead pheasant, but the mark of the feathers revealed the fact that owls had been the murderers. He therefore baited a trap with the partly eaten pheasant, and erected a pole near by, on the top of which he placed a pole-trap. By seven o'clock that night a tawny owl was caught in the pole-trap, and in the morning another was in the baited trap. At the same place a number of ducks were being hand-reared and enclosed by wire-netting, to prevent them straying. The ducklings were fed at six o'clock in the morning, and between nine and ten in the forenoon ten of them were missing. Two keepers concealed themselves, and very shortly a hen gave the alarm which made them look out. So stealthily and noiselessly did an owl glide in, that he was not seen or heard till he was in the act of pouncing on a lot of ducklings which were clustered together, basking in the sun. He was so near his quarry that the keeper could not shoot without killing the ducks, but his sudden movement frightened the owl off, when he made straight for a tree near where the other keeper was concealed and perched above him. Needless to say, his ravages among ducklings were avenged. As I recorded in the *Scotsman* some time ago, a tawny owl picked up a squirrel on the public road at midday; and I have discovered, by placing weasels and short-eared owls together, that the weasels were killed and devoured by the owls. The short-eared owl is a winter visitor, and as it is only on rare occasions that it breeds in this country and has a chance of seeing young game, I would plead for its protection. I would also spare the barn owl, for the following reasons : he is a splendid mouse destroyer, is now rare, and is a beautiful object in nature. Long-eared owls are very destructive among pigeons, and occasionally among young game, but the sparing of them must be left to the good sense of the keeper, who should endeavour to satisfy himself as to how far their destruction would be justified. The same remark applies to the jay, the rook, and the jackdaw.

Legislation has recently been cutting very queer antics. A Bill has passed through Parliament, and been put upon the Statute Book, abolishing the pole-trap, or any trap put on a tree or in an elevated position. It now reads—

(1) From and after the passing of this Act every person who on any pole, tree, or cairn of earth or stones, shall affix, place, or set, any spring trap, gin, or other similar instrument calculated to inflict bodily injury to any wild bird coming in contact therewith, and every person who shall knowingly permit or suffer, or cause any such trap to be so affixed, placed, or set, shall be guilty of an offence, and shall be liable on summary conviction to a penalty not exceeding 40s., and for a second or subsequent offence to a penalty not exceeding £5.

(2) Every offence under this Act may be prosecuted under the provisions of sect. 5 of the Wild Birds Protection Act, 1880 ; and

(3) This Act may be cited as the Wild Birds Protection Act, 1904, and shall be construed with the Wild Birds Protection Acts 1880 to 1902.

This pseudo-humanitarian sentiment has for its object the prevention of cruelty. No one will deny that trapping in any shape is cruel, but a modern pole-trap is more exempt from the charge of cruelty than any other form of gin or snare. Mr. C. M. Pelham Burn, the inventor of the humane pole-trap, used it with great success on his moors in Morayshire. It differs from the ordinary pole-trap in that the jaws strike high and catch the bird by the middle, so

causing instant death. The Bill in question has,
however, now become law, and the trapping of a
sparrow-hawk on her nest, or of a peregrine on a
cairn, is, of course, illegal, so that these tyrants
among bird life, especially the latter, has practically
free scope to butcher our beautiful grouse, which
constitute one of the greatest attractions of our
Scottish Highlands.

It was surprising how this Bill was supported in
both Houses of Parliament by members who possess
a large amount of territory in the Highlands of
Scotland. The many hundreds of thousands of
acres which constitute the rugged background of
our Scottish scenery, and which are in many cases
owned by members of our legislature, might at all
events have been regarded as a sufficient sanctuary
for the protection of rare birds and beasts. Such,
however, was not the case, and the poor lairds who
own a few thousand acres of heather must submit to
their grouse, which in many instances constitute
their bread and butter, being torn to pieces by birds
of prey. We have here an amount of selfishness on
the part of several of our large Scottish proprietors
for which I, for one, feel humbled and ashamed.
Surely they might have protected birds of prey in
their own forests, and left it to the discretion of their
poorer neighbours to do as they pleased. Intoxicated
with their own importance, however, a few pseudo-

humanitarian M.P.'s brought in a Bill which has passed into law abolishing the pole-trap. Whether they will instruct their keepers to act in accordance with law, and refrain from setting traps in "an elevated position," had better be left unasked. In a recent conversation with a keeper to one of those who voted for the abolition of the pole-trap, I remarked he would have to set an example and refrain from trapping hawks. With a peculiar twinkle in his eye, he significantly replied, " Imphm." [1]

After a fall of snow the young keeper should be out at daylight to note his observations of footprints. When the ground is covered as with a sheet of soft white paper, impressions of all birds and beasts are easily made upon its surface, and can then be read as in a book. A study of the tracks of the various kinds of vermin is most interesting, and every keeper should be able to discriminate at once what made the impression. Many traits in the habits of birds and animals, unobserved at other times, can then be accurately noted. A study should also be made of the disturbed cries of every denizen of the wood, as these constitute a valuable guide in detecting the enemies of game. The

---

[1] A new snare instead of pole-trap is a forked stick, forks two inches long ; smear forks with bird-lime. The vermin alights on centre of fork, closes its wings, which get smeared with lime, and has a difficulty in using them again, and is generally found lying close to fork.— A. S. W., P. J. M.

intelligent keeper knows at once if a stray cat, dog, or fox is in the wood. The warning cackle of a cock pheasant, the screeching of a jay, the excited piping of blackbirds and other birds, or the disturbed movements of any living thing, quickly notify to his practised ear that an enemy is abroad.

Properly understood and judiciously carried out, man's dominion over the beasts of the field and the fowls of the air is merciful as contrasted with that of the struggle for existence and the survival of the fittest. In the interests of the food-supplies of the nation, and having regard to the pleasure and profit of mankind, it is the duty of all to preserve birds and animals which are useful by destroying those that prey upon them.

NOTES

NOTES

CHAPTER VIII

THE DOG,—FROM A GAMEKEEPER'S POINT OF VIEW

By Dr. CHARLES REID

TIME was when the dog was perhaps of more importance in the field than it is now, when our grandfathers sallied forth at break of day adorned in those quaint and wondrous garments which still excite our admiration, if not our envy, and with his trusty Joe Manton and all the varied paraphernalia deemed necessary accompanying, with, and by no means least, a dog, most probably trained by himself, and from whose prowess and excellence a large measure of his enjoyment was sure to be derived. And in the evening, over his pipe and his home-brewed, did not the mighty deeds of "Don" and "Carlo" figure fully more prominently in the conversation than in these degenerate days? Most of us can recall and picture the satisfaction of Charles St. John, after watching the futile efforts of a brother sportsman on the other side of the river

Findhorn trying to retrieve in vain several active "runners" in a turnip-field, when, having crossed the river and politely offered his assistance, he, with the aid of his "poodle," brought them to bag. Other men, other ways. Still the conditions are not so changed that we can get through a day's sport without the assistance of our canine friends, and it is in the hope of bringing the importance of this still more prominently before a very intelligent class of men that we are encouraged to write these few pages. The average sportsman is a tender-hearted man, of sensitive disposition, and nothing mars the day's pleasure more than the feeling that, owing to having inferior dogs, a number of wounded animals have not been picked up, and if, as probably he will be, a man who shoots a good deal, he cannot help contrasting the result with such and such a place where he has just been shooting, and which, owing to the superior training of his friend's dogs, was the source of much comment and much satisfaction to the various "guns." How often has the present writer heard in the smoking-room this remark, made too by one who, from his experience, was a capable judge: " I have only known three keepers in my life to whom I could intrust a dog to train for me." This, if true, shows how little the subject is attended to by gamekeepers as a class, and the present writer will sufficiently indorse it by remarking

that the attention paid to this subject by gamekeepers as a whole is far below what it ought to be.
I do not altogether blame them, but, on the contrary,
I believe that owners and shooting tenants are solely
responsible for this state of affairs. Not one in ten
of shooting men takes any interest in this subject, and
it has become so common for tenants to depend on
getting their dogs from dealers at the beginning of
each season regardless alike of their appearance or
their qualifications—in fact, they probably never set
eyes on the animals till they, the sportsmen, arrived
at their shooting quarters. Still, apart from your
peripatetic sportsman, we have a large class who are
more interested in their dogs, and who wish to see
them not only better looked after, but better trained,
who do not wish to have their sensitive feelings
disturbed and their sport marred either by the unnecessary loss of wounded birds, or their minds
haunted by the frantic yells of "Carlo" under the
lash, even though the flagellation was well merited.

Even from a commercial point of view, it is important to consider this question, because the value
of game, *unnecessarily* lost, at the end of the season
may represent a total which would have been many
times the value or keep of a good dog.

It is part of a good keeper's duties to be able to
train a dog both for the moor and the covert, just as
well as he can rear pheasants or trap vermin; and yet

how many do we find thoroughly proficient in these latter who have the most elementary ideas on the subject of the former? By contrast, and not by any means by way of disparagement, we would point out another class, who, with no better material to work upon, if so good, get on the whole better results. We refer to shepherds and their collies. We hear of the sagacity and cleverness of the collie, but feel certain that the great majority of gamekeepers will bear us out when we state that the average sporting dog, pointer, retriever, or spaniel, is capable of a higher education than their much-vaunted canine brother, and that, as a rule, under more adverse conditions. Still the average collie is better trained than the average sporting dog. The explanation is not far to seek. More work is put on him, and so gradually that his brain can absorb and remember—he is kept up to the mark by having to do certain things daily, and not allowed to forget—he is not taken out on a string half a dozen times a year and expected to do a dozen different things of which he never learnt the rudiments. Many readers may suggest: " But we have not the shepherd's time to do this, with so many other duties." Quite true, but it is not necessary. Much can be done at odd times in the spring before the nesting season, and again in the early autumn before shooting begins. A few lessons during ordinary exercise and at odd times have a wonderful

effect, and these, as is a mistake often made, not left
till the shooting day, when the excitement caused
by the appearance of game and the shooting is
sufficient to absorb the dog's whole mind. However,
later on we refer to this subject more fully.

Exhibition of Dogs.

It is not necessary in a work of this kind to discuss
the vexed question of the influence of canine exhibitions on the sporting dog. Much good has been
done by these, but, alas, much evil. The sporting
dog, however, has suffered less than most other
breeds, and on the whole, in the writer's opinion,
distinct benefit has accrued, except in the case of the
spaniel breed. This is due to the fact that these
others have not been tampered with to the same
extent by "fanciers" as the spaniel has, and the
result is seen in the numerous grotesque creatures
which appear on the bench, and with considerable
difficulty are able to walk a few times round the
judge's ring. With these, however, the gamekeeper
has nothing to do. The breed is right enough, but
by selection a non-sporting class has produced an
animal unfitted for work owing to their (the exhibitors') want of knowledge and the apathy of the class
who do know. One must remember, however, that
those are selected specimens, and that it is possible to
find animals of the same breed which are quite fit and

able for field work. The majority of our judges of sporting dogs are men who are good sportsmen, and who judge the animals from a working point of view. So also are the majority of the exhibitors of sporting dogs. For this reason the type of our best animals which win on the bench is an improvement on the dog of thirty years ago, and there is undoubtedly greater uniformity. We would advise, therefore, our readers to attend these exhibitions, not to walk round when the dogs are benched, but to make a point of being present at the judging, to plant himself stolidly down opposite the ring and to scrutinise carefully every animal in it. If in addition he can get a friend with more knowledge than himself to point out the good and the bad points, he will find that his few hours have not been misspent, and have its own reward in the future, when he comes to select a puppy from a litter to train himself. He will then appreciate what a heavy-loaded shoulder, slack loins, or bad feet mean in a hard day's work. This is by no means learnt in a day, though some persons have an instinctive eye for the points of an animal, and are, like the poet, born, not made. Still the average gamekeeper is an intelligent man, and given the interest and the fact that this knowledge is going to be useful to him in his profession, he will soon be able to select an animal whose outward appearance at least fits him for the purpose required.

Selection of Dog.

Without going into unnecessary details, perhaps a few of the salient points which occur to the writer may be of service in choosing a sporting dog, whether pointer, setter, or retriever. Suppose you have the choice of a litter of puppies old enough to train, and therefore of an age to enable one to judge what the future animal will develop into—ask the owner to let them all run free in a paddock, and carefully watch their movements. Assuming that the puppies are all in good health, not only do you learn very quickly which is the best mover, but you note also the disposition and temperament of the various animals. Look at that bold young scamp, full of life, racing round as to the head of the others, chasing every butterfly, leaf, or moving thing, and contrast him with this other timid, nervous creature, afraid of his own shadow. It doesn't require an expert to tell you which will give you most trouble and develop into the better animal. If you find several of the former kind, then so much the better. You can now look over them at close quarters. Let us hope your fancy has a bright, full, intelligent, dark eye. As in the higher animals, including human beings, the eye is a real index of the character. Most judges object to a light yellow eye or a small sunken eye ; and rightly so, because as a general rule you will find the former wild, erratic animals, and the latter dour and stubborn. The head should be big, with plenty of room for brains, and if nicely rounded over the skull proper, preferable to an angular one. The tendency at the present time is to have a long head in all our breeds, but the fallacious and evil part of it is this elongation at the expense of the skull proper. It began with collies, then fox-terriers and Scotch terriers, and has even invaded our sporting breeds. The moment a dog shows some width between the ears, and he naturally gets thicker somewhat as he gets older, then he is supposed by certain breeders to be "past." In the same manner, when he develops some muscle at the sides of his head to use those long jaws, he has become "coarse" and unfit for exhibition. Could anything be more absurd? We, however, have something different in our eye,—we require all the brains we can get in our dog, and we are going, therefore, to select that puppy with the big head, skull nicely rounded, with a muzzle of moderate proportions, terminating in a nose of good size and open nostrils. Whether retriever or pointer, we want a level mouth, neither undershot nor overshot—the former condition is almost never seen, but the so-called snipey muzzle is a common defect in our retrievers at the present time, and a bad one.

The *neck* should be of a good length to give "carriage" to the animal, and set on *shoulders* which slope well back, and the tops of the shoulder-blades should come high up and fairly close together. As in a hunter, you cannot have pace and staying power with the reverse of these.

The *chest*, looking at it from the front, should be narrow; but behind the shoulders should be deep from above downwards, and ribs springing well outwards, giving a good "barrel." This should be continued right back to the free or short ribs. If deficient there and great apparent length in the loins, you have a "slack" animal, without endurance.

The *loins* should therefore be firm, almost slightly arched, with plenty of room from the projecting *iliac* bones to the root of the tail.

The *thighs* should be strong and muscular, with hocks well let down—neither "cow-hocked" nor bending outwards and short below. If your dog is to gallop freely through heather or jump a fence as in the case of a retriever, he must be good in his hind quarters.

And the *feet*, too, are of the first importance. No matter how good he is in the foregoing points, with bad feet he will be a failure. See that those are of a suitable size, compact, toes close, not spreading and arched.

The chief points, therefore, to be desired in a
working dog are a good head and eye, light
shoulders, strong loins, powerful thighs, and compact feet. Given those in our chosen puppy, and
we start well with an animal better than our
neighbour's, and we hope to make him above the
average in other respects.

Training a Dog.

It would be quite impossible in our limited space
to give full instructions on this subject; and moreover, there exist so many capital treatises on this
subject that it is unnecessary. In our opinion,
therefore, it will serve a more useful purpose to
point out some of the errors which many trainers
make in the training of their dogs, and, if possible,
to suggest the remedy. At this stage, we would
like to recall to any novice the importance of an
aid of great value in the hands of our grandfathers,
and which unfortunately, in our opinion, has fallen
into disuse. We refer to the use of the check-cord.
By its means the most refractory puppy can be
brought to reason in a third of the time and with
a minimum of labour, and certainly with greater
comfort to the pupil and his master. We shall
refer to this again.

"*Down*" *and* "*Down Charge.*" — It does seem a

simple matter to put a dog down and to keep him there, but in actual practice what do we find? Not one in ten will do so and remain there till they are ordered otherwise. In the old muzzle-loading days, of course, it was absolutely essential to give the guns time to reload, and, in our opinion, should be strictly enforced, particularly in the case of pointer or setter. In training any dog, including retrievers, by teaching them this habit early you obtain a command early of the animal which makes succeeding lessons infinitely more simple. Begin by putting the puppy down at your feet, gradually increasing the distance; if he moves take him back to the same spot. You may move about, keeping your eye on him at first till you are able to go any distance without movement on his part. On no account must the dog be allowed to move till he gets a command either by "signal or call."

The value of this lesson is appreciated when the dog is taken first among game. The trainer must be consistent, and what is at first very irksome to your excitable and high-couraged youngster in a very short time becomes a mechanical habit. Sometimes you will have difficulty with a timid, nervous puppy in preventing him from running into your feet. In such a case avoid any punishment, but patiently return him to the original spot. If he persists and you punish him, then he probably bolts. Rather than punish, try the cord and hitch it round a peg or post so that when he moves a pull in the other direction will show him what you wish.

From this to " Down charge " becomes a very easy step indeed, again remembering that he is not to be allowed to move till commanded by signal or " call." The advantage of firing some caps or small charges during this early training is twofold ; you decrease the risk of causing gun shyness and you avoid the excitement which it causes in the presence of game. In our opinion a very common mistake is to take a young dog to the second part of his education before the first is complete and endeavour to teach those primary lessons in the field. This is undoubtedly wrong, and renders the task a difficult one, which is otherwise so simple. The advantages of having a dog which drops to hand or " shot " in the field are sufficiently obvious. In practice what do we usually find ? " Duke " or " Don," if he does " down charge," does so only for a moment, and then he is off to have a look at a dead bird, putting up some others on the way, or the repeated shouts of his trainer effectually does this. In extreme cases we perhaps have a race between master and dog who is to get the bird first, and if Don wins the feathers begin to fly.

Use of " Call" or "Whistle." — We cannot too strongly impress also the proper use of a suitable call instead of the human voice. It is too heart-breaking for words to find a whole hillside cleared of grouse, covey after covey of grouse responding to the frantic shouts of " Don," " Don," " Heel," " Heel," or to witness a fine "show" of partridges, which you have with infinite labour driven into the "roots," "clearing" out in all haste at the end. Even more marked is the result of the human voice in snipe-shooting. A dog readily answers, and once he knows its use, if he fails to respond to a second call, a little gentle reminder is necessary. The two most common mistakes made are the *too frequent use of the call*, which causes negligence on the dog's part; and, secondly, failure to moderate the volume according to the distance between master and pupil. Naturally, if the sound is used to its full extent when the animal is a few yards off, it does not impress the animal when he is at a distance, perhaps, of one hundred yards. The most successful trainers of dogs which we have met were very quiet in their manner, and used signs as much as possible—only resorting to the call when impossible to attract the dog's attention by hand.

Range.—Most young dogs will run out freely, and if not, then the example of an old dog will soon be followed. Where many err is in allowing the dog at first to pursue his erratic course, and allow him to believe that he is hunting for his own amusement, and not yours. Make a point of starting the dog

to range to one side or other, and see that he does
it. For some reason or other, many dogs will run
a short distance and then turn sharp to the other
side, thereby missing a particular piece of ground
which you wish him to take. Call him up at once,
and see that he does what you wish. In the same
way get him into the habit of mechanically crossing
his ground thoroughly, and later, when he increases
in wisdom, you may permit him more freedom of
judgment. Neither is it good to allow your dog to
be working half a mile away, either on the beat
below you or the one above which you intend to take
next. By teaching the proper "range" thoroughly
at first you avoid this, nor do you find him at the
far end of a field of "roots" before you have hardly
entered. The nature of the work required will
determine the requisite training; you require a
more bold and free-running dog for a moor, where
birds are few and far between, than for a well-
stocked moor or on low ground, where you are
working in enclosures. For this reason your training will be different on a well-stocked moor on the
mainland, from what it would be if moor shooting
were on the western islands.

Pointing.—As a rule this is not a difficult matter
to teach—most puppies will stand on scenting game,
and the example of an old dog may be useful. Here
the use of the check-cord is of the greatest value, for

it enables you to steady him for any length of time
you wish and effectually prevent chasing birds when
they rise, rendering excessive punishment unnecessary.
A good plan is to find your birds with an old steady
dog, which the young one is quick to observe, then
with the end of the cord in your hand you "steady"
him also for a few minutes—the chances are that he
also gets their scent, then flush your birds, putting
both dogs " down," and carefully mark them down.
Now take up the old dog, go to the place where
you know they are and allow the young one to find
them, taking care that the end of the cord is within
reach. Whenever he winds them, then repeat "Steady"
or "To ho," and repeat the previous performance.
Having done this, the rest is easy. Two lessons of
this kind are often sufficient, and, assuming that this
has been done in the spring, when birds sit so well
before the nesting season, it will only require a few
points before the Twelfth to produce a dog that is
fit to take his turn with the others. The only precaution necessary is not to run him too long and too
much. No man can have really good dogs who
keeps them going when they are tired — nothing
spoils his ranging sooner. When on this subject we
would again point out the importance of thoroughly
teaching his dog those preliminary lessons before
he is taken to game. Very little of the latter is
necessary before he is fit to be shot over—much less
8

than most persons imagine. Many owners and tenants of shootings refuse to allow their keepers to train dogs on their ground in the belief that it disturbs and injures their sport. That it does so undoubtedly if a brace, perhaps, of well-grown lively puppies are taken on to a moor and allowed to career wildly after every moving object, but knowing as we do, and have tried now to show, that so little is necessary if the greater part of the training is done, as it should be, *before they see game*, we think that keepers should be allowed considerably more latitude in this respect, and the benefits to the owner in having better dogs would be the immediate result, with a handsome addition to his servant's yearly income.

"*Heel.*"—It is also unnecessary to give instructions how to keep a dog to heel, but again in practice how unsatisfactory is the observance of this simple rule! As we have already pointed out in the abuse of the "call," the constant repetition produces neglect to obey. The dog is called to "heel," which he obeys, perhaps, for thirty seconds, till he finds something attractive to his eyes, or more frequently his nose— he is allowed to do this with impunity till a little more confidence and freedom on his part attracts attention, and he is again called to "heel." Few things are more irritating to good sportsmen who understand the "game" than the misuse of "heel" and the abuse of the " whistle "; and if the user is armed with one of those instruments usually seen in the hands of our friend " Robert," then good-bye to a pleasant day's sport. And yet the remedy is so simple, viz. a little suitable reminder, or, in the case of a shy, timid dog, the use of the check-cord till the habit is fixed. Again, the importance of this it is almost unnecessary to point out, for how often does not the necessity of keeping to " heel " arise in a day's sport either to save the dog himself unnecessary work or for the welfare of the sport itself.

Running in to " Shot."—Of all errors in the training of our dog this is the most common, and probably the worst. Unfortunately, too, when once become a confirmed habit, it is almost impossible to remedy. Of course in the case of a " setting " dog it is not usually so marked, because, unless he has been taught to retrieve, he rarely bolts in at once on his game, but, even in the case of a setter, it may mean a diminished bag through flushing other birds before the guns have reloaded. By insisting on the " down charge," as we have already pointed out, we find the prevention, and the sole cause is the want of consistency on the part of the trainer. On no account should the dog be allowed to move without word of command, and if he does, then let him be punished more or less severely according to the particular temperament of the animal. The punishment may only be a verbal reproof or something more tangible, *but escape one or other he must not.* Here, again, the check-cord is of great value, and if a dog is interrupted when half-way to his game, the effect is more salutary than a dozen severe thrashings.

Over-training.—Occasionally one sees a retriever trained most thoroughly, who does everything he is commanded perfectly, and yet he is of small value at work. Why? Because he is a machine—the dog has no confidence in himself. If put on to find a bird, he gives in at once and returns to heel ; or the moment he loses the scent he looks to his master for guidance. This is pure habit, of course. Had the dog been allowed to use his own judgment—*i.e.* had his master, even though he knew the dog was wrong, allowed him to find out this for himself a few times, he would have produced a better dog.

Use of Eyes instead of Nose.—Also a common error made by many. To save trouble, or, it may be, from delight in seeing the young dog carry so well, he is allowed to retrieve what he *sees*—he does this, per-haps, thirty times for once that he is asked to find something which he hasn't seen fall, or, worse still, is in his view all the time. Should one be astonished, therefore, that his first idea is to use his eyes, and con-tinue to do so, while that cock pheasant is making tracks for the next country, or that winged partridge had made a dozen sharp doubles in the rank turnips?

Had he used his nose at first, he ought to have had that bird in twenty yards instead of delaying the guns for ten minutes or more, probably losing his game altogether. *Another common fault* is in allowing a *young* dog to run too far out to retrieve his game—he sees the bird fall, and is allowed to go ; in many cases he overruns the spot in his keenness. To remedy this he ought to be taken near the place and given the advantage of the wind before he is told to " seek dead." All this should be done *quietly*, and if too impulsive, he should be cautioned with the word " Steady." Undoubtedly some dogs are from the first better than others at marking birds down, but the chief fault lies more with the trainer in not inculcating this habit of " seeking close " at first till he strikes the trail, and then giving him a chance of doing the rest himself. The less the young retriever sees of " fur" at first the better ; indeed many good trainers refuse to allow their dogs to touch hares or rabbits for at least two seasons, and the practice has much to commend it. Probably one sees better-trained retrievers at covert shoots than elsewhere, because unless he is a wise man the owner does not produce his worst on these occasions, and possibly the temptation to run riot is not so great. To make a really good retriever requires much more time and patience than either pointer or setter. Begin early, but be careful not to put so much work on the animal as to produce the effect such as I have already alluded to under "Over-training."

Temperament.—To be really successful with his dogs, the trainer ought to study their character as he would a human being. Like the "higher animal," he has his peculiarities which must be recognised, otherwise a half-trained animal, or even failure, will be the result. How often do we hear that So-and-so is a "good man," but very severe with his dogs? In every litter you will find no two alike, and to mete out the same treatment to all spells failure at once. The trainer who recognises this early saves himself an incalculable amount of trouble and produces better animals.

Choice of Particular Breed.

It is unnecessary to give advice as to a choice of a particular breed. Owners of pointers advance many reasons on behalf of their favourites as against the various breeds of setter, while the owners of the latter are equally strong on the other side. While it may be that on an exceptionally dry moor the shorter-coated animal has a slight advantage, we do not think that this is of great importance, and fancy is allowed to determine the preference. For similar reasons a decision is made between the curly and the heavy-coated retrievers and between the various breeds of spaniel.

Of much greater importance is to satisfy oneself
that the particular animal springs from a *good kind*,
and that from his structure is fitted for the work
required. There is no reason why a dog should not
both be good-looking and a good worker. Many of
our best dogs on the bench are capital workers, and
it is pure ignorance on the part of those who hold
that the whole of our exhibition dogs are useless for
sporting purposes.

Assistance can be got from Books. — The great
body of our gamekeepers are intelligent men, and
thoroughly capable of understanding what is written
on this subject, and they have scope in the numerous
and inexpensive books published on dogs and their
training. Unfortunately, the majority are content to
follow in the footsteps of the "head" with whom they
served their apprenticeship, who, however capable he
was in conducting a grouse drive or rearing pheasants,
had neglected this branch of his trade. This is not
as it should be, and we would again impress on every
keeper who takes a pride in his work the necessity
and the advantages of being "a good man with
dogs." We would advise him to study works such
as *Dog Breaking*, by General Hutchison, or *Training
of Retrievers*, by Colonel Henry Smith, and not merely
to rest content to teach a dog obedience, but by
patience and perseverance to develop to its utmost
the natural intelligence of the animal. His experi-

ence in course of time will tell him that some of his
protégés will not be capable of attaining a high level,
but he will meet with others which respond to all his
care, and in developing whose good qualities the
trainer will feel that he has had a well-merited return
apart from the many encomiums bestowed by his
confrères.

The More Common Ailments of Dogs.

We have not space to treat this subject as fully
as its importance would justify, but probably if we
mention the more common ailments met with in the
dog, and capable of being intelligently treated by the
average gamekeeper, our purpose will best be served.
In this category we include such diseases as Distemper, Dyspepsia, Rickets, Chorea or St. Vitus'
Dance, Fits, Paralysis, Mange, Disorders of Kidneys,
Heart Disease, Dropsy, Congestion of Brain, Constipation, Diarrhœa, etc.

It may be more convenient at this period to give
some remarks on the ailments of puppyhood, which,
as a rule, are simple and not numerous. Many a
good puppy is lost from want of a little care. Occasionally it happens that a puppy is born "tongue-
tacked," and unable to suck properly, which is only
remedied by a "snip" with sharp scissors. The
writer also has known a whole litter lost within a
week of birth owing to the teats of the dams being

so enlarged that the puppies could not get suitable nourishment. This would be likely to happen only in the case of the dam that had previously several litters ; but if she brought other litters up success-fully, on this occasion the true cause might be more easily missed. The remedy was easily found on a future occasion by providing a foster-mother.

Constipation at this early stage sometimes gives trouble, for which a little castor oil is advisable, and it is good practice at any time during this period to do so whenever a puppy is seen to be restless, whining or not sucking with the others. The common mis-take made is doing so when too late. The use of an enema syringe, even the small glass ear-syringe, with soapy warm water, may be found of great value in an urgent case.

Your intelligent and careful keeper will prevent the ordinary ailments of puppyhood better by attention to the dam before their birth, and we would specially point out the advisability of allowing the dam to run about during at least two weeks before the expected arrival of the litter. If asked, however, to what the excessive mortality in puppyhood is due, we would unhesitatingly say *worms*. Here, again, prevention is better than cure. See that the dam is treated for worms before impregnation ; and also recollect that vermin may be the means of introducing these pests, for it has recently been proved conclusively that the "flea" acts as a host during an intermediate stage of the development of the parasite, and it is obvious how both the dam and the puppies can be thus infected. It may be advisable to wait till the puppies are weaned before treating for these, but if necessary, treatment should not be delayed. The most common worm at this period is the "round" worm, pointed at both ends, whose habitat is the stomach and small intestine. Their presence may be noted in the vomit, or later in the fæces, and it is safe to assume that they are present if the puppy is dry in his coat, more or less emaciated, with abdomen over-distended, or accompanied in an extreme case with fits. Santonin is the remedy, given *fasting*, in doses of $\frac{1}{2}$, 1, or 2 grains, according to age and size of puppy. An equal amount of calomel seems to increase the action of the drug, or followed by a small dose of castor oil. If necessary, this should be repeated in a few days.

Rickets is also another common ailment of puppy-hood, and caused by errors usually in diet, and, secondarily, insanitary or unsuitable surroundings. From our experience the former is the usual cause, *i.e.* the food is given in too large quantities and seldom, instead of *small and often*. A puppy after weaning ought to be fed *at least* four times a day till he is three, or even four months old, and thrice daily till six months. Milk should form the chief portion, and the solids increased with his age. If skim milk can only be used, then the fat must be replaced by the addition of cod-liver oil or other fat; and where size is of importance, as in most sporting dogs, great benefit will be derived by the addition of a preparation of hypophosphates, such as the popular Parrish's syrup or Chemical food. We would here emphasise the importance of using new milk as much as possible; no other article of diet can replace it if you wish to do justice to your puppies. The starchy foods, meat, potatoes, etc., may be introduced gradually, but very sparingly at first. Under the *secondary* cause of rickets we would include a damp or cold bed, want of exercise, etc., and though many breeders consider these as the cause of rickets, still, in our opinion, the primary cause is to be found in errors in diet such as we have mentioned, and these last are often contributory. In many otherwise capital kennels the arrangements for the rearing of puppies are too often defective, and if the owner can possibly manage, we advise him to send them out to "walk" at a farmhouse or with a cottager who possesses a cow. At the critical period—between the second and fourth months—the keeper can inspect the puppies every fortnight at least, and remedy any faults in overfeeding, etc. Where possible, also, board them out in pairs for the sake of the additional exercise which they get in playing with each other.

Distemper is the greatest scourge of the canine world, and, unfortunately, the treatment is also far from what it should be. Again, space will not allow us here to go fully into this matter. As in most things where you find such a difference of opinion, the probability is that the right one is still to be discovered. Vaccination with calf lymph has had many advocates, but the balance of opinion is against it being of any value, though we still live in hope that a serum will be found which will do for distemper what antitoxin now does for diphtheria. We would here point out to keepers that distemper is a specific fever caused by the presence of a poison in the system, that the symptoms vary according to the virulence of the epidemic and the particular animal affected—that therefore, to treat the patient intelligently, one must not pin one's faith to So-and-so's ball or powder, but rather skilfully prescribe for each step of the disorder. When the animal is first affected it is good treatment to give a dose of opening medicine, but not a severe purgative; to feed often with light, sloppy food, chiefly of milk or broth. For medicine, half to one tablespoonful of spirit of mindererus twice or thrice daily, and even more often if fever is high. If powder is preferred, then 5 to 10 grains of nitrate of potash may be given at several intervals. In the majority of cases this is sufficient, and a recovery takes place. If cough is troublesome, or the animal is "wheezy," 5 to 10 drops of ipecacuanha wine may be added to the mindererus spirit. In bad forms you may get head symptoms early, when the dog becomes restless, even delirious, and to treat this you may give 10 to 30 grains of bromide alone or with tinct. of hyoscyamus, 10 to 30 minims. Pneumonia is, however, the usual complication in fatal cases, occurring, too, most frequently *after* the acute symptoms have subsided. The ignorant owner thinks that a walk would do the animal good, or even a wash, and the result is disastrous. Prevention here again is the first essential, but if the presence of such a complication is recognised by the rapid and laboured breathing, then apply hot fomentations—remembering, too, that the animal usually lies on the affected side—mustard and whisky; turpentine sprinkled on the hot cloths may be applied, and if necessary, when the case demands, don't hesitate to remove the hair over that side before applying the counter-irritants. Whatever doubt one may have about giving stimulants at the onset of an ordinary pneumonia, there can be none in this form, and we would give it freely,—whisky, port, beef-tea, eggs, etc., in small quantities and at regular intervals. For medicine, strychnia, carbonate of ammonia, etc., have great value, but the former should only be given under skilled advice.

Chorea, or St. Vitus' Dance, is a very common sequel to distemper, and much more intractable than in human beings. When the spasmodic, jerking movements occur during the attack, bromide of potash, in doses already referred to, would be useful, and recently salicylate of soda in 10-grain doses, with twice the amount of bicarbonate of soda, has been found valuable. This should be given three or four times daily, and the dose gradually increased. Iron and arsenic later as a tonic and the latter alone pushed may cure. Fowler's solution in doses of 2–10 m. is given twice daily and increased till it causes redness of eyes or symptoms of irritation of the alimentary tract, such as vomiting, diarrhœa, etc.

For *Fits or Convulsions* occurring in distemper, the treatment already given above under distemper will suffice, and, indeed, in all cases where the cause is not known. The keeper will remember that these are only symptoms, not necessarily an organic disease, and to treat intelligently he will try to find what is causing them, remembering that worms are a very common cause. Again, if the fit occurs soon after a meal in a dog of gross appetite, the treatment is obvious. If in an old dog, and if he has noticed blindness on one side eye, he may suspect some pressure on brain from tumour or other cause. Therefore, find the cause, if possible. Bromide of potash again will be valuable, and may be combined with iodide of potash.

It is unnecessary to go fully into diseases of the heart, kidneys, etc., which really belongs more to the veterinary surgeon. A simple diuretic, such as mindererus spirit or nitre, is useful in relieving kidney irritation such as dogs often suffer from after hard work.

Mange.—This malady is far too common in most kennels, especially when one knows that it is preventible. The so-called red or virulent form is equally easy to check if treated *at once*, though equally difficult later, and we have found the various mercurial ointments the most efficacious. The green oxide of mercury ointment, one part to two of lard, when applied daily on the appearance of the patch of mange, generally cures, and a dressing of sulphur and oil, followed by a good washing with carbolic or Jeye's fluid properly diluted, generally effects a cure. Paraffin oil is also very valuable, but should be diluted with oil or an emulsion made with soft soap.

Eczema.—For patches there is no better remedy than white precipitate ointment, which may be diluted with an equal part of zinc ointment. If dry and scaly and more chronic, some tarry preparations may be added. The food also should be changed, more vegetables given, and Fowler's solution tried in obstinate cases.

Rheumatism.—The salicylates are now so well known in the treatment of this complaint, that every keeper ought to be able to administer them at once. The salicylate of soda is perhaps the most easily procurable and the most easily administered, both horses and dogs taking it in their food. From five to fifteen grains twice daily, or every four hours in acute cases, will work like a charm. In more obstinate cases, five to ten grains of the iodide of potash given twice daily for some weeks is also good treatment. Milk should also form a considerable proportion of the diet, and mild occasional doses of aperient medicine.

Wounds.—A keeper ought to be able to sew up wounds when necessary, and the addition of a few surgical needles, with ligature silk, horsehair, or stout fishing gut will often come in useful. He should, of course, wash the wound thoroughly with a weak solution of carbolic, Condy's fluid, or other antiseptic, and muzzle the animal to prevent him tearing open the wound.

Eyes.—Inflammation of eyes can easily be treated satisfactorily at the outset with weak lotions of boracic acid or alum—just sufficient to make it perceptible to one's own taste. For more chronic cases, of yellow oxide of mercury two grains to an ounce of simple ointment—a small piece of the size of a pea rubbed along the eyelids—is valuable. Here also the strength of the ointment may be increased considerably if found necessary.

Kennels.

Most owners have their own ideas as to suitable abodes for their animals, but the most common error is that these are often too small, and ventilation is considered unnecessary, and in too many cases the outside run of so many feet is supposed to afford all the requisite amount of exercise. For the greater part of the year, in all weathers, no bedding is provided, and if so, it is not changed often enough. When water is laid on to the kennels, it is used so freely that the floors are constantly damp, producing rheumatism in its varied forms. The expression, " I wouldn't put my dog into it," is a sufficiently common one to justify one in expressing the opinion that the housing of these animals is not what it should be, and we would plead for greater care in diet, exercise, and housing for an animal of so much value to us in our sports. No servant is more worthy of his hire, and we can make him what we wish.

In conclusion, we would again repeat the statement that every good keeper ought to consider it his duty to acquire a knowledge of dogs just as much as he does in the rearing of pheasants, trapping vermin, preventing poaching, etc. In no department of his work will he get more praise and make a reputation more easily than by devoting to this even if it be a tithe of the time and labour which he spends on those other duties mentioned.

9

NOTES

CHAPTER IX

THE MOOR—GROUSE—BLACK GAME—PTARMIGAN

IT is as well for the gamekeeper never to lose sight
of the fact that upon his diligence and skill in
attending to the moor depend to a large extent the
success of the shooting season, in as far as it is
affected by the amount and the condition of the
stock of birds. So clearly is this recognised by all
sportsmen that a well-known authority [1] has laid
down the following dictum: "I have always observed
that where there are really first-rate and honest
keepers, there is always a pretty good stock of game.
Of course seasons will vary, and anyone used to the
moors will know pretty well when to make the allowance for bad weather, etc., but it is astonishing how
lightly moors will suffer from this cause or from
disease when the keeper and his subordinates are
thoroughly trustworthy. Of course you cannot grow
figs on thistles, and when you have a bare, grassy,
waterless, rank heathery moor, it is useless to look
for birds in any amount, but in an average case, with
average conditions, the number and health of the

[1] Mr. A. Stuart Wortley.

birds will be affected by the conduct and care of the keeper in charge."

The main points to be attended to by the keeper in the management of a moor are—

1. The judicious burning of the heather.
2. The regulation of the water-supply.
3. The elimination of vermin.
4. The suppression of poachers.
5. The feeding of the birds in hard weather.
6. The introduction of new blood.
7. The destruction, in the autumn, of old cocks.
8. Judicious planting round and upon lower parts of the moor, useful for sheep and birds.
9. Careful and reasonable control of the number of sheep.
10. The laying down of grit and lime.
11. The removal and burning of all dead matter, such as dead grouse, dead crows, dead vermin of all kinds, but particularly the carcases of sheep.
12. The careful bushing of wire fences and the placing of discs of metal on any telegraph wires that may be near.
13. The keeping down of bracken by cutting in June.

These points may be considered *seriatim* :—

Judicious Burning of the Heather.—The burning of the heather depends, of course, upon the conditions of the weather in different parts of the country in different seasons, but it may be laid down as a

general rule that the best time for burning is as soon
after the legal day, 1st November, as possible.
Heather burns better in the autumn than in the
spring; though it may appear green, there seems to
be an oil that keeps it alight, and one can burn
against the wind, the flame eating up everything as
it goes. On no account put off to the last few days,
as many keepers do. During this period advantage
should be taken of every dry day. Heather-burning
is controlled in Scotland by an Act passed in 1773,
whereby any person setting fire to heath or moor
between 11th April and 1st November is, on conviction, liable to a penalty of £2 for the first offence,
£5 for the second, and £10 for the third and every
subsequent offence, or, failing payment, imprison-
ment. The owner, tenant or occupier of the said
lands shall be found guilty unless he can prove that
the fire originated on other lands, or was caused
neither by his tenants nor members of his household.
An extension of time may be obtained by proprietors
of wet or high moorlands which are in their own
occupation ; if the lands are let, they may authorise
their tenants to burn under the terms of this extension. The authority must be in writing, and a notice
must be sent before commencing operations to the
sheriff-clerk of the county, along with a fee of 1s.
Landlords should, in granting leases, stipulate that
the tenant shall only burn the hill or moor after

obtaining his written consent, or that of his factor, and
that the burning must take place under the direction
of his gamekeeper.   Keepers should never be off
the moor in time of heather-burning.

When a moor has been badly neglected and is
covered with acres of thick, old, and rank heather,
burning should be carried out in a more radical
fashion than is necessary on ground that has
been carefully attended to in the past.   In the
former case, heather may be burned in long narrow
strips of a width of some 25 to 30 yards.   These
strips should, if possible, be spread fairly equally
over the moor.   In exceptional and very bad cases
it may be necessary to burn a very large tract
of old rank heather.   But, excluding these badly
neglected cases, the best principle is to burn the
heather in small patches, uniformly, all over the moor.
The reason for this is fairly obvious.   The necessary
cover must never be at too great a distance from
the feeding-ground of the young birds, which is
generally young heather of some few years' growth.
Justice is necessary for the younger birds, who are
liable to be evicted from their feeding-ground
amongst the young shoots by the older birds, when
the heather has been burned in long strips.   When
small patches of heather are burnt, it is more difficult
for the old birds to see their younger brethren, or
cousins or nephews or nieces, as the case may be,

when they are feeding and sunning themselves. In proceeding to burn the heather, the keeper must take into consideration the dryness of the moor and the direction of the wind. He should always be accompanied by two assistants to control the fire and to prevent it from extending too far.

The keeper must always remember that the danger lies not in over-burning but in under-burning. Old heather, whether dry and rank, or, as is usual, very damp underneath, is a plague to any moor, supplying healthy food neither for birds nor sheep. It hardly seems necessary to add that it is also liable to produce many a curse from the tired sportsman who is either patiently following the dogs or is "finding" his own birds. On no account is the burning to be left to the absolute discretion of the shepherd.

In regard to heather-burning, it may be added that if the moor is to be chiefly shot over dogs, the heather may be allowed to grow a little longer than in a moor used for driving purposes. In the former case it is more necessary to preserve good cover than in the latter, and there is no doubt that the radical heather-burning practised on a "driving" moor tends to make the birds wilder.[1]

2. *The Regulation of the Water-Supply.* — There

---

[1] A useful heather burner, sold by MacPherson, Inverness, is now on the market ; it answers admirably, and ensures a great saving of time and trouble compared to the older methods.

is no subject so much neglected by gamekeepers as that of the efficient water-supply of the moor. On the driest moor the keeper hesitates to be seen with anything but a gun, whilst during certain weeks of the year he should carry nothing but a spade. In fact, it may be laid down as a general rule that, omitting the pairing and nesting seasons, the spade should be a constant companion of the diligent and skilful keeper. Springs and streams need continual clearing. Streams have to be dammed here and diverted there, so that an equal distribution of water may be supplied to the moor, for there is no greater handicap to the preservation of game than a deficient or an irregular water-supply. Every keeper should remember that this subject is as important as the burning of heather. It is a question upon which he will have to utilise as much brain as he possesses, for it is a matter that requires the careful application of varied methods to individual cases. Here, for example, is a spring that is absolutely clogged by undergrowth, there is one that is obscured by heather and other overgrowth, whilst here again we find a stream that has too free a fall and that requires judicious damming, so as to supply the small pools experience has taught to be necessary as water-troughs for the birds. It must not be forgotten, too, that a series of well-cleared and generously flowing springs adds much to the pleasures of a

shooting party, and often indicates to the sportsman
the competency and efficiency of the keeper.

Not only do the springs require attention and
consideration, but the condition of the larger
streams must be carefully inquired into. It
may be necessary to divert the flow of a stream
on to a tract of ground that requires water. It
may also be required of the keeper to get rid
of those many deep undermining pools which are
apt to form in the course of streams and which
are death-traps for young birds, not to mention
sheep. The undermined parts must be filled in and
the sides of the pool shelved. This should really
be done by the careful shepherd, but they don't
like the spade any more than the keeper. The
question of the efficient draining of the moor is
of equal importance. No definite laws can be laid
down as to the nature and extent of the drains.
Each case must be judged on its individual merits.
Many keepers are apt in this matter to proceed
upon some stereotyped line, and to miss the
idiosyncrasies of the moors under their control.
Drains should, as a rule, be wide and shallow,
and should be formed with sloping sides. They
should never be too deep.[1] On no account must

[1] Deep drains may be "roaded," which is done by making an incline
at right angles to the main drain, at intervals of a hundred yards. The
" roading " is of assistance to the birds in getting to the water.

there be over-draining ; but this is not a danger that need generally be feared. We have tramped over many a moor that has been swampy and boggy and besotted, and upon which we have observed the gradual disappearance of the heather, moors which were destined to become useless as breeding or holding ground for birds.

3. *The Elimination of Vermin.*—This subject is dealt with in a special chapter by Mr. Tom Speedy, than whom no one can speak with greater authority.

4. *The Suppression of Poachers.* — The laws in regard to poaching must be carefully remembered. They are summarised in Chapter V. The greatest care must be observed at two seasons : first, at the nesting season and for some time afterwards, and, secondly, just before the Twelfth, when marauders are apt to be abroad to procure an early supply of grouse for the market.

5. *Feeding of the Birds in Hard Weather.*—The stock of grouse on a moor depends to a great extent on the supply of food. In addition to plenty of young heather, grouse are very fond of blaeberries and bilberries ; these should be encouraged to grow, and roots from woods and rough ground lifted and planted at intervals on the moor. Women and children should be prevented gathering the ripe berries on the moor. The artificial feeding of the birds in hard weather is a question that

is not only considered as unimportant, but from what experience has taught us, seems a point that is absolutely neglected. Its necessity is chiefly found on high ranged moors, the tendency being for birds to emigrate to the lower reaches during severe weather. Mr. Stuart Wortley writes on this point: "It is quite worth while to feed them a little at such times. It is chiefly when the snow is caked or frozen over with a very thin coating of ice, and they cannot scratch through it to get food, that they are most pinched and may leave the ground, never to come back. I remember Mr. Walter Stanhope telling me that in the very hard winter of 1859–60, the grouse on his Dunford Bridge moor left the grounds in hundreds. Many were killed in the fields in a half starved state, and even one or two in the Barrack Square at Sheffield, some fifteen miles off. He then sent men up to the moor with long rakes, and as they raked the snow off, the grouse followed them close, as gulls will follow the plough. Your keeper should see to these methods of helping them to feed in severe weather, and not, as is too often the case, helplessly gape at the half-starved packs sitting on walls or scratching at the ground in the fields below the moorland, until, forced by hunger, they rise and fly clean away in search of milder conditions."

Of course, the feeding of the birds must not be carried out unless under dire necessity, for there is a probability of some uncharitable neighbour considering the action unsportsmanlike, in so far as it may draw away the birds from his moor. But there is not much danger of this misunderstanding taking place. Stooks of corn judiciously planted in the most desirable places is the best method of supplying food. It is an ill wind that blows nobody any good, and at such a time the keeper may be in a position to judge of the number of old cocks left on the moor. Their greed will be easily discernible, and an apparently mean advantage might be taken to rid the moor of these voracious, ill-mannered, domineering tyrants. It is a practice recognised by all experienced poachers, and it is well that keepers should learn from the skill of law-breakers. There is much to be learnt from rogues and vagabonds.

6. *Introduction of New Blood.*—The evil effects of interbreeding must be remembered, and there is much to be said in favour of the occasional introduction of new blood, either by interchange with other owners or, in Scotland, by the purchase of Yorkshire grouse and *vice versâ*. In putting down the new birds, the long feathers of a wing may be clipped. There is, however, one very serious warning that must be repeated here. If birds are introduced from strange moors, on no account should they be

purchased from suspicious sources. The important correspondence that took place some time ago in *The Field* as to the dastardly manner in which certain moors were depleted of their grouse by netting near the marches ought to make every true sportsman suspicious of the dealer in live game. If the practice of introducing live game from other moors be followed, it should be carried out on the principle of exchange with or purchase from *legitimate owners*, and *not* from those irresponsible persons who have small moors in the vicinity of large ones, and who indiscriminately attempt to net every grouse that flies across the marches. Considering the evils of the system and the difficulty of keeping the imported birds on the ground, it is better that eggs should be exchanged. One or two placed in each nest is the most reliable method of laying them down, though it entails more trouble to the keeper than placing a larger number in one or two nests; or they may be put under domestic hens. (*See* Artificial Rearing.) Another method is the exchange of coveys with moors eight or ten miles off. In July, when the coveys are fairly strong, the keeper should take a steady pointer (on a hot day when the birds will lie close), and having located the covey, should throw a net over same. Carefully catch all the birds in the covey, and transport them in a basket, laying them down on a part of the moor, which, if it be at all possible, should not be shot over that year. Birds were transported from Ronachan in Argyllshire to Jura in this way with success some years ago.

7. *The Destruction, in the Autumn, of Old Cocks.*— This, one of the most important of the gamekeeper's duties, is nowadays so neglected as to be almost an unknown quantity. It is universally recognised that the presence of a large number of old cocks is in every way detrimental to a moor. Old cocks are pugnacious and quarrelsome, and they seem to take a special delight in interfering with the domestic arrangements of the younger birds. They are, in every way, undesirable tyrants. They drive the younger birds from their selected nesting grounds, and thus interfere with breeding. It is on this account that so many authorities advocate driving as a cure for such ill-fated moors, although many old-fashioned keepers are averse to driving. In driving, the old cocks are killed off in much greater numbers than in shooting over dogs, as it is a matter of the commonest observation that the old birds and cocks lead the packs, and it is an established fact that a driven moor generally gives better breeding results than a moor that is worked by dogs alone, for in shooting over dogs the guns are apt to take the nearest birds, which are generally hens. No better example of this can be found than the Moy moor, which is about 11,000 acres. When The Mackintosh started driving in 1871, the bag was 2836 birds,

while in 1893 it had risen to 4480, in 1901 to
7127; what it was over dogs before the driving
began we are not told. But whether the moor
is driven or dogged, the keeper should be allowed
in the late autumn, after the systematic shooting
days are passed, to take occasional walks over his
ground and endeavour to shoot down as many
old cocks as he is able. How much this precaution is necessary may be emphasised by an
instance which came under the notice of one of the
present writers in the month of January 1903. He
was one of a party of guns in an improvised partridge
drive in the county of Ayr, and in one of the beats,
being an outside gun, he was stationed at the end of
a field which lay on the fringe of the moor. He was
surprised to find, as the beaters came towards the
guns, that the air seemed filled with the calls of old
cock grouse, and on looking to the right he could
see them rising and going away every half-minute
or so. The climax was reached when the beaters
were entering the last field, when, instead of partridges, six or eight old cock grouse came over his gun.
He hesitates to prophesy what the condition of that
moor will be in a few years. When the tenant
discussed the point with the keeper, the only reply
he received was the futile one that he had tried for
years to get near the cocks to shoot them, but not for
a moment did the latter realise that their presence
10

was a reflection upon his capacity as a keeper. This matter of the killing of old cocks is one of the questions upon which the owner of a moor is himself generally ignorant or careless, but every keeper who has at heart the prosperity of the shooting under his care should see that attention is paid to the matter.

Of course it must be understood that this shooting down of old cocks is no child's play. It requires both patience and skill. In the majority of cases the birds must be stalked. The stalker must go on to the moor alone, his trained dog being well under control, and behind him. He must proceed in absolute silence, taking advantage of any cover the moor may possess in the shape of old dykes and ditches. He will find that a well-choked barrel is best for his purpose, although it may even be necessary to use a rifle. He should never hesitate to kill the birds sitting. Some years ago on a moor in Strathtay, one of the present writers indulged in a series of these stalking expeditions, and he was very content, after a day's careful working of the ground, by creeping up burn sides, or crawling alongside old dykes, or often by coming upon his bird unexpectedly round a favourable knoll, to return at night with two or three brace of old cocks. He counted such a bag as of much more import to the future prosperity of the moor than if he had returned with a larger bag of younger birds.

But even despite all these stalking expeditions, there is often left on the moor a large number of these unwelcome "chronics." Where there is much hilly ground, they are to be found on the tops in late autumn and winter, from which fortresses they descend to the detriment of their younger brethren in the plains. Even where driving is not practised as a general rule, it is as well that one or two drives at least be arranged over these tops. Such drives are not easy to manage, but a competent keeper, keeping in view the general law of driving which refers to the customary flight of birds, and observing the point at which the old cocks come nearest to possible "butts," can select his stations accordingly. This is a matter worthy of the careful consideration of master and keeper, but it is a matter generally neglected on a "dogging" moor.

It is even to be recommended that the old cocks on the tops be regarded as vermin and trapped. If such trapping were carried out on the very high ground alone, there would not be much danger of harm coming to the younger birds.

8. *Judicious Planting.*—It is advisable, where there is little cover of the nature of forest growth or shrubbery near to the moor, that there should be a certain amount of planting on the lower parts of the ground to act as cover for the birds in bad weather.

9. *Careful and Reasonable Control of the Number*

of Sheep. — A separate chapter is devoted to the
relationships between keepers and farm tenants. It
is only necessary here to emphasise three facts—(1)
the one already referred to, that in no case must the
heather-burning be left to the discretion of the sheep
farmer ; (2) that shepherds' dogs must be kept
under control in the breeding season ; and (3) that
the keeper should, if necessary, indicate to his master
the palpable fact that the stock of sheep is too
large and interferes with the feeding material of the
grouse.   Most moors are habitually over-stocked
by the farmer, which condition is the chief factor in
the high death-rate among sheep, as well as being
highly detrimental, not only to proper shooting
(especially when this is practised over dogs), but
also to the food supply of the stock of game on the
moor.   The danger can be avoided by the owner of
the farm limiting the number of sheep in drawing
up the terms of his lease.   When the adjoining land
is well stocked with sheep it is altogether desirable
that the moor should be fenced off.   Some of the
best managed moors suffer not inconsiderably from
the depredations of sheep from neighbouring lands.
The feeding capacities of the moors under consideration may be, and in the event of there being only a
small stock of sheep are sure to be, better than those
of the adjoining lands, and on this account the sheep
will naturally migrate to the best grazing-grounds,

and will as a result injure their feeding capacity. Also the moors will be constantly disturbed by the shepherds' dogs driving back the sheep to their legitimate ground. Along the march of a moor which is not fenced, it is advantageous not to burn the heather, but to leave it long and rank. Where such a condition exists, the sheep will not stray across the march.

On the question of sheep and grouse moors Mr. Tom Speedy writes : "Let us assume that there is a good stock of game, and the nesting season all that can be desired. About the 20th of May hatching has commenced, and large broods are by this time following the parent birds. This is also the period for gathering the sheep, with the view of marking the lambs. Shepherds and their dogs are out betimes to the marches of their respective hirsels. The process commences, and the flocks are driven in a homeward direction. Eventually the shepherds meet and the sheep are concentrated in an immense flock, sometimes amounting to thousands, and driven towards the 'fanks.' Those who have witnessed the gathering of a flock as described, and have seen them driven in a solid line many hundreds of yards in width across a heathery hillside, must at times have speculated as to the probable fate of grouse eggs and newly-hatched chicks. With this end in view, we have devoted many hours, accompanied by a dog,

to the trail made by the flock, and have found both
eggs and young game in large numbers trampled
and destroyed. In the second week of June a
similar course of congregating is adopted, for the
purpose of clipping the old stock. Again, in the
beginning of July, gathering is unavoidable for
clipping the milk ewes." During these repeated
operations the sheep are generally driven over the
same route to the fanks. We strongly advise keeping
the heather short on the route, so as to facilitate the
progress of the lambs. The shepherds will always
select this way, and thus be a cause of saving many
birds. This is a point the shepherd should be
consulted upon.

Besides sheep, damage is often done by cattle lying
down on nests, and we have known the eggs of both
grouse and black game destroyed in this manner.

10. *Improvement of the Feeding-Ground of the Birds
by Introduction of Grit and Lime.*—Grit is an essential
and important part of the food of the grouse. It can
be obtained by the birds in very small quantities by
the sides of streams and on other watercourses, but
it will be found to the advantage of the moor, and
the trouble will be fully repaid by the results, if a few
cartloads of grit, as well as a little lime, be taken on to
the moor every year and deposited in suitable places.

11. *The Removal and Burning of all Dead Matter,
such as dead grouse, dead crows, dead vermin of all*

kinds, but particularly the carcases of sheep.—It has been recognised from the earliest ages on record that nothing leads more to pestilence than leaving dead animal matter exposed to the air, and in contact with the food and water-supply of mankind and other living creatures. Accordingly, this recognised fact must be borne in mind by the keeper in dealing with any dead matter that may be found on the ground under his control. Dead grouse, dead crows, dead vermin, are dangerous enough in their power of contaminating the air, the soil, and more particularly the watercourses, but dead sheep are infinitely more capable of mischief, not only to living sheep, but also to game. It will be found, on careful observation, that a high death-rate of sheep is due to two causes—(1) to overcrowding, and (2), and more specially, to the presence of, or the effect of the former presence of, the rotting carcases of sheep. Some years ago an experiment was made on a certain moor in Scotland. The carcases of two sheep were left to rot in the open. After decay had well set in, two sheep (a two-year-old wether and a ewe) were temporarily fenced in at different parts of the moor, each sheep being given two acres of good hill ground. Both the sheep died within six weeks, and there appears to be no doubt that death resulted from the sheep eating grass contaminated by the carcases of the dead sheep. In these latter days when the destruction of vermin is carried out with some thoroughness, the ravens and hoody crows, the natural scavengers of the moors, have not the chance of making a meal off any sheep that may have died, and so the carcases are left to rot. Not only are the watercourses contaminated (courses which may be bringing water to the farms), but in wet districts great areas of the moor may be fed with decaying matter, to the detriment of the sheep farm, and, what is more important for us, to the grouse. The keeper should therefore impress upon the farmer the danger that threatens his stock by any neglect in removing this dead material. Shepherds, as a rule, will laugh at this warning, partly from ignorance, but chiefly because a belief in it will give considerable trouble; but they ought to be *made* to meet the wishes of master and keeper on the subject. To make it as easy as possible for them, they should be allowed the loan of a pony to bring the carcases from the hill. At Glenrisdell, Argyll, an economical furnace has been erected in the flue of the cattle meat boiler, and the shepherd, on finding a dead sheep, takes up a hill pony, brings the carcase down, skins it, and then places it on the gridiron, lighting a fire of coal and wood beneath; when the burning is complete the remains are buried. To this furnace the keeper should also bring the bodies of dead game, dead crows, and dead vermin of all kinds.

12. *The careful Bushing of Wire Fences, and the Placing of Metal Discs on any Telegraph Wires that may be near to the Moor.* — The great mortality that often occurs from birds being caught in their flight by wire fences or telegraph wires is known to every keeper, and yet the means to counteract these evils are not consistently carried out. All wire fences that are likely to be in the line of flight should be "bushed" with heather, care being taken to see that the bushing is not removed. We have known instances of its removal by shepherds, one confessing to having picked up sixty grouse in one season along a line of several hundred yards. Notice should also be given to the Post Office authorities if it be found that birds have been killed by coming in contact with their telegraph wires. The authorities named will meet the wishes of the sportsman in having discs of metal put at intervals along the wires to warn the birds of their danger. In driving along a moor road in Argyllshire this spring, the present writers observed within half a mile three or four dead grouse and black game lying in the ditch side in the line of the telegraph wires, and on examination there could be no doubt as to the cause of death.

13. *The keeping down of Bracken.*—The increase of bracken is a serious matter in many moors. The best

way to get rid of this pest is to cut the bracken down twice yearly with the scythe, when it is about a foot high and before it seeds. If this is continued for some years it will die down, but if left alone it is certain to spread, and ruin the hill both for sheep and game.

Artificial Rearing.

Excellent reports have been received from various sources as to the success attending the "hand" rearing of grouse. Game-hens, and sometimes bantams, have been used for the purpose, and the coops are placed on short heather, where a fresh shift can be got every day. "When the chicks are hatched," says Mr. Speedy, "they should at first be fed on hard-boiled eggs, with an admixture of "Standard" meal, that firm making a special preparation for the rearing of grouse and black game. Rice and seed may be added later, and maize—of which they are very fond—when they are large enough to swallow it. It is desirable to rear them in places where, besides heather, as much natural food as possible can be got, such as blackberries, cranberries, ribwort, bracken, etc. Hand-reared grouse keep well together during the autumn and winter months, and are easily known, so that they can be spared by the careful sportsman. On the approach of spring they spread over the moor and pair off to propagate their species, thus disseminating broadcast fresh blood

over the district." No doubt some difficulty will be
experienced in procuring the eggs of grouse. One
solution of the difficulty is to obtain them from deer
forests, where the removal of eggs would be regarded
more as a benefit than otherwise.

Shooting the Grouse.

I. *Over Dogs.*

There are several important points to be remembered by the keeper in shooting over dogs. Some
of these are dealt with in the chapter on dogs,
others may be recalled here. As to whether pointers
or setters are preferable on a grouse moor depends
largely on the moor, and how it is watered—setters
require much water,—but as a rule pointers are more
steady than setters.

1. "Guns" must be kept in line, and should be
warned not to walk too quickly.

2. Outside beats should be worked first, so as to
drive in birds on to the lower grounds for the
afternoon shooting.

3. The direction of the wind must be continuously
studied, and the beats arranged accordingly.

4. A knowledge of the habits and habitats of
the grouse must be taken into consideration. In
the early morning the birds are found on their
natural feeding - grounds — that is, on heather, three

to four years old. On the approach of the dogs
the grouse generally seek cover in the thicker
heather near. After feeding-time they return to
their roosting-ground, where they remain during
the middle hours of the day. In the evening they
return again to their feeding-ground, and after that,
a little before dusk, return again to their roosting-
ground. In very hot weather the birds frequent
the sloping sides of burns and streams, or seek the
cover of mixed bracken and heather, or shelter themselves among the bog-myrtle. In wet weather the birds
ascend to the higher grounds. In boisterous weather
they are generally found on the sheltered sides of hills.

5. Strict silence should, if possible, be maintained
as the " guns " proceed. There must be no superfluous
speech-making either to men or dogs. The attention
of the guns should be drawn to a point by some
simple ejaculation, such as " Mark, sir," or " Steady."
The question of arresting the attention of the guns
is important. Nothing is more tantalising to the
keen sportsman than to be told in a casual, indifferent, languid voice to " Look to your right,
sir," and to find that a bird has gone away some
hundred yards before the sentence is completed.
When a bird rises independent of a point, the
keeper should call out emphatically, " Mark, sir,"
indicating " right " or " left " or " behind," as the case
may be.

6. The ground should be worked systematically. Towards evening every piece of ground must be carefully searched. The largest bags of the day may be made when the birds have retired to their roosting-ground.

7. In addition to what is said in the chapter on dogs, the following points may be remembered :—

(1) Pointers and setters should not be overworked. To secure this, they should be changed at least every three hours.

(2) It is best to have one man whose duty it is, primarily, to hold the non-working dogs in leash. This man should walk some eighty yards behind the guns, and should act as a marker for the flight of coveys and for fallen, especially towered, birds. Where the number of men is limited, he receives the picked-up birds, and after carrying them for a sufficient time to allow them to cool, he hands them on to the man with the horse and panniers.

(3) Retrievers must be kept well in leash.

(4) If the scent is bad, the dogs must not be allowed to range too far, and the ground must be worked very slowly and carefully. If the point habitually fails, or if the birds are so wild as not to sit to the point at all, it is best to withdraw the dogs altogether.

(5) Plenty of time must be allowed for dogs to drink, but they must be discouraged from habitually

taking to water. Where the ground is destitute of water and the day is very hot, water should be carried on to the moor for their benefit, in the panniers.

(6) Dogs should be given some slight refreshment in the shape of a sandwich or a bone at the luncheon hour.

(7) It is as well, at the beginning of the season at least, to soak the feet of the dogs in strong brine or other hardening fluid, after the day's work. Plenty of experience on the roads before the Twelfth hardens their feet.

(8) When a dog comes to a point, there should not be any "to-hoing" to it. If it has been properly taught, it should "hold up" without any words from the keeper; an uplifting of the keeper's hand should be sufficient. If a dog has a habit of drawing too close on the birds, the keeper should come quietly to its side and hold it gently back till the guns are ready, directing, of course, the attention of the guns to the point. If the dog be too slow in drawing on the birds after the guns are ready, it should be encouraged by patting it on the back or even by dragging or pushing it on.

2. *Driving.*

The keeper's duties in regard to grouse-driving may vary from the conducting of several improvised drives on a moor that is free from butts and which is chiefly "dogged" or walked or stalked, to the arrangement of systematic and elaborate drives. In preparing for the former little is necessary but a study of the wind, a knowledge of the general flight of the birds, and the selection of points which might be used as natural butts, such as dyke or burn sides, rocks or the backs of the crests of braes and hillocks. In dealing with the business of an elaborate drive, however, he is concerned with a very different business and a campaign which will require most of his arts and all of his resources. But there are three important pieces of information, knowledge of which must underlie the whole of his plan of campaign.

(1) Accurate observation of the lie of his land. The keeper must carry in his mind a veritable Ordnance Survey map of the moor.

(2) The habits of the birds as far as the question of their customary flight is concerned.

(3) The principles underlying the forming, the marching, and the evolutions of the corps of beaters.

These three pieces of knowledge will lead him far to a successful outcome of the issue before him, which is how best to get the stock of birds over the guns. To successfully carry out a series of drives to their most perfect issue will, however, require not only careful consideration, but much

elaborate manœuvring, and on this account he will
have to take into his consultation, more closely than
in most of his duties, the man who should know a
great deal about the sport he wishes to enjoy, namely,
his master. Besides this, the keeper, who desires to
learn the art of grouse-driving thoroughly, must
seek information of a more elaborate nature than this
book pretends to supply. If he desires to bring his
results—comparatively, of course—to the perfection
attained at Moy Hall, at Bromhead, at Gannochy,
High Force, or Studley, he will buy or borrow from
his master the writings of Lord Granby, Lord
Walsingham, Sir R. Payne Gallwey, Mr. Tom
Speedy, Mr. Horace Hutchinson, and Mr. Stuart
Wortley,—more particularly of the last. All these
writers deal with their subject tersely, simply, and
graphically, and any intelligent keeper will rise from
the perusal of these authors with a fairly definite view
to the last and the best word on the subject. As we
have said, we cannot pretend to deal with the matter
on the principles of elaboration so excellently and
vividly carried out by Mr. Stuart Wortley. We can
only absorb the best views and present them with the
modifications of our own experience.

Let us then further deal with the three points
enumerated above—

(1) Accurate knowledge of the conformation of the
land. From this knowledge the keeper will be able

to lay the plan of his drives, so as to meet efficiency
with economy of time and of space. He will learn
what parts of the moor should be driven first, so as to
keep the birds on the ground for future drives, and
how best to work the moor so that the birds may be
driven in from the outlying beats for the final flush
over the guns. On hilly and rocky grounds he will
discover where best to place the butts so that these
different parts may be effectively worked. With a
knowledge of the usual flights of the birds, added to
the general information he possesses as to the lie of
the land, he will be able to judge as to the best
general distribution of the butts.

(2) It is only by continuous and careful observation that the keeper will be able to gauge fairly
accurately the general direction taken by the birds in
their flight. On this important information depends
the question as to where the butts should be placed.
Where driving is practised on a moor, the initial
drives can only be regarded as experimental, and
even when fairly accurate knowledge has been
obtained, further experience may require the alteration of the position of the butts. The fact cannot be
unduly emphasised that no hesitation must be shown
in making new lines of butts, or in shifting old ones.
On many moors the butts of primitive days are
treated like eternal monuments, not to be interfered
with by any law or experience on earth. Truly these

11

old stagers may be monuments—of ignorance,—but quite useless for sport.

(3) The principles underlying the formation, progression, and evolution of the beaters. The art of driving is not easily learned, and the details are only perfected by experience. There are keepers who, despite the fact that birds are continually breaking back over the drivers or escaping at the flanks, persist with their primitive fashion of a more or less uncontrolled line of drivers, who are possessed with only three ideas,—firstly, to make their way by a bee line to the butts; secondly, to keep in line with their neighbours; and, thirdly, to yell "Mark" whenever birds arise. Let it be reiterated for the hundredth time that the formation of the drivers should never be a straight line, but should be horseshoe-shaped, and that the length and the disposition of the flanks must vary according to the ground and the direction of the wind.

Having enumerated the three main points which must serve as the basis of the keeper's knowledge, let us glance for a moment at some of the practical duties which are the natural outcome of this knowledge.

The first thing to be considered is the placing and building of butts. The practical points connected with this procedure may be enumerated—

(1) The butts must be placed in the general line

of flight of the birds, which, as we have shown, is discovered by the keepers, after careful observation from experimental drives.

(2) Butts should never be placed on the skyline. There is no exception to this law.

(3) Butts should be so placed that some eighty yards or so of gently sloping ground stretch in front of the guns, this ground constituting the main field of action. The best possible situation is just over a brae or small hill—the edge of the hill being about eighty, and never more than a hundred, yards from the line of butts. But never, no never, on the skyline!

(4) Butts should never be placed where experience has shown that the birds usually fly too high for the guns,—for example, at the bottom of a deep gorge between hills. Birds only dip their line of flight in traversing wide, shallow valleys. In passing over a deep gorge, they maintain their flight at the height of the first peak crossed, and will be out of range of the guns at the foot of the gorge.

(5) The distance between the butts should be regulated according to what experience has shown to be the width of the flight of the birds after concentration by the drivers and flankers. On level and undulating ground they should be closer than on rougher and more hilly ground. The old fashion of having butts at intervals of some eighty to a hundred yards is going out of vogue. The other

extreme is practised by The Mackintosh at Moy
Hall, where an allowance of only fifteen yards is
made between the butts, on the principle that the
concentration of birds is more marked than is
generally believed, and that much good shooting
material is thrown away when the butts are wider
apart. The only objection made to closely placed
butts has been the one of the possible danger of
accident. Where the nature of the ground necessi-
tates that one butt is out of sight of the proximate
one, a stake, or better, a white stone, should be placed
to indicate the fact of the proximity. This practice
discounts any chance of temporary forgetfulness,
which has been known to occur to the best of sportsmen. On rough and hilly ground the spread of the
flight is wider, and here the butts should have a
greater distance between them—a fair distance being
fifty yards.

(6) Butts must be as invisible as possible, and,
except in very rocky and very marshy country,
practically flush with the surface of the moor.
The old-fashioned high-walled " batteries " should be
in general discarded. The best way to construct a
butt is to dig a hole in the ground with a diameter
of some five feet at the bottom and six feet across
the top. The "gun," in standing in the hole, should
be just able to see and shoot over the slight
parapet at the top, which should be almost flush

with the moor, and never more than two feet above its level, the outside being so arranged with heather hags as to slope gently up to the mouth of the butt. It may be useful, for the sake of firmness, to line the inside of the butt with wire netting, and also the outside of the slightly elevated portion above the level of the moor. In the latter case, the netting should not be exposed to view, but may be covered with a layer of heather-covered earth. About a foot in front of the butt, a drain may be cut, which, if not too conspicuous, may be left open, or it may be covered carefully, so as to maintain its capacity as a drain. The draining of the butt itself is of importance. An opening in the butt with a drain which leads to a lower level than the floor of the butt will answer the purpose. The floor of the butt should be covered with wood. This ensures a fairly dry base for the shooter and his loader to stand upon. A board of wood supported on two posts as a seat at one side of the butt is also advisable. A stake may be inserted to tether a retriever.

7. Butts should be well built, well drained, well in line, and kept in good repair. On no account must a very prevalent fashion be permitted to continue of allowing the butts to take care of themselves, or leaving their repair to any energetic or practical hands that may exist among the " guns." How

often, oh, how often! have we found ourselves
crouching behind a small turf dyke, or in badly
built, tumbled down, drafty, rakish - looking butts,
flooded with three or four inches of water, from
which we had to go scouring the land for stray
slabs of peat or heather hummocks on which to kneel,
for in no other fashion could we hide from view our
cold and restless bodies. How we have shivered and
groaned in these pits of stupidity and gross carelessness — built probably in the early seventies, and
instead of growing dignified in their old age, sink-
ing to a miserable decay under the dissipations of
accident and weather. If we are not to have newly
built, newer fashioned butts, then in the name of all
that is decent, let the keeper or his men patch up
and drain the old ones, and save the " guns " from acute
rheumatism, pneumonia, or shattered tempers. Let
the " guns " at least have a chance of doing even their
second best. It is on moors that are let to shooting
tenants for short periods that such immoral neglect
of duty chiefly prevails. Often it is the owner
himself that is to blame. He knows he will have
little difficulty in letting his shooting, and if he is not
a keen or unselfish sportsman he is never particularly
anxious for a lengthy lease of his moor. Accordingly in such cases the duties of a keeper are often
allowed to slacken to an appalling extent, and in the
decline of the sense of duty, the butts suffer first,

after the butts the springs and the drains,—everything, in fact, that seems to the lazy or half-stupid keeper to have little bearing on the number of birds killed.

(8) It has been suggested by some writers that the heather should be burnt for some distance round the butts, so that the birds may be found without difficulty after the drive. The two great objections to this are—(*a*) that the butts would stand out more conspicuously than when surrounded by heather; and (*b*) the birds are apt to be badly broken up in falling on to hard ground only protected by burnt heather.

The Drive.

There are general principles in regulating the disposition and movement of the drivers which may be enumerated—

(1) Where men are easily obtainable and it is proposed to carry out the drive in as complete and elaborate a manner as possible, two companies of drivers should be employed, one taking up their position at the far end of the second drive, ready to come forward as soon as the first drive is over and the birds are picked up.

(2) In a first-rate drive there should be sixteen to twenty drivers, the best men being on the flanks. The centre man of the horseshoe should also be an experienced man, while, to save expense, the main

curve of the horseshoe may be made up of intelligent boys.

(3) If the head keeper goes with the drivers he should be on that flank which it is necessary to control more. Otherwise he may act as a stop near to the line of butts.

(4) Drivers should walk slowly and silently, keeping their eyes open to receive directions from the man under whose control they work. There is no earthly use in yelling "Mark" when the birds arise—this only frightens them, and is apt to make them break back.

(5) When birds arise and show a tendency to break back or to pass over the flanks, the drivers should quietly stoop so as to keep out of sight for the time, and then slowly rise again as the birds approach them. This plan is much better than the common one of shouting and gesticulating, and the probability is, if the former plan is observed, that the birds will sweep round in front of the drivers and go over the guns.

(6) In driving ground which is high on one flank and low on the other, the drivers on the lower ground should be a little more advanced than those on the higher ground.

(7) When there is a strong wind blowing across the drive, the downwind flanks should be well advanced. They thus form a screen to turn the

birds. It may also be advisable to put more men on the downwind arm of the horseshoe, at the expense of the upwind one.

(8) Different coloured flags should be used by the different members of the drive. For instance, plain white for the rank and file, red for the centre or head man, and red and white for the flank men and points.

(9) Drivers should come to a halt about fifty yards in front of the butts, and stay there till all the birds are picked up by the keepers and their dogs.

PICKING UP AND PACKING OF BIRDS.

(1) Where dead birds can be seen they may be picked up by hand before the retriever is loosened, but in doing so, care should be taken not to spoil the scent for the dogs by tramping all over the ground. On no account should beaters be allowed to pick up birds for this reason—this should be left to the keeper, with his well-trained retriever or spaniel. The man who owns a well-trained spaniel or retriever should never go to a grouse drive without his dog.

(2) Birds should never be put in panniers and carts at once, but should be allowed to cool.

(3) The packing into the panniers or carts should be carefully and systematically carried out, the birds being put in singly, and so arranged as to form a compact mass.

HILL PONIES.

In selecting ponies for hill work, whether for carrying panniers, deer, or men, the truism must be stated that the main point to observe is to select ponies that can climb. They should never be Lowland born or bred, and their chief qualifications should be strength and sureness of foot. They should possess these qualifications along with that of being good climbers, at the expense of speed, paces, and style, which should never be looked for. They should not be too small—size and substance is what is needed. The shoulders should have a moderate slope—this ensures sureness of foot—and breadth of loin and substance of bone should be demanded. In working the ponies they should be allowed as much as possible to have their own way, and to pick out their own stepping ground. They should be allowed to go slowly. How often have we seen a pony fall, simply because the rider or the leader would persist in jerking its head backwards.

BLACK GAME.

There are a few facts as to black game which may be recalled for the benefit of the keeper "who does not know."

With regard to the stock, there are certain conditions which are conducive to a good supply of birds.

(*a*) Delay in killing till the birds are in full plumage and capable of good flight, *i.e.* black game, except old cocks, should never be shot till the middle or beginning of September.

(*b*) Absence of vermin and plenty of rough ground.

(*c*) Judicious burning of heather and furze on the fringe of the moor.

(*d*) The neighbourhood of corn and turnip crop to the black-game ground.

(*e*) Killing of old cocks, as discussed when we were dealing with grouse.

(*f*) A limitation of number of grey hens to be killed.

With regard to the time for killing black game, we think the keeper is perfectly justified in indicating to the ignorant or the very young sportsman the fact that it is a recognised rule, despite the present unsatisfactory state of the official close time, to leave young black game entirely alone in August and the beginning of September. If a young blackcock gets up in August and trundles slowly away in front of the guns, the keeper should call out, " Ware blackcock," or simply, " Blackcock, sir." In the latter case, the tone of the voice indicates the fact that *of course* the guns understand that the bird is not to be killed.

As to the killing of old cocks, the keeper will

recall what we have said about grouse. The old blackcock is equally as tyrannical and disturbing as the old cock grouse. In attempting to rid the ground of these pests, the keeper has not the same difficulty, however, as in the case of the grouse. Black game are very conservative in their habitats, and generally select a particular spot for their fighting matches and carousals. The keeper will soon discover some place on the fringe of the moor where the birds congregate in the early morning. It will probably be an open space in some old wood, and, by getting up early and planting himself in cover, he will have an excellent opportunity of "potting" the old cocks. When the blackcock is to be stalked as it sits on the top of a dyke on the moor, it is to be recommended that, if the keeper is accompanying one of the guns for the purpose, he should take a different route from the latter, keeping far away from him and yet in sight of the birds, the gun in the meantime creeping up unobserved from an opposite direction. This practice distracts the attention of the victim from the main danger.

Black-Game Driving.

In driving black game there are several very important points to be observed—

(1) The drivers must be absolutely silent. This is even more important than in driving grouse.

(2) Like partridges, black game cannot be forced to fly contrary to their customary line of flight. On this account they are difficult to turn, and flank men are not of so much value as in driving grouse. However, the rule we have indicated, when speaking of grouse-driving, as to the drivers first stooping and then gradually rising as the birds come near, sometimes meets with success in turning the birds.

(3) The line of flight of black game is very constant. On this account, in driving a wood, the keeper is soon able to discover at what parts of the cover the birds usually pass out, and should place the guns accordingly. It is useless, as a rule, to line the guns at equal distances, as in grouse-driving. They should be fairly close together at the places indicated by the keeper.

(4) Black game will not drive well under the following conditions :—

(*a*) When all the corn is not cut.

(*b*) When the day is wild and blustering.

The best day on which to shoot black game is a dull misty day when there is little wind. The mist hides the "guns" from the fine long-ranged sight of the birds. High wind is apt to scatter the packs.

(5) The keeper should not hesitate, unless he is dealing with experienced black - game shooters, to

remind the "guns" of two or three very important practices in black-game driving:—

(*a*) On no account should a hare, breaking away at the opening of the drive, be fired at, nor should the first birds, which generally come singly and are in all likelihood grey hens, be shot. This is an unvarying rule. To fire at these "scouts" is simply to set the whole army flying away in all directions, while, if these single birds are left alone, the rest of the pack will sail grandly over the guns.

(*b*) "Guns" must keep absolutely silent, well hidden, and as immovable as is compatible with nature.

(*c*) Of course the keeper must warn any very ignorant "gun" that grey hens must not be fired at, unless the stock is so great that it is desirable to reduce it.

Poaching Black Game.

In addition to the general principles recognised for the suppression of poachers, long stakes, with a nail driven into the top at right angles, may be planted at intervals over the black-game ground, when poaching by netting is common. This practice is also valuable for the protection of grouse, but, owing to the general limitations of the black-game ground, it is easier to carry out than in the case of grouse.

PTARMIGAN.

Every gamekeeper should be aware of the fact that ptarmigan are like woodcock in one respect. They always lie as to the wind. They are therefore to be found on the lee side of the hills. This fact is to be carefully recalled when they are being looked for. If, unfortunately, the march stretches along the summit of a hill and the wind is blowing from this side, the birds will be on the other side of the march, and there is not much use undertaking a mountaineering expedition to find them, unless the wise course is followed of arranging with the neighbouring owner or tenant to shoot ptarmigan on the same day. By so doing, the recognised method of killing ptarmigan will be followed, that is, by shooting in two parties. When the "tops" are on the keeper's own ground, the two-party principle enables him to get over the great difficulty of ptarmigan-shooting, which lies in the fact that the coveys fly from one "top" to another. If there is a single party, the guns will have only one chance at the broods, unless they descend again to the "plains" and make another ascent to the other "top," which procedure is apt to become monotonous, even to the most vigorous sportsman.

It goes without saying that there is no use taking out the guns on a misty day. In all forms of sport where there is thick mist, there should be no firing, and when on a fine day, the guns being on the "tops," mist begins to collect, shooting should cease. On this account it is to be recommended that in ptarmigan-shooting the keeper and all the guns should each possess a pocket-compass. This, together with the fact that in all cases of difficulty one should follow the course of streams, will do much to counteract the disagreeable probability of being lost in the mist.

It may be necessary for the keeper to remind the young sportsman of the possible danger of not having his gun at "safe" while in the act of climbing or in groping his way over boulders and rocks.

The keeper should neither take with him pointers nor setters. They are inclined to be much put out by the presence of blue hares ; but an old retriever is of the greatest possible value.

NOTES

CHAPTER X

THE PARTRIDGE

OF the many services rendered to sport by Mr.
Stuart Wortley, none can be valued more highly
than the continued emphasis he has laid upon the
fact of how neglectful has been the general attitude
of the owner, tenant, and keeper in regard to the rearing and the preservation of partridges. Mr. Wortley,
in discussing this important question, finds the explanation of the fact in the recognition of the
pheasant as having the primary, often the only,
claim to attention. Where pheasants are reared to
any great extent, this is notoriously true, but there
are other conditions, especially in Scotland, which
have acted to the detriment of the breeding and
protection of partridges. In the Highlands of Scotland the partridge has become almost a negligible
quantity, not from any choice on the part of landlord or sporting tenant, but from the fact that the
stock is so comparatively small that it is almost
disregarded. In this instance it is not the pheasant
that serves as the unwilling cause of offence, but

the grouse. As in the case of large covert shoots
in the south, so in the case of moors in the north,
the keeper has been (metaphorically speaking) in
the past, and seems likely to be in the future, a
snob. The pheasant and the grouse he regards as
high in the social world of the bird, and worthy of
pampering and adulation, whilst the poor vagabond
partridge is left more or less to grub for himself.

The blame for this condition of affairs, of course,
reflects to a marked degree on the owners or tenants
themselves, but does not entirely release the keepers
from their responsibilities. Many sportsmen only
stay at their shooting boxes as long as they are
able to get sport on the moors, and return south
practically indifferent to the fact of the possibilities
of good bags of partridges from the cultivated
land that stretches down the strath in front of their
very lodge doors. And even when this indifference
is not so marked, there can be no doubt that the
general run of sportsmen would prefer to bag their
ten or eleven or even their four or five brace of
grouse in the late season, with the joy of a tramp
on the hill, than spend a weary day, dragging their
muddy boots through wet turnips and potatoes, with
the prospect of a larger bag of the autumn bird.
This is but one side of the question. There is a
more important reverse. Many sportsmen in the
Highlands of Scotland are indifferent to partridge-

shooting, not because of the more absorbing claims
of the moor, but because of the general poorness
of the partridge stock, and such being the case,
and granting, of course, the necessary ground conditions, the blame is to be laid largely at the door
of the gamekeeper. The present writers, with their
sporting imaginations stimulated by a fine picture of
well-cultivated agricultural land, stretching from the
edge of the moor, in rich variegated tints, down
to the edge of the river, wending its rapid way
through the spirals of the strath, and interrogating
the head-keeper as to the prospects of partridges,
have had their imaginations often curtailed by being
told in an indifferent tone, that there may be a
few coveys, but nothing to speak of. And such
information has been conveyed to them as if the
fact finally settled the responsibility of the keeper.
Let it be our duty to emphasise the fact that it
has only determined the existence of wilful neglect
of opportunity on the part of the sportsman, and
the absence of a due sense of responsibility on the
part of the keeper. If there be good partridge
ground, the partridges ought to be there. If there
be none, or if there be only a poor stock, it indicates
an indifferent sportsman or a casual keeper.

Of course these remarks are made with a full
recognition of the fact that the keeper's department
may be undermanned. But that fact is to be

taken into account in all we have to say as to
the keeper's duties. But we intentionally leave out
of account those rare cases where one keeper has
perhaps in his charge a fairly extensive moor, a
rabbit warren, and several stretches of good cover,
and whose time is fully taken up on these pre-
serves, trapping, draining, and watching. Such conditions, being rare, need not trouble us. It cannot
be said, as a rule, that keepers are overworked.
Their duties and responsibilities are great, and there
is no more popular fallacy than to imagine that
their occupation is but a very pleasant form of an
idle country life. But the care and protection of
a stock of partridges, although requiring considerable
time, patience, and skill, need not prove irksome to
any keeper who is at all interested in his profession.

In the majority of cases the partridge ground is
at his very door, and more easy of control than the
moor, which may stretch miles beyond his immediate
circumference. And, although such be the case, it
is a notorious fact that on many shootings the information one can obtain as to the number, position,
and condition of partridge nests and eggs is lament-
ably poor, and a desire for specific information is
dismissed by a few inconsequent and often mislead-
ing general statements. And it is curious to observe
how glibly the indifferent keeper will, season after
season, talk of the drowning of the young birds

and of the smallness of the coveys, apparently indifferent to the fact of the ways and means to
counteract these conditions. In the case of Highland shootings, the keeper, perhaps, is not so
much to blame as the men whose care is chiefly
with a semi-wild bird of the hand-reared pheasant
type. The imagination of the former may be stunted
by the fact that his work is chiefly with birds which,
to a marked extent, look after themselves, and which
receive but slight artificial assistance compared with
the hand-reared pheasant. But, although this be a
fact, it ought not to serve as an excuse, and it will be
the first duty of the sportsman who realises the possibilities that he may have missed, to remind the keeper
of the artificial processes that are necessary for the
proper rearing and care of a good partridge stock.

Having said so much in regard to the partridge
ground attached to shootings where the moor is the
first consideration, we return to the conditions to
which Mr. Stuart Wortley has specially directed his
remarks. "Most English manors," says this great
authority, "have not anything like the stock of
partridges which they ought to produce. This I
attribute to three causes. First, the keeper's work
is not, as far as partridges are concerned, well understood or properly carried out. Second, which is a
result in part of the first, there is a good deal more
egg - stealing and poaching than there should be.

Third, the stock, being low, is too much reduced by hard shooting." In dwelling on these facts this writer selects a particular shooting, "The Grange," to illustrate how the partridge stock may be improved, and dwells at length on some of the practices observed. "The high average maintained at The Grange is due to a combination of . . . conditions (favourable) and the system on which the keeper's work is conducted ; and it is here that I think a lesson may be learned by other owners and keepers. First and foremost, the latter are taught to treat partridges, and not pheasants, as the first consideration. Partridges require a better and more watchful keeper than pheasants. The old-fashioned system of leaving partridges to take care of themselves in the nesting season, while your keepers are devoting themselves exclusively to the pheasantry and the coops, must be abandoned. Everything must be done to watch and thwart egg-stealers and poachers. *To arrive at this, it follows that the whereabouts of every, or nearly every, nest must be known, and these must be watched and visited practically every day."*

The rule which we have printed in italics must serve as the basis of the keeper's conduct. In no other way will he be able to attain to satisfactory results. To those who have become accustomed to the go-as-you-please philosophy, this may seem at first an irksome addition to their day's work, but we are concerned, not with the likes and dislikes of keepers, but with their duties.

As in dealing with the question of moors, we may categorically enumerate the various points that must be regarded by the keeper for the proper preservation and improvement of his general stock.

(1) The supply or improvement of cover.

(2) and (3) The careful watching and protection of eggs and nests and artificial rearing.

(4) The improvement of the stock by the introduction of eggs from other districts, and the importation of foreign partridges.

(5) The destruction of vermin.

(6) The suppression or the frustration of poachers and poaching.

(7) A tactful understanding and sympathy with the farmers.

(8) The killing of old cocks.

1. *Cover.*

Many estates are fortunate enough to possess so much well-distributed cover as to call for little innovation of a radical nature. Some are ideal in this respect, the various fields of potatoes and corn being flanked and intersected by rough ground of broom ("whin") and gorse, with here and there additional growths of birch, juniper, and other classes of trees. How notoriously this kind of cover is used by part-

ridges can be proved by the fact that on the first
of September in Scotland, long before the crops are
cut, small bags of partridges are to be obtained by
simply walking through these patches of cover. As a
rule these strips of "rough ground" are considerably
elevated above the cultivated land, and in preparing
artificial cover based on the principle of their construction, the question of elevation must not be lost
sight of. In proceeding to lay out this nesting cover,
common sense must be used in distributing the
patches of ground equally about the estate, avoiding,
if possible, too close proximity to the pheasant coverts,
which must naturally be kept as quiet as possible till
the day of the first pheasant shoot. In preparing
these strips of cover, or banks, it is as well that
considerable care be taken with regard to judicious
sowing. If the banks be sown with young broom
and left unwired, there is a likelihood of the young
growths being eaten by rabbits, hares, and foxes;
but if the wiring be too high, there is a danger of the
hen partridge not being able to get her young brood
on to the slopes of the banks, on those occasions
when stormy wet weather urges her to seek protection for her young. This remark only applies,
of course, to the very early days in the life of the
covey; but it is important, nevertheless, for it is at
this very stage that young birds are apt to be washed
away by driving storms, or to be drowned in ruts and

furrows. With regard to the depredations of foxes, Mr. Wortley rightly points out that " they will not be entirely kept out by wire netting after it has been up a year or two, but they will always be loth to trust themselves much inside it, and any little alteration, such as an extra strand of wire along the top, will make them suspicious of a trap, and in all likelihood keep them out altogether."

It seems necessary to point out here, what seems to have been omitted by most authorities, that the cover must no more be allowed to take care of itself than heather on a moor. It will require from time to time judicious pruning, supplanting, and re-planting, so as to maintain its value as a feeding and rearing-ground. It is not necessary to add, after the observations we have made, that, in this consideration at least, rabbits and hares must come under the category of vermin and be treated accordingly.

The question of expense will naturally arise in dealing with this matter of sufficient cover for partridges. In many cases the owner will be satisfied with a considerable improvement of the existing cover, in fewer cases he will be prepared to meet the outlay necessary for the planting of new ground, and where expense is no object he may advocate the laying out of sanctuaries or pre-serves. These may be as elaborate as the King's covers at Sandringham, or may simply consist of stretches of corn or rye plantation preserved in the midst of other cover for the special use of the partridge.

2 and 3. *The Careful Watching of Nests and Eggs and Artificial Rearing.*

We have already laid down the ideal principle for the protection of nests and eggs from the depredations of poaching. Any slacker method can only lead to disastrous results in so far as the size of the coveys is concerned. Egg-stealing is a very profitable business, and is conducted with ease, owing either to the carelessness or the dishonesty of the keeper or his underlings. This carelessness is a form of neglect of duty that should bring any self-respecting keeper to his senses, and if not, should bring him to the right-about. Of course, as in other matters, the criminal neglect of duty by the keeper is merely a reflex of the casual indifference of the master—here again, we touch on a matter of explanation, but not on a matter of excuse. In the matter of the depredation of nests and eggs the keeper has to deal with six types of enemies, each of which must be watched closely and frustrated. These are —(1) vermin—including foxes, (2) farmers and farm labourers, (3) casual poachers from neighbouring villages, (4) professional poachers, (5) stray dogs, and (6) mowing machines. Each of these enemies is dealt with in individual chapters treating of the specific subject concerned. As for the general habits of a great number of keepers, all that is done to prevent the stealing of eggs and the poaching of young coveys seems to be an occasional sleepy stroll slantways across a field that may contain six or seven nests or young broods, and the occasional slipshod "bushing" in the grass fields. Every corner of every field should be gone over carefully at the beginning of the season, until a thorough knowledge of the whereabouts of nests and the number of eggs be obtained, and then the rule followed as to watching which we have printed in italics. Any diminution of the number of eggs must be carefully noted and the cause traced to its source.

With regard to the protection of partridges and their nests, it must be observed, in addition to what is said in the chapter on vermin, that the destruction of the latter is naturally easier in cover which is not too redundant. Accordingly, the "rough ground," "the whins," the banks, and the fences must be loosely planted. If already thick, they must be thinned out. Trees and shrubs must not be too closely planted together. In other words, shelter, or as it is termed, "cover," must be sparse and well distributed, full of young vegetation, and well protected from vermin. Where nests are found in the open, it is recommended that "a single strand of wire, about ten inches above the ground, be stretched from stout pegs." This will prevent any fox from crossing the field. Bushing must be carefully attended to, the bushes being liberally distributed and well planted, and careful observation made of any tampering with the position in which they were first placed. The attention of the factor should be called to see that the farmers keep their ditches cleaned, as otherwise, in times of flood or spate, water does not get away, and is apt to flood out the nests. Keepers should prevent the birds from nesting in ditches so foul with undergrowth that water cannot get free flow.

After any rainstorm, or during it, if necessary, the keepers should be out and making observations as to the safety of their nests and small coveys. Some artificial help is often necessary to protect the eggs from destruction, and a wise keeper will often discern a chance to interfere for the benefit of his broods, although it must be remembered that human interference is soon detected by ground vermin, especially stoats, and the future safety of the eggs may be in peril. "If a sad mishap," says Mr. Macpherson, "has befallen a clutch of eggs, and some of the number have actually come to grief, the misfortune can best be redeemed by such eggs as happen to have escaped destruction being placed under the charge of a domestic fowl. When the little

fellows emerge into the world, they soon learn to
take care of themselves, but the pupæ of ants are
requisite for their successful rearing." For it is
notorious that the hen bird hesitates to return to its
duties if its nest has been partially destroyed or
interfered with. That distinguished observer, " A Son
of the Marshes," indicates in the *Pall Mall Magazine*[1] the methods of procuring the pupæ. "Two
very different kinds of ant-hills supply the eggs or
ant-pupæ to the young of game birds, and of partridges in particular. First, there are the common
emmet-heaps or ant-hills, which are scattered all
over the land ; go where you will, you will find
them. These the birds scratch and break up,
picking out the eggs as they fall from the light
soil of the heaps ; the partridges work them easily.
But the ant-eggs proper—I am writing now from the
game-preserving point of view—come from the nests
or heaps of the great wood ants, either the black
or the red ant. These are mounds of fir nettles,
being in many instances as large at the bottom in
circumference as a waggon wheel, and from two to
three feet in height—even larger where they are very
old ones. They are found in fir woods, on the warm,
sunny slopes under the trees, as a rule, pretty close
to the stems of the trees. The partridges and
their chicks do not visit these heaps, for they

[1] *Pall Mall Magazine*, 1893, p. 737.

NOTES

would get bitten to death by the ferocious creatures. The keepers and their lads procure the eggs of these, and a nice job it is! A wood-pick, a sack, and a shovel are the implements required for the work. Round the men's gaiters or trousers leather straps are tightly buckled, to prevent, if possible, the great ants from fixing on them, as they will try to do, like bulldogs, when the heaps are harried. The top of the heap is shovelled off, laying open the domestic arrangements of the ant-heap, and showing also the alarmed and curious ants trying to carry off their large eggs to a place of safety ; but it is all in vain! Eggs and all, they go into the sack. In spite of every precaution, the ant-egg getters do get bitten severely, for the ants would fix on anything. They spit, as the men term it, their strong acid venomously. . . . These heaps are harried for the home-bred birds,—that is, home and hand-fed ones, both pheasants and partridges hatched by small game - hens — game - fowl kept specially for that purpose—from the eggs that have been taken from the outlying nests." Or, as we have shown, from the destroyed or partially destroyed nests. "Other strains of the domestic fowl are used, but the game-hens are the favourite foster-parents. When the birds are fed with the eggs, as many of the ants as it is possible to get rid of are kept out; but some are sure to be mixed up

13

with the eggs, and these fix on the birds, making
them jump off the ground. The common emmets,
the creatures that the wild birds feed on — their
young broods particularly — are harmless, but the
large wood ants are not."

But it is strongly to be recommended that the
chicks which have been placed under the care of the
game-hen should be transferred as soon as possible
to a brood of partridges of much the same age as
the chicks. Artificial rearing and feeding presents
many difficulties and risks, and there is no difficulty
in the way of a parent partridge receiving the little
strangers into her home, granted that the domestic
hearth is not already too crowded.

For the guidance of the keeper, it might be useful
here to summarise the circumstances under which
he is entitled to lift eggs and transfer them to the
game-fowl :—

(1) In those cases where a nest has been disturbed
by a dog or a casual intruder, and there is a reasonable fear that the parent partridge may desert its nest.

(2) Where the parent birds have been killed or
frightened away either by mowing machines or by
other intruders.

(3) In cases where the eggs are found nested
in positions of danger or where in the judgment
of the keeper they are lying in too exposed a
position.

(4) In cases where two hens have laid in the same nest and quarrel as to the right of taking sole control of the eggs.

There are circumstances where a very careful and observant keeper may be able to say definitely that certain eggs have just been laid. If he can trust to the accuracy of his knowledge in such cases, and if he be faced with any of the four conditions mentioned above, he may transfer the eggs to the nests of other birds which have not begun to brood, and which have not already their full supply of eggs—that is to say, not more than eighteen or twenty.

The eggs for artificial rearing may either be eggs collected from the nests of partridges on the estate or may be bought from recognised English game farms. In the former case it is sometimes necessary, in the latter always so, to test if an egg is still fertile. This is done by putting the egg into water. If still fertile it will sink to the bottom of the vessel used, if addled it will float. It will be observed that occasionally the larger end of the egg tends to point upwards and not to be quite flat at the bottom. This indicates that the egg is rather stale. The old adage may be quoted, *the fresher the flatter*

When the eggs have begun to chip they should all be removed to the incubator, except two or three,—never less than two. When hatching has taken place, the chicks are put into the drying-box, but not kept there very long before removal to the game-hen who is acting as foster-mother. It is wise to see that the hen is well fed before she receives her hatched brood. Chicks are always carefully turned into the coops at nighttime. After six weeks of artificial feeding they are turned into the cornfields.

Attention must be drawn here to the practices which have proved so successful at Sketchworth Park. They are described in detail by Mr. Argus Olive in *Country Life* of November 14th, 1903 : " The partridges are allowed to go on laying until they have started to incubate their eggs, then about the third day of sitting their treasures are removed from them and sham eggs are given in their places, so that the birds continue to sit until their own eggs that have been put under eggs are chipped. The process is not completed until twenty-five of these chipped eggs are brought to the sitting partridge, whereas probably only fifteen or fewer were taken from her. She is easy enough to deal with, and if she objects to the hand that introduces the eggs and takes away the sham ones, she will not move more than a yard or two, and will come back directly she is allowed to do so.

" It is not supposed that she would, from the start, incubate twenty-five eggs, but it is a different thing when the young are so far self-sustaining as to be able to chip the shell; and it has been known, even before the period of the process of incubation, that a desertion and absence of outside heat for twenty-four hours has not killed the embryo. At anyrate, without arguing the case, the hen partridge does hatch off these twenty-five chipped eggs. It will therefore happen that three old birds will care for all the eggs of five, so that two birds out of five are not kept sitting upon sham eggs, but have their nests destroyed. The object of this is that they should start laying again, and in order that this should be certain, these two are robbed before incubation begins, for it is a questionable point if partridges that have once become broody very often lay again; if they do, how early or rather how late they do it. Personally, I do not believe many ever lay again that season if they have once started to sit. At anyrate, the risk is not worth running, and as these two birds will each be good for about eight second nest eggs, if the first are taken in time, the moral is obvious. In practice, this seems to be the utmost improvement that has proved successful. Its gross result for the five birds may be stated thus—Safety from thunderstorms and from vermin for the incubating eggs, and besides, ninety-one eggs instead of seventy-five for every five birds."

Feeding of the Young Birds.—We have already spoken in former paragraphs as to the feeding of the young chicks which have been placed under the care of a foster-mother. It is only necessary for us to add a few remarks here on the general feeding of the young partridges when they are reared artificially.

It is essential that the young partridges should have a good supply of the pupæ of ants during the first fortnight after hatching. When these are not obtainable, Mr. Carnegie recommends bruised wheat soaked and then fried. "About the third or fourth day, some custard may be given mixed with lettuce, chickweed, plantain (the unripe flower), groundsel, rice, broken small and boiled, and small quantities of any small bird-seed. The best way is to make a thinnish custard, and mix some of the other food material with it, always giving preponderance to the green food. Any insects which may be obtainable may also be given, in addition to the ants' eggs, which, it is necessary to remark, ought not to be offered the chicks till the other food has satisfied their appetites." "Boiled rice, custard or hard-boiled eggs," says Lord Walsingham, "well crushed, will certainly ensure the saving of a fair proportion of the chicks; but these alone are by no means equal to the same with the addition of ants' eggs. It is a good plan to sweep the rough herbage on the borders of some neighbouring field or wood with a coarse bag-net made of canvas or calico on a stiff iron hoop fixed on a strong handle. By this means a large number of insects of various kinds are easily collected, and can be conveyed in a bag to the coops, and thrown down for the birds. When the birds are three weeks or a month old, the same food that is given to young pheasants may be provided for them, but grain should in no case be given, unless first soaked and crushed."

The coops for artificially fed partridges are best placed in fields where the grass has been cut. The young chicks are then able to take advantage of the new grass as it grows. The coops should be moved not infrequently, so as to ensure a new feeding-ground, with its potentialities of grass and insect life. A supply of water is necessary for all partridges, whether artificially reared or in a wild state, and it is as well, in a great drought, to distribute small drinking-troughs over the estate. In this way the lives of many young or even old partridges have been saved.

In making these remarks on the artificial rearing of partridges, it is only necessary to add that it is much more important that the keeper should give his time and sense to the careful watching and protecting of the wild birds in the nesting season, than that he should be concerned in the processes above described. Very few sportsmen go in for artificial rearing, and it is practically unknown in Scotland.

4. *The Improvement of the Stock by the Introduc-*
   tion of Eggs from other Breeding-Grounds,
   and the Importation of Foreign (chiefly Hun-
   garian) Partridges.

Enough has been written with regard to the
criminal abuse of the practice of buying eggs for
the purpose of improving stock, and it is again
referred to in another chapter. Far and away the
best method is to obtain the eggs from a friendly
sportsman. Rather than buy eggs from strangers,
it is better to lay down Hungarian partridges or buy
Hungarian eggs. This remark, of course, is made
with the object in view of counteracting the dishonesty that is apt to be associated with the trade
in eggs. It is most necessary to state that eggs
obtained, for the purpose of being placed in the
nests of parent partridges, must be freshly laid ; if
incubation has commenced, they are best dealt with
under foster-parents. For the improvement of the
breed of stock, an interchange of eggs is made
recourse to, either simply by transferring eggs from
brood to brood on one's own ground (where this is
extensive), or by dealing with a friendly neighbour.
A similar interchange or transference of birds may
be recommended. On one's own property birds may
be captured, while at feed, by coops. Two out of
three cocks should be killed and the remainder

removed to the ground indicated. Here they are
kept under coop for a few days, fed sparingly,
and then turned out. The same process is
followed when exchange is determined on with
birds from neighbouring properties or from a
distance.

With regard to the introduction of Hungarian
partridges a few remarks are necessary. They
should be turned down sparingly—a few every year.
On this point Messrs. Tudway and Hall write: "The
earlier they are turned down the better. Birds
should always be turned down at night, in the
neighbourhood of their water and food supply. If
this does not exist, supply both. On the night
that the keeper turns them down, let him first
separate the sexes, and then place about four hens
in one spot, and the same number of cocks at a
distance, repeating the process while the birds last.
This will give them the chance of mating with
English birds the same season."

The practice followed by one of the present
writers who has for years dealt with Hungarian
partridges is as follows: He erects enclosures—
each eight feet by five feet—at various parts of his
partridge ground. The enclosures are about three
feet high, and are made of wire netting fixed on
stout poles, covered at the top with packsheet
to prevent the birds hurting themselves in their

attempts at flight. One end of each enclosure is moveable, and is virtually a wired gate. Inside and all round each enclosure are placed fir branches, which act as excellent cover. From six to eight birds are placed in each and are fed on barley and hay seeds for eight days. At the end of that time they are settled down. Food is then scattered outside of the enclosures, and on a dark night the "gate" end is opened. Lord Walsingham's modification of this plan, as far as it affects the letting out of a few birds at a time, is probably an improvement.

But whatever method be adopted, on no account should the practice—which we have observed on more than one occasion—be followed of letting the birds out on the night of their arrival and after being hustled about for days in the process of travelling. Where such a procedure is practised, the birds immediately take flight, and, flying hard, fall exhausted many miles from where they were laid down.

The questions of (5) The Destruction of Vermin, (6) Poachers and Poaching, and (7) The Good Understanding with Farmers and their Employees, are dealt with elsewhere. It is only necessary to conclude this part of the subject by referring to the question of the killing of some of the cock birds, which are nearly always in excess of the hens in each covey. The

keeper should get the consent of the master to kill
a few cock birds at the pairing season.

Note.—It has been recommended by some authorities, that at the pairing season the keeper should
scour the grass fields and drive the birds into the
corn fields, so as to urge them to make their nests
there instead of in the more exposed grass or lea
fields.

Shooting the Partridge.

Walking Up.—In shooting partridges by walking
them up, pointers and setters are used in those
cases where there is not too large a stock of birds
and where economy of time and energy is desired.
In the majority of cases, however, they are dis-
pensed with. Some of the main points to be
remembered by the keeper in the shooting of
partridges by the walking-up method may be
enumerated.

(1) It is very advisable, before the shooting
commences, that the stubble and lea fields be well
beaten in the early morning, for the purpose of
driving the birds into the covers of potatoes and
turnips—the former for preference. The keeper
should send out boys for this purpose, or he may
gallop on a pony over the fields, driving the birds
in and noting their destination.

(2) A good deal of time will be saved, and a

large amount of important information gathered, if a marker or markers be posted on high vantage grounds to note and indicate the flight of coveys. Any piece of high ground near to the scene of action may be used for this purpose, or the marker may even use a tree from which to " look out." Even when hands are scarce it is better to utilise a marker at the expense of the number of beaters and attendants than to dispense with him altogether, unless the lie of the land be such that he is either useless or superfluous. This will be found a very exceptional condition of affairs. There must be no "halloing" between keeper and marker. A code of signals may be arranged, a whistle being used for preference. It is well, however, for the keeper or one of his underlings to interview the marker from time to time and thus be able to obtain accurate information.

(3) It should never be suggested that guns should go into a turnip field unless birds have been seen to go, or are known to have gone, into it.

(4) Before the guns and beaters begin to cross a field, the keeper should see that the hedgerows at the beginning of the beat are thoroughly searched, and that all the fences are explored before the field is finally abandoned.

(5) The keeper should be particularly careful to

warn the guns to keep a sharp lookout at the end of every beat. Guns are apt to slacken their attention as they approach a hedgerow or the corner of a field. It is at such places that birds, which have run ahead in front of the guns, are apt to rise.

(6) If it be left to the keeper to decide how the guns and the beaters are to advance, he may choose one of several methods, the most usual being the advance in line and the "half-moon" principle. The former plan is the more common, especially when the field is at all extensive, but it is as well to recommend, when this practice is followed, that when the end guns are close to a hedge one or two of them should be flanked, that is, a little in advance of the others. When a strong wind is blowing across the field, it would be better that the line be flanked in every beat. The keeper's attention must be constantly kept to the formation and evenness of the line of guns and beaters. If the "half-moon" pattern be used, it is necessary to drop a polite hint as to the danger involved. If this be done judiciously, it will be well for the whole party and will not cause offence.

For an elaborate description of this form of advance, and for information as to other less used methods such as the advance by echelon, the keeper is referred to Lord Walsingham's excellent account in the volume on *Shooting* in the Badminton Library.

It is hardly necessary to add that in approaching a covey in a stubble or lea field, never by any chance should the guns be advised to advance directly on the birds. They must be flanked, and approached by a wide horseshoe pattern, which tends to become a circle as the guns proceed.

(7) If in beating a field there be no desire to drive birds in one particular direction, then the guns and beaters should wheel, but if it be desired to force the birds ahead, the line should come back to the original starting-point.

(8) When a single bird is killed, the place should be carefully marked by the keeper or by one of the beaters, and the line should continue to advance till the place is reached. Where several birds have fallen, sticks should be planted at the nearest points possible to the places where they are likely to be found. When a bird towers or falls at a great distance, an attempt should be made to mark the spot by selecting some object in the field of vision that will give the line of the bird,—a tree at the end of the field, some outstanding piece of growth in the field, or a gap in a hedge, may be useful for this purpose.

(9) In working the retrievers for picking up birds, the following instructions should be carefully remem-

bered. (*a*) First pick up the birds that have fallen behind the guns. (*b*) Leave alone all consideration of runners till the dead are picked up. (*c*) Never allow a dog to go on to fresh ground. Runners or birds that have dropped far out may be picked up in later beats, care being taken to remember their line. If, in the later beats, there be any difficulty in finding, a man may be left behind with a retriever, while the guns proceed to another cover. (*d*) Only send a dog immediately forward to a killed bird if you can absolutely trust him. (*e*) In picking up a bird, let the dog have the wind of it. Dogs work better alone, and not with men near them to spoil their scent. Men carrying hares or rabbits are especially to be warned off.

(10) The keeper should remember the unvarying law,—the line must move slowly, evenly and silently.

Note.—It is in every way to be recommended that, where partridges are habitually killed by the walking-up principle, an occasional drive should be arranged. In this way the coveys are dispersed, there is an interchange of blood, and old barren birds are killed off.

Driving Partridges.

There are several important points in connection with a partridge drive that the keeper should keep in his mind :—

(1) The question of fences is of importance where partridge-driving is regularly practised year by year. The keeper should, along with his master, try to use persuasion with the farmers not to cut their fences too low. If the good relationships referred to in Chapter III. be maintained, this should be easy. Shooting from behind a good high hedge is quite a different matter than from behind a low-clipped one, or from behind an artificial " butt " in the shape of an improvised hurdle.

(2) In the majority of cases the keeper will find that the guns will take up their position for shooting guided by their own knowledge of the sport, but he may be called upon to indicate to the less experienced the best positions to assume. He will keep in mind the necessity for good cover, and remember the rule of experience that guns should stand near to the hedge in up-wind drives and well out from the hedge in down-wind drives. From a high fence in the latter case the guns should stand far out.

(3) The law of making experimental drives, as laid down in the chapter on Grouse, must be followed. In this way the line of the general flight of the birds will be learnt, and it must be carefully remembered that partridges will not be driven the way they are not accustomed to go.

(4) It is best to preface a drive by ordering the

beaters, in the morning, to drive the birds from off any outlying ground.

(5) It is advisable to have the first drive with the birds driven down wind.

(6) The beaters on moving forward to a drive should pass along a boundary fence.

(7) In bringing back the birds for another drive, the knowledge of their flight is important. It is useless to attempt to bring back birds from directly behind the guns if the birds have not flown there. This seems a truism, but it is necessary to indicate that such foolishness is often practised. Remember the seemingly simple, but oft forgotten, rule : Bring back the birds from where they have flown with the wind.

It is advisable in bringing back birds against the wind that some of the guns should walk with the beaters, as a great many birds in this case break back.

(8) The head-keeper should form the centre of the line of beaters, to guide and warn the flanks, and he should, for preference, be mounted.

(9) The law of flanking is the same as in the case of grouse-driving. A screen, well thrown forward, should always be formed on the down-wind side. Flanks should be enlarged and increased according to the wind, and it is as well that good guns be placed along with the flanks who are

14

on the down-wind side. When there are no guns on the flanked side, or when their presence is discounted, there should be a good deal of shouting and waving of flags on that side.

(10) In addition to the keepers, who stand with their retrievers behind the stationary guns, there should be a keeper or two at the other end of the field in which the guns are standing, to mark and pick up towering birds, and those that have dropped far out.

(11) All birds should be picked up on the day of the drive. Scouring the fields on the day following disturbs the birds too much. Partridges should always be allowed a day of rest after a drive.

Poaching the Partridge.

Where it is possible, there should always be extra hands engaged in the nesting season, and every care should be taken to systematically watch the fields where there are nests. Bushing must be carefully carried out. "An excellent plan" (writes Sir R. Payne Gallwey) "to check the operation of poachers who net partridges, is to procure three sticks of thorn, each two feet long, tie them across in the centre, with wire or tarred string in the form of a cross or star, sharpen their ends, and place one of the points lightly in the ground. This arrangement cannot be seen at night, and on being touched by a net rolls up in it end over end like a wheel.

The sticks can be kept from year to year ready for use, and be quickly placed in position in the fields."

Another plan is to drive oak posts, about an inch square and three to four feet long, into the ground at various points over the fields. It will add to their usefulness if a few nails be driven into the posts near to the top.

But whether bushing, poling, or other method be carried out, such practice must not supersede careful day and night watching.

CHAPTER XI

THE DEERSTALKER

By Captain HENRY SHAW KENNEDY

To my mind, for an outdoor servant, there is no
more delightful occupation than that of a deerstalker.
His life is generally spent in wild and magnificent
scenery, and though the house or lodge he lives in
may be isolated—perhaps twenty miles from the
nearest town or village—yet there is a charm in the
isolation, and there is a slight romance in living out
of the world far from human ken. What can be
more delightful than to feel that the " wild red deers,"
as they call them, are your only neighbours for miles
and miles. Well, if these are not to the stalker's
liking, I should advise his taking to some other
trade.

But now to business. Every man is not fitted to
be a deerstalker—in fact, very few men are. No
man need attempt to take on this job with success
unless he is sound in heart, lung, and limb, with sight
of the very best. The stalker must be a first-class

walker—never know what it is to be tired; and, above all things, his soul must be in his work.

It is no easy task to outwit a large herd of deer, over ground they have lived on for years, with tricky winds blowing up the corries, and take your "gentleman" safely up to shooting distance.

My experience of the deerstalkers I have met and crawled with, and they are a goodly few, I look back upon with the greatest pleasure. I have invariably found them most delightful companions and keen (in fact, sometimes too keen) sportsmen, and I may say that some of the happiest days of my life have been spent on the hillside in their company, and I don't think I am wrong in calling them Nature's gentlemen.

Now and again one comes across lazy and indifferent stalkers (men who, in many cases, have become degenerate by the too frequent use of the black bottle), but, as a rule, they are few and far between, and for them I have no use, and have nothing to say.

These few little hints I am now writing are not meant in the least to serve as advice to the old deerstalker—he has nothing to learn, and is as wise and 'cute as the red deer himself or an old cock grouse on a mountain-side; but it is for the *young* stalker learning the practices of his trade that I write these few lines of simple advice, which may possibly be of use to him. For, looking back on old stalking days, how well I remember many a long and difficult stalk and crawl magnificently planned and carried out by the stalkers, marred at the last moment by some trifling error arising from want of experience. Instead of the stalk being a red-letter day in the forest, a day crowned by the prize of a goodly stag, it has ended merely in a long, dreary walk home in the dark, with your "gentleman" low and depressed in spirits, and fully aware that he will be well chaffed over the *miss* when he returns to the lodge.

We will now imagine ourselves in front of a forest lodge, time 9 a.m. (I am all for stalkers being "early astir" as the sporting papers term it, for late autumn days are short). Stalkers, gillies, and ponies with deer saddles, the number of the latter varying with the number of rifles to take the hill, all are preparing for the start.

Now, young stalker, the first thing, we presume, is that you are suitably dressed. Nothing to my mind can be better than *Lovat* mixture, but there are one hundred and one different patterns of cloth equally as good, and in several forests they have their own particular brand that they swear by, which is worn by stalkers, gillies, and the "gentlemen" themselves. However, these are matters of detail. Of course, the nature of the ground makes some mixtures much more suitable than others.

Of one thing I am certain : it is always best to have the whole of your suit and your cap made of the same material. I have often watched a line of grouse drivers on a hillside through a glass from a distance, and have always found the most conspicuous were those who wore mixed suits,—that is, coat of one material and knickers of another.

As regards boots or shoes, I prefer the former, as they give more support to the ankles; and spats when wet are apt to make cold feet; but this is entirely a matter of taste.

As each "gentleman" is told off to his beat by his host, this is the time, stalker, young or old, to be observant. If you are to take the hill with a sportsman you have been out with before, you have little to learn; but if he is a *new-comer*, you must try and find out for yourself, unobserved, what he is made of before getting him up to deer. In all probability you will have a mile or two to walk up the valley or up the hill before you come to the first spying-ground. As a rule, your "gentleman" will walk with and talk to you, and now is your chance; he may be an old *shikari* and know every card of the game, and be able to walk as well as, perhaps better than, yourself, and may be able to teach you a wrinkle or two; but this you will not be long in finding out, and *vice versâ*.

Should your "gentleman" be elderly, or you find

that he is not a good walker, you must at once
suit your step to his pace as much as possible, for
many a good day has been marred and many a
good stag missed by young stalkers not keeping
this fact particularly in mind. They bring their
"gentleman" up to shooting distance faultlessly,
having made a magnificent stalk in treacherous
wind over most difficult ground. But too fast! too
fast! they have never turned to look at the panting
object behind them; the rifle is pulled out of its
cover, shoved into the sportsman's hand, and the
whisper, "Tak' 'im noo, tak' 'im noo, Captain—
the big black one." But alas! the sportsman's sides
are heaving, his heart is throbbing, and his hand
is shaking from excitement and fatigue, and getting
up, he draws an unsteady bead, which results in a
miss and remorse for the rest of the day.

Now all this might have been different had you
adapted your pace to that of your " gentleman," which,
if deer are *settled*, it is just as easy to do as going
at your own pace. Of course, there are times,
when deer are on the move, that you *must* go
fast — in fact, race — for a shot, but the stalker
should always remember that there is not the
slightest advantage in his being one hundred or
two hundred yards in front of his "gentleman"
(a condition of affairs I have seen). The two
should be in close touch with one another.

But let us now hark back to the spying-point. Now, young stalker, we will presume that you are thoroughly acquainted with *a glass*, and before you have sat down two minutes to spy you will know if your "gentleman" is *at home* with it or not. He may be a first-class man with the glass, but you must not think you are a better man than he because you pick out deer first, as this results from the fact that you know the ground and exactly where to find them. The sportsman, on the other hand, is heavily handicapped, being a stranger and not knowing the likely spots to put his glass on; but in two minutes, as I said before, you can tell if he is at home and of any use with the glass. The *novice* you will detect at once; he is quite at sea with it, and has not the slightest idea of putting himself into a spying position, nor of keeping the glass steady—one minute he gazes at the sky, the next he plunges into the heather Now, having discovered your "gentleman" is a *duffer* (you need not tell him so), but seems anxious to learn, do everything you can to show him the best spying positions—off your knee, or off a stick, etc., and above all things be patient—suit yourself to the occasion. Of course, it is a thousand times better and far less trouble for you to find your "gentleman" an accomplished stalker. You may then very often pick up little hints from him if you are attentive

and observant, and you can both work so much
better together and consult one another as to the
stalk.

But let us suppose you have found deer from
your first spying-point, and a stag among them fit
to shoot, and your "gentleman" a novice, then take
plenty of time to explain matters to him, make
him have a good look at the deer through his glass,
point out to him the way the wind is blowing, and
how you intend making the stalk. This procedure
will be far more interesting to him than if you
shut up your glass, telling him nothing, as some
do, but simply let him follow you like a shadow
as you crawl and creep over rocks and wade through
burns.   It is far more exciting for him to know
the spot you are making for than to treat him as
a nonentity.   Therefore explain to him that when
you are crawling he must crawl, and when you are
slithering he must slither, and when you lie flat
he must lie flat, and should you *suddenly stop* (an
action prompted perhaps by an old hind looking
up), he must stop at once also, in however disagreeable a position he may be, and not move a muscle
till he gets the " office" from you. Sometimes you
are caught with one knee in a green spring and
the other on a sharp rock, which is anything but
pleasant ; but such are the ups and downs of
deerstalking.   When you are crawling with an

inexperienced "gentleman," it is always best to look round every now and then to see if he is acting in conformity with you or not, for sometimes a stalker cannot conceive what has put deer off the ground till he looks round to find his "gentleman's" head buried in the ground, but his heels in the air, or some part of his body showing.

Now, having walked, run, crawled, wriggled, slithered over fearful ground, sometimes in sight of deer and sometimes not, you have arrived safely within a few yards of where you expect to get your shot—now is the time for you, of all others, to keep *perfectly calm*. Nervousness and excitement are very infectious, and you are very apt to infect your "gentleman," especially if he be a novice, and very often if he is not. I cannot imagine any more exciting moments than those spent as you are just crawling up to the last little hillock or rock, knowing there is one of the finest harts of the forest within one hundred yards.

Have the cover of your rifle unbuckled and all ready to be pulled out in a second, and, above all things, do not take the best, and perhaps the only good spot to shoot from yourself. Make your "gentleman" creep alongside of you, or even a few inches in advance; let him have the front seat now, and choose the position he likes best to shoot from. I have often seen good, experienced stalkers take the front, and only possible place to fire from, themselves, pull the rifle out of the cover, thrust it into his "gentleman's" hand, and expect him to shoot as best he could.

There are a hundred and one little, trivial circumstances that cause *a miss* at the last moment, that could be so easily avoided.

Crawl close up alongside your "gentleman"—do not let him fire till the stag is offering a good broadside chance. If the deer have not "taken you up," there is no hurry whatever, unless the light is failing, when the sooner you shoot the better. Now, having given your "gentleman" the hint— "Tak' him noo, Captain," he will at once place his forefinger round the trigger in the shape of an "'ook" (as our old drill sergeant used to teach us), "and, without moving the ''ead, 'and, or heye,' press the trigger gently until the 'ammer falls"; and I think, if he follow out these instructions to the letter, the stag will also fall—and thus ensure a successful stalk.

But other little trifles very often cause a miss, such as blades of waving grass or heather being in front of the foresight. Now, to avoid these, the rifle must be raised to clear them, with the result that it is then found difficult to secure a good rest. To overcome this difficulty, if the ground is suitable, lie face downwards in front of your "gentleman," and give him

your shoulders as an excellent rest to shoot from.
It will, of course, be necessary to gradually raise or
lower yourself until he gets the right height. A short
stick is also very handy to shoot from if used carefully, but, of course, you run the risk of its being
"taken up" by the deer. Another point I would
advise all stalkers to be most careful of, and that is,
having got their "gentleman" safely up to the last
shooting-point, be sure that he takes the *right* stag.
I have often seen terrible disappointment by his
taking the *wrong* one. Nor is it always the sportsman's fault. Perhaps, for over an hour he has been
crawling behind the stalker, his nose glued to the
latter's boots, and has never had a chance of looking
at the deer he is stalking, till in the last hurried
moment he has before firing ; and it is not always so
easy to pick out the *best stag* amongst a big lot,
wildly scattered, unless there is something very dis-
tinctive about his head or body. Now, the "gentleman" having taken his shot, and you have seen
that the stag has got it in the right place and is
lying dead on the hillside, it is best to remain still
for a minute or so, as the herd of deer are much
more likely to settle again soon, and not go over
the march, than if you rushed in before they are out
of sight.

Having "gralloched" your stag, put him on the
pony, and started him for the lodge, and had your

lunch, and the day being still young, you can commence again, spying fresh corries and finding fresh deer, and may, perhaps, have one or two more successful stalks before night; but on no account should you be bloodthirsty—it is much better, to my mind, to have a blank day than to bring in an *unshootable* stag; it spoils the average weight of the year, and, if many of these sort are shot, it spoils the reputation of a forest. A stalker should know exactly his master's wishes as to how many stags one individual " rifle " should bring in on one day. I have known a " rifle " go out and, being carried away by his own excitement and his stalker's encouragement, bring in five, or even six, stags in a day, which were not worthy to hang by their heels in the larder.

Now, to my mind, that " gentleman " need not think himself hardly used if he is not asked to shoot in that forest again, and the stalker need not think himself a martyr if he gets the " Royal Order of the Boot." These " Waterloo " days, when several indifferent stags are killed, spoil the sport for others, as later in the season, when real good stags come on the ground they cannot be shot, as the *limit* may have been reached beforehand, which, to put it mildly, is a most annoying fact.

Now I am going to tread on very dangerous ground. A stalker cannot be too careful how he acts with regard to the forests that march with him. I don't think I am exaggerating when I say that, as a rule, there is more jealousy, more rivalry, and more cool feelings (may I use the words?) among the neighbours on deer forests than in any other locality. I find it exists not only among the owners, but among the stalkers and the gillies, and this jealousy is as infectious as the grouse disease itself. Again, Mr. Stalker, I offer my humble advice. If it be possible, do all in your power to keep friendly with your neighbouring forests and foresters. I am sure it will pay you best in the long run, for, in adverse winds, your neighbour can do incalculable damage to your sport.

Now we will jump from the neighbouring forests to your glass—not the glass of *Glenlivet*, but to your telescope,—to my mind by far the greatest friend a deerstalker has got, for, when he fails, you may as well "put up the shutters." It is the one great pull you have over the deer, as you are able to pick them up long before they, even with their keen eyes, can detect you. Now, you cannot be too careful of this said glass. In very bad weather, it is very apt to get fogged and be quite useless until taken to pieces and dried. Remember, then, when your glass is "bunged up," you are badly handicapped, and, to my mind, you lose half the pleasure of stalking. If it is a very wet day, use your glass as little as possible.

A good plan for you and your "gentleman" is to take it in turns to spy, so that, if one glass gets out of order, you have the other to fall back upon. Always take your glasses to pieces every night and have them well dried in front of the fire. This rule applies also to the case, which, if damp, is apt to fog the glass.

I will not go into all the "pros and cons" of different rifles — you could write volumes on this subject, and every man knows what rifle he prefers. The great thing, to my mind, is to hold them straight. I have often heard the very best of rifles abused for inaccurate shooting, when the real cause was "stag fever" — a very common complaint. As a stalker, you will most likely be provided with a rifle of some sort to shoot hinds with in the winter, and, with a little practice, you can soon suit yourself to any rifle. Remember always that, like your *glass*, you cannot be too careful with your rifle or that of your "gentleman." They should be cleaned immediately after you return from stalking, and hung up. Some sportsmen of my acquaintance clean their rifles themselves, and do not trust anyone else to touch them. Of course this is the safest plan, and no blame can be attached to the stalker if anything goes wrong.

The stalking season over, the sportsmen having all gone south, you are left a good deal to your own devices. You have the long winter to get through, which, of course, must be more or less monotonous in your isolated lodge, but, if you are a good man, you will find plenty to keep you occupied—watching your deer in the heavy snowdrifts, and doing what you can for them. You will also very often have hinds[1] to kill, and, next to stalking the stag himself, what better sport could you wish for? Then, when the New Year comes round, you can spend many an hour watching for good stags to shed their horns, for these, and many other little items, such as skins, etc., are looked upon as the stalker's perquisites.[2]

On the Deterioration of Heads.

Before concluding, I would like to make a few remarks on a subject that hardly comes under the heading of " The Duties of a Stalker," but yet must

[1] This question of hind-shooting is of primary importance in its applicability to the improvement of stock. We leave out of count altogether the question of good venison, which ought to be secondary to the desire to assist the general welfare of the forest. In keeping this in view the main point to be attended to is the destruction of old hinds, whose calves are in ninety per cent. of cases feeble and unhealthy, and in the opinion of many authorities, chiefly females. The stalking gillie is too apt to lose sight of the primary object of his work, and to select well-conditioned hinds, instead of the decrepit females before mentioned. " It has been proved," says one writer, "that ninety per cent. of yeld hinds killed would have had stag calves in the ensuing season. Thus, every ten yeld hinds killed mean a loss of nine prospective stags to the forest." On this account yeld hinds should be left alone.

A. S. W.—P. J. M.

[2] Every young stalker should procure, if possible, a *small* copy of Mr. Grimble's excellent book on *Deerstalking*. In it he will find a fund of information.

15

be a most interesting and useful study for him, and
that is the growth and development of the deer's
horn, from the time it commences to sprout from
the stag's skull (covered with velvet), till later it
develops into what I consider one of the most picturesque and most prized and valued trophies a good
sportsman can possess, and that is a finely matured
stag's head. I feel I am treading on dangerous
ground when I write on this subject, so many
abler and more experienced men than myself have
made a lifelong study of deers' horns, and a great
many most interesting and instructive articles have
been written regarding them, and yet, in spite of all
this writing, and in spite of all this study of animal
life, there is no disputing the fact that of late years
the heads of Scottish red deer have been deteriorating
greatly, and " all the king's stalkers and all the
king's men " cannot put a stop to this and make
them pick up again. I think I am correct in saying
that this deterioration is going on in almost every
forest in Scotland, and I think all old stalkers will
corroborate with me in this and tell you the same
tale,—" Heads are going back, back, back ! " What
is to be done ? Money will not stop it, artificial
feeding in winter will not stop it, and the introduction
of fresh blood and park deer seems of no avail,
though I do think that good wintering in a small way
helps deer to grow better heads. But in my very

humble opinion, and I trust I will not bring a
hornet's nest of deerstalkers about me for what
I am going to say — to my mind, the key to this
deterioration of late lies in the wholesale killing
year after year of the very stags that should be
left to reach maturity, and produce good stock.
But how is this to be prevented? It is next door
to impossible. The majority of forests are let to
yearly tenants who pay very large prices for them,
and very naturally wish to make the most they can
out of them, which, of course, means killing off the
finest heads in the said forests. As this continues
year after year, a good forest goes from bad to worse,
till at last it becomes a wilderness of wretched,
miserable stags, with heads that no good sportsman
would care to hang on his walls.

Now, to be brief, the best possible cure for this
deterioration is, of course, to spare as much as
possible all six, seven, or eight-year-old stags with
promising, well-shaped heads, and so give them a
chance, when they are ten or twelve years old, of
carrying magnificent heads such as one sees in
old drawings of Landseer and Crealocke.

There is one great drawback to this attempted
preservation of young stags with promising heads,
and that is, that although you do everything in
your power and skill to save them, your neighbours
may kill anything or everything that comes within

reach of their rifles, and so ruin all the good you are trying to effect.

Now, Mr. Stalker, it is very often in your power (though not always) to prevent the class of stag of which I have been writing from being shot, and when you save one of these you contribute your mite to the improvement of Scottish red deers' heads.

Deer-stalking Notes by Editors.

In addition to what has been said in the body of this chapter, the following points should be observed by the young stalker :—

(*a*) Never attempt a *down-wind* stalk.

(*b*) Always try to stalk *down hill*, as deer seldom look up the hill, and always try to have the sun at your back and shining in the eyes of the deer.

(*c*) Remember the general rule, that deer move up wind when they are feeding.

(*d*) In fine weather the biggest stags are on the highest hills ; in wet and stormy weather they are on lower ground.

(*e*) Remember that whatever wind may be blowing across the hills, there is always a current moving *up and down* the narrow glens. It is therefore wise to carefully spy out the ground near to where the deer are grazing, and notice the movements of the grass in their vicinity, and make your stalk accordingly.

(ƒ) The distance one may approach near to a herd varies. When there is a strong wind it is not safe to pass within a mile of the herd.

(g) In making a stalk, be particularly careful to avoid any outlying herds of deer; if these take you up they may move and upset all your calculations.

(h) Every stalker should have a first-class telescope, and should never be without it. There is nothing better than those supplied by Ross Limited, New Bond Street, London.

> " The best laid schemes o' mice and men
> Gang aft a-gley."

CHAPTER XII

THE RABBIT

THE gamekeeper is called upon to regard the rabbit in a variety of aspects, and these may be thus categorically enumerated—(1) as vermin; (2) as a comparatively unprotected and unpreserved occupant of a shooting estate; and (3) as a member of a carefully preserved and systematically protected warren; and in dealing with him in the latter capacity the keeper has to view him either as part of a farm — that is, when the rabbit is preserved mainly for market purposes,—or as part of a sporting property — that is, when he is preserved for the purposes of shooting.

He will most likely be called upon to view the rabbit as vermin in the following cases :—(1) On a good moor, generally; (2) proximate to good partridge cover ; (3) and near to special cultivated ground—as, for instance, farms, gardens, lawns, and the like.

Many owners have no objection to a stock of rabbits existing on their moors, but in every way they are to be regarded as a pest, especially in those cases where shooting is practised over dogs, or by simply walking up the birds. Many a brace of birds has been missed owing to the fact that the barrels of the shooter have been loosed on a rabbit. On this account it is as well that the rabbit should be exterminated on a moor, and not only on this account, but also in view of the voracious habits of the beast, and more particularly on account of the fouling of the ground by its excretions. There are cases, however, on small and badly stocked properties, where the chance of an occasional rabbit affords some consolation to the weary shooter, who, after tramping for hours without a shot, regards the furtive bunny almost in the light of "game." The presence of rabbits at least ensures his return with something in the bag.

To the keen and experienced rabbit shot, nothing affords better sport than rabbits in heather, but where such are desired it is better that a certain part of the moorland be reserved for the rabbit stock. On most shootings there is a considerable acreage of ground near to the lodge where rabbits are plentiful enough for such purposes, and where birds do not generally breed. But these facts do not upset the general rule that on a moor the rabbit is to be regarded primarily as vermin. (2) In regard to good partridge cover the same remark is to be made, although in this case the

main objection to its existence is in relation to the
feeding capacity of the ground. As a rule, there is
not so great an objection to its presence as in the
case of the moor, especially when the cover is
extensive and is used as shooting ground. A day
among the "whins" would lose half its attractions
were it not for the rabbits which afford such excellent
practice as they dart between the bushes, and the
escape of a covey of partridges means merely, as a
rule, a flight into turnips or potatoes, the best and
natural cover in which to kill them. But if the cover
just referred to is required for a good stock of
partridges, and if its food possibilities are limited,
and especially if the birds are not to be disturbed till
the first drive, it is better to get rid of the rabbits. (3)
The destructiveness of rabbits is notorious, and the
keeper will often be called upon by his master to
protect his garden and his flower-bedded lawn from
their encroachments; and a farmer has a right to
protest in those cases where rabbits are laid down to
such an extent that they overrun and materially
damage his crops.

So much for the rabbit as vermin. In considering
him as a comparatively unprotected and unpreserved
occupant of a shooting estate, we are regarding him
in his most popular and most general aspect. We
use the word "comparatively" advisedly, for in nearly
every case some protection is necessary both for the

sake of the rabbit and for the sake of proper shooting, and however little attempt is made to convert a small rabbit shoot into the proportions of a warren, yet it is necessary, if rabbits are to be all healthy or numerous, that the rule as to the addition of new blood be observed as carefully as in the case of the latter. *The unvarying rule is, that new blood should be introduced every year.* This is a rule, however, that is almost invariably neglected. The law of inter-marriage is the same throughout the whole animal world. Inter-marriage amongst peoples tends to the deterioration of the race. An uncrossed grouse stock tends to disease and death. A rabbit stock which is left to itself accumulates diseases of the most virulent description. The danger is far greater in the case of rabbits than in that of birds, owing to the migratory habits of the latter. Many people refuse to eat rabbits owing to a suspicion that disease is likely to be present. This may be an extreme and an un-necessary caution, but the mere fact that it exists indicates the truth that such disease is *apt* to be present.

It is difficult to lay down a general law as to the number of rabbits to be put down each year, when we are not dealing with a warren, but merely with scattered rabbit burrows, but we should say that about three or four to every hundred acres of ground would be sufficient. The best time is when the

shooting is over, but not later than the middle of
January. This is late enough to permit of the
Christmas shootings. When there is sufficient
evidence to prove that the rabbit stock is dimin-
ishing from any cause apart from the destruction
by gun and trap, the whole stock should be obliter-
ated and an entirely new one laid down. Great
care should be taken in the selection of the ground
from which the new blood is taken. It should come
from districts at as great a distance away as is
consistent with convenience, and should be from
ground where the laying down of new blood is
consistently and habitually practised, and, if possible,
from ground where rabbits are not too numerous.
In selecting the rabbits, bucks should preponderate.
In the majority of cases it is easy enough to arrange
an interchange of blood. For this, it is, of course,
necessary that the health of one's own stock should
be above suspicion.

The unenclosed burrows with which we are now
dealing are, in the main, used for the purposes of
ferreting, and it will be the duty of the keeper to see
that there are convenient arrangements made for the
purposes of the guns. It is often necessary to
do a little clearing in the vicinity of rabbit-burrows,
especially when there is much undergrowth. When
the burrows are in thick wooded cover, rides may
be made—not only the wide-open rides as used in

pheasant coverts, but smaller ones not open to the sky. Rides should also be made on bracken ground and on the heather land that is used for rabbit-shooting. In the latter case, the rides are most useful, for where the heather is thick, old, and long there is little or no chance for the gun to spot his rabbit, until perhaps he sees it disappearing over the edge of a knoll, or into a hole, a hundred yards away. If the heather has been well attended to, and this is very exceptional on land that is near to the lodge and is used primarily as rabbit-ground, the rides are not so absolutely necessary, and sporting shots might prefer to take their chances without their aid.

It is often desired to lay down stock on ground that is at present untenanted by rabbits. When this is done outside a warren and chiefly for the purposes of ferreting, suitable ground will, of course, be chosen—that is to say, ground which combines the necessities of food and good opportunities for shooting. This ground should be temporarily closed in by wire fencing, and should be scooped out here and there to assist the rabbit in the process of burrowing. After the ground has been sufficiently burrowed the fencing may be removed.

The Warren.

A warren may be an extensive stretch of ground a quarter of a mile or more in length, as exists at

Stenton, Mr. Graham Murray's place in Perthshire, or may simply be a three-acred field. In the former case, no change of venue is necessary; in the latter, it is usual to change it from time to time, say once every five or six years. The ideal warren must be well drained, well supplied with food, and well enclosed. The soil should be sandy and porous and free from the possibilities of flooding. Good natural warrens stretch along the banks of rivers, but have a considerable elevation above high-water mark, and slope gently upwards towards the pheasant covert, which stretches in almost parallel lines with the windings of the river, and are enclosed at each end, either by natural fences, protected by wire netting, or simply by this netting erected on wooden palings. A good warren of this type has varieties of cover, bracken, broom and gorse, heather and hussocks of grass, and here and there small juniper trees, and varieties of shrubbery. But although such a warren is described as a natural one, it is liable to the same laws as the ones we may term "artificial." The extinction of vermin must be thoroughly looked to, the cover must be regularly supervised, wiring must be carefully examined, draining carried out, and, if necessary, lime occasionally scattered to counteract the fouling of the ground, overcrowding avoided, and evidences of disease carefully noted.

Where no such natural warren exists, and it is

proposed to construct one, it would be to the advantage of a keeper if he visited some well-known
warren, and took into view the natural conditions
which he proposes to imitate. In selecting his
ground, he should keep in view the following points:
—(1) The lie of the land; (2) the condition of the
soil; and (3) the capacity for cover. The land
chosen should in no case be on clay soil or be
rocky ground. Sandy soil is the best, although
peaty ground is not to be sneered at. The place
chosen should be fairly high, and of an undulating nature. Great trouble will be saved if ground
can be found which has been already well burrowed,
so that the new stock laid down may soon find a
home. Where these burrows do not exist, the
keeper and his underlings must assist nature by some
preliminary digging, as we have described before.
Where nothing but a clay soil can be obtained,
artificial mounds may be constructed of a looser
and more porous earth, sown with grain seeds, and
containing holes which can be readily converted
into burrows. An excellent form of warren can be
made by simply enclosing a piece of moorland where
the heather is not too rank and thick, which lies
well, and which already contains rabbit burrows, and
a certain amount of isolated trees and shrubbery.
This land, if well cut with rides, is both excellent
feeding and shooting-ground. It is important

that the burrows be distributed pretty evenly
and generally in the warren. Where it is found
that rabbits have collected in one area to the
exclusion of others, and there is a danger of an
insufficient food supply, it might be as well to construct temporary enclosures within the warren, in
which the rabbits may be placed, and these
enclosures kept up till such a time as burrowing
is complete. Great care is necessary in regard to
the cover available. It may be necessary to scatter
fern or gorse seed, or even to plant or transplant
trees and bushes. Most good warrens have, here
and there, large flat heaps of the branches of trees.
These afford excellent cover, and are especially to
be recommended when the warren is used for
shooting purposes. Where the warren is a permanent one, or where there is a suspicion that
temporary ground has become stale and tainted,
some addition to the natural food must be made.
That great authority, Mr. Lloyd Price, recommends
that portions of the ground should be fenced with
wire netting, and crops of clover, oats, or beans
grown within the enclosures. When these have
been carried, or partly so, the wire netting may be
removed and the rabbits allowed access to this
reserved ground. By changing the position of
these plots, the rabbits get access periodically to
fresh, untainted ground, and thrive accordingly.

During the winter, it is always wise to give the rabbits artificial food by scattering corn and good hay here and there over the warren. Some authorities recommend swedes, but these are better avoided, for, although they agree with some rabbits when they are associated with corn and hay, they are apt to produce intestinal and other troubles.

It may be as well to quote a more elaborate, yet simple enough, method mentioned by Mr. Lloyd Price, for constructing a warren (*Encyclopædia of Sport*, p. 174):—" Find a field or rough open space, either partially or wholly surrounded by woods, in which rabbits live and breed. Let this be walled round, and let holes be made in the wall at regular intervals, and closed by wooden or iron shutters at will. Encourage the rabbits to feed in your walled-in ground. Of course, the beasts soon get quite at home in your enclosure. A night or two before you shoot, shut down the shutters and the thing is done. An improvement would be to make the shutters of light iron bars, to swing outwards from the cover into the preserve shambles, or whatever we choose to designate the field of slaughter; the rabbits would soon learn to use these, and as the gratings would swing back of themselves, preventing the return of the tenants, your enclosure would soon fill itself without any particular attention on the part of the keeper. Care must be taken, however, not to leave the huge trap too long without emptying, or else to supply plenty of food inside, or the rabbits would starve." It is perhaps as well to impress upon the keeper that great care must be taken with the fencing. This must be thoroughly carried out at the beginning, and examined carefully afterwards, in case any destruction may have been made by sheep or other animal pasturing in ground approximate to the warren. A single or a double strand of barbed wire outside of the warren fence is useful to prevent such inroads. Wire netting must, of course, be turned over both top and bottom, for rabbits are good climbers. It might be as well that a single barbed wire be stretched across the curve at the top. The points at which the wire netting is turned over must be strengthened by fairly thick wire, to prevent bending.

In summarising the facts to be remembered by the keeper for the prosperity of his warren, we might tabulate the following, which must receive his earnest attention :—

(1) The proper food-supply of the warren. Where cut hay is supplied, care must be taken that it is kept dry and healthy by some form of covering.

(2) The careful and habitual restocking of the ground. This must be done annually, with healthy rabbits from other warrens, as rabbits breed rapidly. Kill down stock in winter hard, especially the ones that lay out, these being generally the weak ones expelled from

the burrow by the stronger does and bucks, who keep possession of the stronghold, these being useful for breeding healthy big stock. As rabbits are subject to interbreeding and remaining about the same burrow, ferreting is useful in order to change the habitat and encourage interchange of blood.

(3) Proper fencing.

(4) The elimination of vermin.

(5) Draining, if necessary.

(6) The occasional scattering of lime and salt to prevent fouling.

(7) Avoidance of over-stocking. In a case where a warren is used for profit, about one hundred rabbits to the acre is a good average, but only about ten to the acre where it is used for shooting purposes.

Where a warren is small, great pains must be taken with the care of the ground. If the venue of the warren be not changed, careful liming and artificial feeding must be had recourse to. It may be even dressed with some phosphatic and lime mixture, of which, perhaps, dissolved bones is the best. But it is strongly to be recommended in the case of small warrens, that the venue should be changed every five or six years, so as to secure new feeding-ground and to give the old ground a chance of recovering its food capacity and its healthy condition.

16

Shooting the Warren.

The main point to be observed in this connection is to assert, once and for all, that on no account must ferreting be used for making the rabbits lie out. Gastar is the only thing to use. Let every hole be blocked about five days before the shoot, and let the thrown-up earth be sprinkled with the tar. Next day go round the holes again, and block as before. Do this every day till the time of the shoot, and the process is complete. Your whole stock is in the warren, eating in the open, or lying among the bracken or round the foot of trees, or under the heaps of faggots. Let this method be tested once, and such processes as ferreting, smoking, and the like will pass into the limbo of archaic ignorance.

With regard to a warren shoot, it is only necessary to remind the beaters that they must prod, and not beat out the rabbits. Every foot of the ground must be carefully probed, faggots must be thoroughly overturned and explored, dogs must be kept well leashed and brought up to the line. There must be no stragglers. The whole party of guns and beaters should move across the warren like a battalion of infantry advancing in line. There must be no dangerous rushes forward by beaters or dogs.

Never attempt to suggest that rabbits be driven to the guns. That is a fool's suggestion.

Ferrets and Ferreting.

The main point to be remembered by the keeper is that ferrets are as liable to disease from bad hygienic surroundings as he is himself. Accordingly, the ferret should be assured of cleanliness, fresh air, and good food. The days of dirty, badly-ventilated boxes ought to be at an end, and as much care should be taken of the ferret-runs and hutches as of the kennels. Ferrets must therefore be allowed plenty of pure air and sunshine. To secure this, there must be connected to their sleeping-saloons a sufficient open-air run, which should be on dry, porous, well-drained soil. It is best that these runs should be tiled over, so that they may be well sluiced with permanganate of potash solution, sanitas, or other antiseptic fluid. It is easy to arrange these tiles so as to secure sufficient drainage. The sides of the run should be high enough to prevent the ferrets escaping, yet not too high to interfere with the easy entrance of the keeper for cleaning and other purposes.

The hutch, which is pierced with holes for the proper exit and entrance of the ferrets to and from the runs, may be a box, the top and sides of which lift bodily from the ground. In many cases the box consists of but one department, but recent improvements are much more elaborate, and even go so far as to secure three compartments—one for sleeping pur-

poses, one for feeding, and one for the calls of
nature. Where such an arrangement exists it is as
well that each compartment should have an easily
removable "tray," so that it is not necessary to
disturb the whole flooring for the purposes of cleaning, and so that the ferrets may be confined in one
compartment whilst the other two are being cleaned.
This cleaning must be carried out once in every
twenty-four hours, and must be thorough. The runs
need not be cleaned so often, but require careful
inspection. Either sand or sawdust may be used
for the floors of the trays.

" The food of the adult ferret consists in the main
of bread and milk, or porridge, or rice, but on no
account should it be too sloppy. Meat is given
occasionally. It must be fresh, and may consist of
liver of deer, mice, rats, birds, or a piece of freshly-
killed and warm rabbit. This should be tied to a
staple with a bit of string to prevent the ferrets
from dragging it into their sleeping-place, and thus
soiling the bedding."—(HARTING.[1])

Ferrets should not be fed too often ; once in twenty-
four hours is all that is necessary.

Working.—Ferrets should never be carried in a
bag, but always in a ferret-box, and on being brought
home should always have their feet washed. It is

[1] *Encyclopædia of Sport*, p. 239.   See also his volume on *Rabbits* in
Fur, Feather, and Fin Series.

always best, where possible, to have at least two keepers out while ferreting. If one ferret sticks, the guns may proceed to the next burrow, while the second keeper waits till the "stuck" ferret comes to the surface. If this does not happen after some time has passed, a dead rabbit should be laid at the mouth of one of the holes; if this does not succeed, the rabbit should be disembowelled and the entrails laid at the mouth of the hole, or a cartridge may be emptied of its shot and fired into the burrow. If all these plans fail, the ferret may be dug out, or nets or harmless traps may be set at several of the holes.

Neither the "guns" nor the keeper should be seen by the working ferret. They should, if possible, stand down-wind and out of sight. We hold firmly that a ferret should never be muzzled, and seldom coped. A rabbit is driven to the surface better by a ferret that is free, and a coped ferret is only capable of worrying, not killing.

Diseases of Ferrets.—The commonest complaint is *sweats*, with symptoms of abnormal temperature, thirst, running from eyes and nose, loss of appetite, and dulness. The affected ferret should be isolated, and bathed in some antiseptic fluid, as mild boracic acid and water, or permanganate of potash. It should be well dried and placed in a clean, fresh, dry, and warm hutch. The animal should be fed on slops—fresh warm milk, arrowroot, soup, and similar foods. Whatever is used, there should be a very gradual addition of solid food to the diet as the ferret improves. A good thing is a newly killed sparrow or other small bird, given a piece at a time sprinkled with a pinch of sulphur, once in twenty-four hours. All discharges should be carefully washed from eyes and nose, and the latter anointed with vaseline.

Foot-rot—Therapeutics. — Creosote or nitrate of mercury ointment applied once a day.

Worms. — Areca-nut or Filix-mas, followed by castor-oil.

Eczema.—Cleanliness and change of hutch, washing with antiseptic fluid, careful drying, and the use of nitrate of zinc lotion.

Itch.—Some form of mild sulphur ointment.

Keeping down the Rabbit.

The rabbit may be kept down by (1) shooting, (2) ferreting and shooting, (3) catching by a pitfall, (4) trapping, (5) snaring, and (6) netting. Of the last four methods there are endless modifications, and it will be found that most keepers have their own pet method, from which they are very loath to depart. As long as the method is legal, effective, comparatively painless, and economic, nothing can be said in its disparagement. The legality is of importance, for no one can use a spring trap to catch rabbits except (*a*) in the mouth of a burrow, and (*b*) unless the rabbits are taken by an owner occupying his own land. Many methods employed to take rabbits are completely ineffective, and should be immediately disregarded. Failure often results from the keeper leaving the traps exposed to view. Unless soil is sprinkled over them to hide them from the keen sight of the rabbit, they will be as useless as a piece of dead iron. Another cause of the ineffectiveness of a snare or trap, is the taint of anything that has come from human contact. The smell of man, dog, powder, rabbit, game, hanging around a trap, is a handicap that can only point to failure, therefore the keeper must see that his hands are perfectly clean before he sets his trap, and that the latter does not come in contact with his clothes. Mr. Harting recommends that after the hands have been well washed in soap and water, they should be rubbed with mould scraped up near the place where the snare is to be set. "When it is time to put the wire into shape, and smooth out any bends or kinks in it, this should be done, not with the bare finger and thumb, but with a bit of wash-leather between them. It is easily carried in the waistcoat pocket, and a snare rubbed down with this will be found to run as smoothly as possible when touched by a rabbit. Moreover, this intercepts any scent from the bare hand. To secure the effectiveness of snares, they should be set in the morning. The evening dews are apt to preserve the scents of the keeper."

The "humanitarian" side of the question must not be neglected. Any trap or snare that catches a rabbit and causes it needless suffering and a long and painful death, must be avoided.

It will be to the advantage of the keeper to be cognisant of the best traps and snares that have been recommended by authorities on the subject. Their modification is endless, and from a description of some twenty or thirty, we select three or four which appear to us to meet the requirements of the keeper in the most effective, the most painless, and the most economic way.

(1) *Cruickshank's Trap.*—This, the latest of all traps, is manufactured by Mr. A. A. Cruickshank, Craighall Warehouse, Glasgow. The body of the trap is exactly the same in form as that of the ordinary rabbit trap. It is of Dorset type, fitted with brass mounts. It is lighter than all other traps we have handled. The spring distinguishes it markedly from other traps. It is made of fine steel, and each spring is constructed so as to fit any trap, and can be detached or attached by hand without a tool. The spring does not need a railway

rail for a base to prevent buckling, as the entire pressure on removal of load passes right through the spring into the air on account of the loose socket attachment. In addition to this, as the spring terminals come close together when set, the spring, whenever the plate is touched, starts off more readily than in other types. The danger of a broken lever during frost is largely if not altogether removed by the coil spring. Experience has shown that this is altogether an excellent form of trap, and being of excellent workmanship, light, strong, effective, and durable, is certain to become popular.

(2) *Burgess' Spring Trap.*—This is recommended by Mr. Carnegie in his volume on *Trapping*, who appends to his recommendation this clear description of its qualities :—" The spring is the most important part of the trap, is thoroughly well tempered and strong, but, nevertheless, easily pressed down when the trap is set. The flap and catch and other important parts in which most makers fail are of copper, and do not wear away like iron, nor do they rust, which would clog the trap and prevent it acting. The plate is square, with the four corners taken off, and is of zinc, being so fitted as to be level with the jaws when set. These latter are thick and rounded, the teeth fitting one into another, though not closely, a space of one-eighth of an inch being left between. The teeth should on no account be sharp or pointed,

as their being so tends to break the leg and cut the sinews, thus liberating the rabbit ; nor should the teeth be continued round the turn of the jaw. . . . In order to prevent the rabbit, when caught, drawing the trap away, the back piece of the gin is furnished with a hole at the end, through which a chain about a foot long is attached by means of an S hook. The chain should have about eight links, with a swivel in the middle, and a ring of one and a quarter inch diameter at the end. It is purchasable apart from the trap, and should be well tested, as the weakness will be found where least looked for, viz. in the swivel, and this should always be examined. The ring is for a stake, which is driven to hold the trap. The best wood for this is ash, which should be cut in lengths of eighteen inches, and split, then rounded off to the required size, fitted tightly to the ring, driven on to within one and half inch from the top, and be over-lapped by this part, which ought to be left unrounded as far as the ring comes."

(3) *Brailsford Trap.* - - This is a trap to catch rabbits alive, and is manufactured by Messrs. Arling-stall & Co., Warrington. The following description is taken from *The Field*, being an extract from a letter from Colonel Butler, of Brekenham Park, Suffolk :—" It consists of a wire cage, very strongly made and open at both ends, the door being kept up by a simple method of setting. There is a treadle

made, and as soon as that is touched the doors close and the victim is imprisoned. . . . In setting them in runs, under shelving banks, or by the side of wire netting, I usually make wings at each end of fir boughs, or something of that kind, to guide the animal in ; but when set at drains or holes, it is only necessary to make a wing at the end farthest from the hole, the trap at the other end fitting close up to the entrance of the drain." This trap, it may be added, is extremely useful not only for catching rabbits, but all forms of vermin.

(4) *Mr. Lloyd Price's Snare.*[1]—" Select the narrowest part of a frequented run, one well covered with herbage, if possible, to conceal the apparatus, either on the flat, or better still, on the side of a hill. Drive the big peg firmly into the ground at the side of the run, let this be well hidden by the grass, heather, or what not ; then give a hitch or bend to the centre of the wire to hold the same in a loop just four inches in diameter. Next, stick the carrying peg in the ground to hold the loop (which should just easily go round your closed fist) at an acute angle to the run, also in the grass at the side, or otherwise concealed, four inches from the ground, and with the runner of the noose on the low side, so that the loop may run easily along the wire. Properly set, the catch-loop should stand up at right angles, or nearly so,

[1] *Encyclopædia of Sport.*

from the support peg, elevated above the surplus wire. If the latter be at the top, the noose will not run so freely; this can advantageously be hidden with bits of cut grass, leaves, etc., as also may the string which connects the wire with the holding peg."

Netting may be practised either by the small bag net attached outside a rabbit-hole, or by the long net. The first is used, of course, with a ferret. The long net is familiar and needs no description. It is used outside covers and is worked at night.

Poaching the Rabbit.

The planting of thorns near to rabbit runs is of value in counteracting net poaching. Where the long net is used by poachers or farmers, it is as well for the keepers to forestall them by arranging a shoot in this method:—Have a shoot with the long net and let the rabbits away, then a second shoot on the same principle, and it will be found that fewer rabbits appear. The third shoot can be safely left to the poachers or farmers, for they will get nothing.

Note.—The keeper should never forget that it is inadvisable to put fur and feather into the same game-bag or pannier. He should also remember to empty the bladder of the rabbit immediately it is picked up.

CHAPTER XIII

THE PHEASANT

THE science of rearing and "showing" pheasants has produced such an extensive literature, and has become such an elaborate affair, that it is absolutely impossible for such a book as this to attempt to deal with the question in any but a summary way. To enter into the details of "showing" pheasants alone would require the whole of this book and more, and we can only repeat what we said when dealing with grouse-driving,—that every man who desires to reach to any perfection in the art and science of the matter, must have recourse to the books of the great authorities. In the rearing, showing, and shooting of pheasants more than in any other branch of sport, it is advisable that a small reference library be at the command of the head-keeper, and it is for the master to see that advantage is taken of the privileges of this literature. Although we have indicated more than once the leading writers on sport, it may not be out of place here to enumerate the books of reference which we have found most useful in our study of pheasants.

(1) Experience—by far the best book.

(2) *The Encyclopædia of Sport.*

(3) *Shooting*, by Lord Walsingham and Sir R. Payne Gallwey (Badminton Library).

(4) *The Pheasant*, by A. Stuart Wortley and others (Fur, Feather, and Fin Series).

(5) *Practical Game Preserving*, by W. Carnegie.

(6) *Sport*, by W. Bromley Davenport.

(7) *The Gamekeeper at Home*, by Richard Jefferies.

(8) *Pheasants*, by W. B. Tegetmeier.

(9) *Letters to Young Shooters*, by Sir R. Payne Gallwey.

(10) *Shooting*, by Horace Hutchinson and others.

(11) *The Forester*, by Brown and Nisbet.

(12) *Sport in the Highlands and Lowlands of Scotland*, by Tom Speedy.

(13) *Birds of Norfolk*, by Henry Stevenson.

With these at his command, no keeper can say that he has not heard the best words on the subject, and will hardly require the more or less superficial study which we propose to make.

The keepers' duties in relation to the pheasant differ enormously. They may be connected with a shooting in which the pheasant is only regarded as part of a mixed bag, or they may be concerned with rearing and "showing" on an elaborate scale. It is in the latter case that the keeper's knowledge of the literature of the subject will be of importance. In the former case, where he is only possibly concerned with a few head of wild birds, he will have little to learn, and there will be small need of elaborate studies in rearing and "showing." In these cases his beating will be simpler than the beating of partridges, and he will only have to bear in mind the general rule affecting flanks and stops. But it is altogether a different matter when covert shooting is conducted on a scale of great elaboration.

Pheasant-Rearing.

Bearing in mind what we have already said as to the impossibility of dealing with the question at any length, let us take a view of the main points that have to be taken into consideration.

(1) There are several ways advocated of dealing with the question of the proper supply of eggs for the next year's sport. (a) In some estates the procedure is simply to attract the hens that are left after the shooting is over, by a little judicious feeding, and to allow breeding to take place in a semi-wild condition, and then simply to collect the eggs that are laid. (b) Another plan is to utilise a particular covert as the breeding-ground ; this covert only being protected in the sense that a certain amount of wire

fencing surrounds it; otherwise there is no penning nor other form of artificial enclosure. (*c*) A third and more general way is to collect a certain number of hens before the shooting begins, and either enclose them in the kind of covert mentioned last or in enclosed pens. (*d*) A modification of this is to leave the collection of the hens till the shooting is over. The great objection to the latter practice is that some of the hens may have been "peppered" by shot, and may have received injuries to the maternal organs. There is also another point in favour of taking hens before the shooting begins. By so doing, one is rid of the incessant fear that too many hens will be killed, and that there will not be enough left for the mews.

Whether it be required to secure hens for the mews or not, every keeper should ascertain the condition of his stock as soon as the shooting season is over. This is easily done by a little regular feeding. If there be too many cocks, he may exchange them for hens with a neighbouring keeper, and *vice versâ*. If this practice be not convenient or possible, the keeper should indicate to his master the fact of this superabundance, and if a large number of hens are not to be procured to counteract this disproportion, some more cocks should be killed.

But whether there be disproportion or not, the general game law as to the value of fresh blood must be remembered, and as much care taken in procuring pure breeds as in the case of rabbits or partridges. Crossed breeds or weaklings should on no account be introduced. Lord Walsingham supports the contention that "there is no better breed than the true *Phaseanus Colchicus*, commonly known as the old-fashioned dark variety without a white ring on the neck. These are free layers and good mothers—straying less from home than the paler plumaged varieties more recently introduced. They are quite as hardy, and fly at least equally as well. There are few places in England now where some traces of a cross with *P. Torquatas*, the ring-necked Chinese bird, are not to be met with, but, in the opinion of the writer, the cross-bred bird is not so worthy to be encouraged and propagated as are those of the old, dark, pure breed." The exchange of birds and eggs should be frequent — if possible, of an annual occurrence.

If the hen birds are to be kept in mews instead of being allowed to breed in coverts, more cocks should be supplied than in the more natural state. There should never be more than six hens to each cock in the mews, and there should be every facility for the wild cocks to get to the enclosed hens. The mews, therefore, should not be shut in at the top. In constructing the mews, the main point to be remembered is that they should be absolutely

17

closed in for at least three feet from the ground,
so that the pheasants may be free from disturbance
and annoyance from without. The birds should
have plenty of space, air, and light, and the ground
on which the mews are constructed should have a
light, porous soil. If the latter condition be not obtainable the ground should be dusted with sand and lime.
Pens are constructed either as separate domestic
establishments, containing one cock to several hens,
or are made to hold as many birds as one requires,
the proportion of cocks and hens being maintained as
in the small pen. Half an acre of ground accommo-
dates about forty hens. If the pens are constructed
in covert, the place chosen should have plenty of good
undergrowth ; if they are placed in the open the
ground should be planted with shrubs of varied kinds.
Spruce and privet are generally recommended.

In feeding the birds in the mews, care should be
taken that this is always done by the same person.
He should on each occasion be dressed in the same
type of clothing. No strangers should be admitted,
and whether feeding the hens in mews or covert, or
the young broods at a later period, there must be
no attempt to call the birds by whistling to them
when about to distribute the food. This bad habit
tends to domesticate the birds to a marked degree.
It is to be remembered at this point that if open
coverts are used, on no account must birds be put

into coverts in which they will not naturally stay. Select a covert which they naturally draw to and stray to. The general law that it is the duty of the keeper to assist, and not to thwart, the instinct of the bird must be observed. It will be found that pheasants naturally select coverts which have plenty of light, plenty of shelter, that are dry and warm, and have well-drained, porous soil, and which face to the south or south-west. This fact will lead the keeper to understand that he must on no account select ground which is cold or damp, which is exposed to the north or the east, and which is dark and dreary. The law which applies to pheasantries also applies to the ground on which the coops are placed.

The food of the penned hens should be of soft consistency—the ordinary poultry food (barley-meal and biscuit-meal) in the morning, and dry mixed grain in the afternoon. Some green food should be given occasionally. All food, whether for old birds or for young, should be mixed in the morning. On no account should the keeper perform this duty at nighttime. Stale food is a marked cause of disease. Too much maize should not be used, it makes the birds heavy, yellow-fleshed, and not agreeable to eat —vary feeding with light barley and oats and very little maize.

Great care should be taken that the ground of the pheasantries (and likewise the ground on which the coops are placed) is free from vermin, and is not allowed to stale. In the case of the pens and mews, these should be purified by a sprinkling of lime and sand, and if feasible the ground should be changed every few years. Stale ground is an important cause of mortality. Some authorities recommend that powdered oyster shells be placed in every pen.

About the beginning of April the keeper begins to collect his eggs, and he will continue to do so for about a month, and he can turn out his penned birds by the middle of June. By that time he will have his foster-mothers ready. Game-hens are the best, and of these the black-red game-hen is to be preferred above others. If these are not to be obtained, small hens should be selected, of which buff Orpingtons are probably the best mothers. They should all be strong birds, absolutely free from disease. He should carefully retain the eggs of these hens for some eight or ten weeks before the pheasant hatching season, for the purposes of food for the pheasant chicks. The roosting of the game-hens is of importance, care being taken of them as consistently as of the pheasants. The sitting hens must be allowed an early morning run on the wet grass, so that they may damp their breast feathers. This markedly assists in the hatching process. Some authorities recommend that where the hens are kept in closed yards the eggs should be sprinkled with tepid water at the time of the morning meal.

In collecting the eggs it is wise for the keeper to mix some "wild" eggs, and some purchased or exchanged eggs, with the ones collected in the pens. All nests that have been built in exposed or dangerous places should be denuded of all their eggs except one or two. Leaving the latter is a stimulus to the wild bird to go on laying. Otherwise she would as a rule desert her nest. Of course when the nests are left they should be carefully watched.

Suitable ground for the coops having been selected, the eggs are put under the game-hens, whose nest should consist of a square of dry sod or turf. On no account must the ground have been used the previous year. *Ground for coops should be changed every season.* Lime, gravel, and sand should be freely scattered about, and a liberal supply of cover in the shape of fir branches be placed at intervals, to afford temporary shelter to the chicks from the inroads of their enemies. The presence of the "cuckoo-spittle" should be noted. It contains an insect which is deadly poison to the young chick. One acre is sufficient for a hundred birds. The sitting hen should not be confined to the coop. This method of confinement, being a severe tax upon the nature of the bird, is unnecessarily cruel. Not only is this so, but the method deprives the chicks of their natural protector, and prevents the hen from cleaning and dusting itself, with the result that it becomes infested with vermin, which are conveyed to the chicks. It should be tethered with a cord about a yard and a half long. This allows sufficient room for the hen to move about and to perch on the top of the coop. When vermin approach, the hen is able to warn the chicks by her cackle, and they have a chance of running under her wings for protection. The hen must, of course, be shut into the coop at nighttime. When an incubator is used, the eggs are removed from the game-hen as soon as they begin to chip and are placed in the incubator, and when hatched the chicks are removed to the tray above. All the eggs must never be removed from the nests at the same time. In putting back the chicks there is no need to select special chicks for special hens. Chicks must never be let out very early if there is frost or heavy dew on the grass. Remember, covers should be kept quiet, or birds will leave them; no stray dogs, or shooting rabbits round covers at evening; no broken fences to permit of cattle straying in them. Keepers on their rounds need not leave the rides for fear of disturbing the game.

Encourage plenty of undergrowth and wild berries for natural food. Where there are none transplant in autumn or spring. How many keepers trouble about this?

Mr. Carnegie's Table of Food for Young Pheasants is as follows :—

Age of Pheasant.	Morning Feed.	Mid-day Feed.	Evening Feed.	Remarks.
Up to 3 days	Custard.	Custard.	Custard.	A slight sprinkling of oatmeal may be added if thought desirable.
3 to 7 days.	Custard and meal.	Custard and meal.	Custard and meal.	The meal to be gradually increased.
7 days to 3 or 4 weeks.	Custard, crushed wheat, millet seed, chopped lettuce, burned hemp, chopped potatoes.	Custard, barley-meal, boiled rice, onion, Dari seed, chopped artichoke.	Custard, oatmeal groats, buck-wheat, rape seed, dry dough.	But two of these need be added to the custard, or the separate diets can be altered day by day or every three or four days.
1 month to 2.	Wheat and (or) barley.	Custard and meal.	Wheat and (or) barley.	
2 months to 6.	Maize, barley, beans, green food.	Custard and meal, Dari, oats, maize, green food.	Maize, peas, wheat, green food.	These can be given on alternate days or changed week by week.

Other authorities recommend hard - boiled eggs passed through a sieve with a little specially prepared biscuit-meal or oatmeal, as the food of the young birds. No water should be given at any time. The moist food supplies enough. No food should be given to the chicks for the first twelve hours after hatching. A good supply of insect food, as in the case of young partridges, is of great benefit, and when this is not obtainable maggots may be given. These may be obtained from the bodies of dead crows.

But whatever plan of feeding is adopted—and the variations are too elaborate for us to dwell upon them in detail — war should be severely waged against the habitual extravagance connected with pheasant - feeding. Overfeeding and waste are rampant in most places where pheasants are reared. Most birds get 40 per cent. more food than is necessary, and the keeper must combine a sense of responsibility with his judgment in discovering the right mean. No encouragement should be given to the practice of habitually buying " patent " foods. The keeper should make and prepare his own food.

When the young pheasants are old enough the coops and chicks are removed to the covers.

Poaching the Pheasant.

Watching must be carefully carried out by night and by day, and the possible depredations by foxes and poachers dealt with. If trespassers or night poachers are suspected in any covert, threads should be stretched in the evening across any likely paths of access, twelve inches or so from the ground. Their condition in the morning will warn the keeper as to the presence of poachers, and a careful lookout must be kept for the next few nights.

Alarm guns, bells, etc., may also be used. Artificial pheasants nailed to the branches of trees afford a good plan of thwarting the poacher.

A strict lookout should be kept for any suspicious carts that may be loitering about the ground. It is as well that the keeper should gallop on horseback round the roads and over the estate every evening.

Depredations by foxes or dogs during pheasant-rearing can be frustrated by stretching several lengths of string, with small bells hung on to them at intervals, about nine inches from the ground, all round the approaches to the coops. The fox is sure to scent a trap and clear off. If the string is soaked in carbolic, renardine, tar, or some other high-smelling liquid, so much the better. In hunting districts, where foxes are plentiful, this plan is very necessary, and is thoroughly efficacious.

An excellent plan to trip up poachers is to have wire instead of string stretched across all approaches to the rearing - ground. Another practice is to surround the coops with a stout wire, and to attach to it one or more dogs, so that each dog has a free range over a considerable stretch of ground.

On some estates one of the night watchers carries a horn, and blows on it every quarter of an hour or so, for the purpose of driving off foxes.

It is very wise for the keeper to occasionally go round the hedgerows with a spaniel and drive in strayed birds.

Shooting the Pheasant.

There are four cardinal principles in the beating of pheasants to the guns which must be carefully imprinted on the memory of every keeper—

(*a*) Push pheasants as far as possible on their feet and bring them back on their wings ;

(*b*) Drive pheasants on their feet away from home and then flush them homewards ;

(*c*) Flush pheasants at a considerable distance from the guns ;

(*d*) Flush pheasants from a higher ground than that on which the guns are placed.

Now these cardinal principles are enumerated on the understanding that the keeper is expected "to show" his pheasants in the best way possible. That is, he is to bring them to the guns flying high and fast; he is not to present a number of "flap-doodlers" and low-flying birds. The latter may please certain people who are quite satisfied if they bring the thing they aim at to the ground, but it is not sport. The great boast of every keeper should be that his birds fly higher than most and require some "stopping." Accordingly let him remember that to produce such a result he must do something more elaborate than send his beaters in at one end of a covert and march them in a straight line to the other. He must, in fact, push his pheasants on their feet to a flushing-point and then allow "the trouble" to begin. In saying as much, it will of course be at once recognised that this can only be done by careful arrangement of covert, beaters, stops, and guns, and will require considerable study and patience.

Now to obtain the desired result on the cardinal and classical principles we have summarised, he must first think of the flushing-point, which may be—

(a) A detached piece of covert like the famous Scarborough clump at Holkham ;
(b) A specially planted piece of covert at one of the corners of the main coverts ;
(c) A turnip-field some little distance from the main covert.

The Scarborough clump at Holkham produces such excellent results that the practice followed there is to be recommended to the consideration of all keepers, and in following the Holkham methods he should remember certain important rules :—

(*a*) The detached covert must not be larger than the main covert;

(*b*) The end of the main covert must be thinly planted and must not be fenced in; if it is fenced there must be an open space immediately in front of it.

(*c*) The undergrowth in the detached clump must be good, and not hollow at the bottom. Birds are thus prevented from running and crowding together and rising all at once or in great numbers.

Having these conditions, the beaters must enter the main covert at the end farthest away from the detached covert, flankers must be placed, both men and guns, and the beaters must advance. As the birds are pushed forward on their feet, the beaters must not get too close to the running birds. Pheasants can be driven anywhere if kept on their feet. If there is a danger of too much squashing together, or a threatened flush, the beaters must be halted. As the beaters advance, all thick cover must be properly beaten, especially bramble bushes. Beaters have a habit of neglecting these from fear of injuring their clothes. Every beater should therefore wear a smock and gaiters. In driving the birds from the main covert, the beaters stop about one hundred and fifty yards from the end of the covert, which should be quite open, and begin to make a great noise ; this drives the birds across the open space to the detached covert, and they are now ready to be flushed. Stops are placed around the detached covert, each man being ordered to beat two sticks together to prevent birds collecting in his vicinity, and for his own safety. Guns are placed in single or double rows as desired in the space between the two coverts—not nearer than eighty yards to the detached covert—and the flushing begins by one or two men entering the clump and putting up birds one by one or two or three at a time. After this has gone on for some time, all the beaters enter, and, moving slowly across the covert, drive out the birds, which, passing over the guns, take their height pretty much at the level of the trees of the home covert, from which they had been beaten. A modification of this plan is for some of the beaters, after leaving the main covert, to cross the open space and be lined facing the detached clump, that is, some distance in front of the guns. This will ensure the birds passing over their heads, and gives the guns a better chance of high and strong-going birds.

(2) Where it is proposed to follow the method of driving the birds into a corner of the main covert, the latter should be worked in a series of beats until the whole of the birds are at the flushing-point. The cover of the flushing-point must be

attended to as carefully as in the detached clump, and from it there should run a narrow strip of similar cover along the whole face of the wood. In this case there must be a drive or open space made inside the cover, where most of the guns are placed. The birds on being flushed will fly homewards, as in the first case. Stops as before.

(3) The third method we have indicated consists in driving birds into a turnip or potato-field some hundred yards in front of the main covert, stops being placed at the end and sides of the field. The guns stand in the open between the main covert and the field, and some beaters advance into the field some sixty or seventy yards and halt. The rest of the beaters then go round and bring the field back in the homeward direction. The birds rise, pass over the heads of the stationary beaters, and make for the covert, passing in their flight over the guns.

These three methods of "showing" the birds may serve to illustrate the cardinal principles we have enumerated, and will suggest to the keeper, who is ignorant of the matter, the advisability of modifying methods which are now regarded as prehistoric. He will find the details of each of these methods described, with some slight modifications, in Mr. Stuart Wortley's epoch-making volume on *The Pheasant*. Even where there is no artificially arranged flushing-point the birds may be so driven as to secure them being flushed from a higher plane than that on which the guns stand. For instance, where the covert is lying on the side of a hill or gentle slope, the birds should be flushed from the highest point, never the lowest. In those cases where coverts are very much on the same plane, and no particular flushing-point is used, it might be suggested that a line of stops should stand in the open, close to the covert, in front of the guns, who should stand much farther back than when the birds are pushed from a flushing-point—say some 100 yards or more.

When it is absolutely impossible to conduct pheasant - shooting on these scientific principles, from want of suitable coverts or from other reasons, it might be as well that near to the end of the coverts three parallel rows of wire netting be arranged, with an opening in the centre of the two posterior ones. As the pheasants are pushed forward some will collect behind the first netting, some behind the second, and some behind the third. Each division can then be flushed separately.

In some places, where they have small pheasant shoots, matters are improved, and pheasants are shown better, by prefacing the first covert shoot by a dummy shoot, a sort of dress rehearsal, a few days before. Keepers are placed with blank cartridges, and the birds are sent over the guns once. By this method the head-keeper is able to note the flight of the birds and deduce therefrom the proper position of the guns, and in addition to this the birds fly higher when the real "trouble" begins.

In addition to what has been said, the following practical points may be indicated :—

(1) Sewin may be used as an excellent form of stop, both for hares and pheasants.

Sewin is made by fastening white feathers and scarlet tape at intervals of a yard, and ferret bells at intervals of five yards on to white or yellow cord, which is placed on sticks some two and a half feet high, firmly planted in the ground. The sewin is continually jerked by a beater, specially told off for the purpose. It may be used both inside and outside of the coverts. The sewin is kept on a reel, and is wound round an iron frame. The reel, the frame, and the sewin are supplied by well-known firms.

(2) Late in the season stoppers are even of more importance than beaters. All stops should, of course, get into position in the early morning, long before beaters start and guns begin to fire.

(3) Always shoot the covert that has the most birds in. Do not keep to a stereotyped habit of shooting coverts whether birds be in or not.

(4) Always shoot the exposed coverts early, as birds stray to warmer quarters on the fall of the leaf.

(5) All things being equal, outlying coverts proximate to other shooting-ground should be shot early to prevent the loss of birds by straying.

(6) No wild or untrained dog should ever be allowed in the coverts.

(7) All birds must be picked up as they fall. One or two keepers with dogs following a mixed line of guns and beaters are useful. A keeper or keepers, in fact, should always be behind guns. In the clump or detached covert system they should be just inside the main covert.

(8) The coverts should be searched carefully with dogs, preferably on the same day, or the day after the shooting, for the purpose of finding any wounded or dead bird that may not have been picked up. The keeper should be allowed to take a gun and shoot any birds that show signs of being wounded.

(9) All birds should be counted at the end of each beat. This will counteract any tendency to theft on the part of the beaters.

18

CHAPTER XIV

WILD DUCK

By Lord DOUGLAS GRAHAM

DURING the past few years we have seen what large bags of wild duck it is possible to obtain by careful rearing and good management. Although the number of wild fowl can hardly be said to have decreased, yet there is little doubt that in some marshes where, many years ago, large flocks of wild duck used to collect there is scarcely one to be seen. The reasons for this are numerous; the most important of which probably is, that as our population increases, wealthy sportsmen and landowners are tempted to seek seclusion and build their mansions in far-away spots which have always been the haunt of the wild duck. These birds, being of a shy disposition, seek other pastures, and the only way to lure them back is to breed and rear by hand others, which will act as decoys to their more nomadic brethren. At Netherby and other places enormous bags have been realised, the size of which

would hardly have been credited ten or twelve years
ago; moreover, the trouble taken is well repaid by
the excellent sport these birds afford; and the
difficulty involved in killing a really high duck is
sufficient to satisfy even the most exacting sportsman.

The common wild duck are fairly plentiful all over
the British Isles; they are generally to be found in
lakes, ponds, rivers, or other watery places. The
male, commonly known as the mallard, is a singularly
beautiful bird. The head and upper part of the neck
are of a dark green hue; the lower part of the neck,
which is separated from the upper part by a white
ring, is of a greyish brown colour; the breast above
is of a deep chestnut, below of a greyish white; the
back is greyish brown. The wings, which extend to
nearly three feet, are of a rich purple colour merging
into black; the greater wing coverts have tips of a
velvet-black, with a bar of white near the end, and
the lesser wing coverts are of a greyish brown. From
the end of May till the beginning of August the male
adopts the dress of the female, and does not completely assume his own brilliant plumage till the
beginning of October. The female is smaller than
the male and is of a brownish hue, the back being
blackish brown and the breast pale yellowish brown;
the wings brown, with a little green. The male bird
has a tail of twenty feathers, the four centre feathers
of which are curled up: they are of a greenish black

colour, the others being greyish white. The female has a tail of brown, the feathers margined with reddish white. The young birds, male and female, known as flappers, resemble each other till after the first moult.

The young wild duck is easier to rear than the young pheasant, and the expense is small, but certain precautions have to be observed, or the result will mean failure. The eggs can be bought nowadays at comparatively low prices, and having once been bought, there is no necessity to purchase more for the next season, as the females reserved for laying will lay quite sufficient. But supposing, as will probably be the case, that the eggs are to be collected on the estate and along the marshes, it is not necessary to consider the question of purchase. The eggs are usually to be found in the rushes along a river bank or in an open field. The nests have even been found in thick trees, and this is not such an uncommon place for a wild duck to build in as might at first be supposed, especially if the trees are situated near a river bank. I have found a nest two years in succession in the same tree as a jackdaw had built hers. To secure the eggs, in this case, is, however, rather a severe test of the agility of a keeper. The eggs, by the way, are of a pale green colour, and are usually eleven in number.

Having procured the eggs, the treatment is much

the same as it is for pheasants, but ducks' eggs require to be damped with water more frequently, as is natural, considering that the female duck would always return to her nest with her breast feathers wet. They take twenty-eight days to hatch, and on hatching the hens, ducklings, and coops should be placed on some sheltered grass field. The ground selected should be dry, and should be wired in, as the ducklings are inclined to wander. After a fortnight or three weeks the hens may be removed, but the coops should remain, and the young birds should be regularly cooped up at night, and also during the day if it be very wet. It is important to ensure that they have plenty of ventilation when in the coops. It is essential at this time that the ducklings should not get into any water for swimming, as they will be found to develop cramp and rheumatism : large pans for their drinking - water should also be avoided, in case they get into them, and, when the water is done with, the pans should be emptied. As regards feeding, it is important that they should have plenty, but it must be of the right sort ; they must be fed regularly when very young—five times a day, three times in the morning and twice in the afternoon. The food which is most highly recommended is a meal specially prepared by Messrs. Gilbertson & Page, Hertford. It should be mixed with a little water and given to the birds warm for the first fortnight ; after that they may have it cold. No other form of nourishment is required, and if given regularly the birds will be found to thrive on it and grow rapidly. After a fortnight, three times a day is sufficiently often to feed them, and this may in turn be decreased to twice a day. When eight weeks old, the birds may be taken to the stream or water which is intended for their permanent home, and fed twice a day as before. After a time they will become accustomed to their new surroundings, and then they need only to be fed once a day, in the morning. The soft food should, however, be continued for some time after removal to the water, and a few coops should be taken to the water's edge. It should be borne in mind that everything possible should be done at this time to accustom the ducks to their new surroundings, to give the place a homelike appearance, and to ensure their remaining in it. A few pinioned ducks and good food will do more to attain these objects than anything else ; moreover, other birds will be attracted by their calls, and later on in the season, about evening feeding-time, many may be shot coming in to join their companions. After the ducks are a month old, oatmeal may be added to the prepared food, to make up a more substantial meal, and the birds should always be let out of their coops early in the morning before the dew is off the ground, as they will then amuse themselves by catching the worms and slugs. After it is desired to give up the soft food, Indian corn or maize will be found the most suitable diet. This should be supplied regularly once a day, in the morning, and thrown near the water's edge. There are many other forms of food, however, such as acorns and the dried insides of rabbits, which if chopped up will be found most appetising and a pleasant change of diet. The great enemy of the duckling is the rat, and these voracious animals are sure to be found wherever there is maize ; great pains, therefore, should be taken to kill them before putting down the ducks. About the time of the harvest the ducklings will be able to take care of themselves and will fly away in the evening to feed on the corn. If the keeper blows a horn when he feeds them, they will get into the habit of returning to their old feeding - ground when they hear the sound, and this custom may be of use later on, when the horn will summon them to sterner realities than those of their morning meal.

It is about sunset that some of the best sport with these birds may be obtained. The wild duck will congregate at dusk in some pond, and if the right place be found, the air will be thick with them flying to and fro for about twenty minutes. This period of flighting, as it is called, rarely lasts for more than half an hour. The best way to find out the haunts of the duck at night is to walk round the leeward

side of the ponds by day, and observe if there are
any feathers lying on the edges. A field of stubble
in flood is a certain place for the duck to feed in. As
wild duck always settle in the water against the wind,
it is generally found best to stand with one's back to
it, as a good shot is then afforded as the bird comes
down to alight. Excellent sport may also be obtained
in the same way at dawn. The duck all fly back to
the lake or water where they live, from the fields or
marshes where they have spent the night in feeding.
It is necessary, therefore, to find a spot where they all
cross over, to select a good place behind a stump
or some other natural cover, and to be there about
twenty minutes before sunrise ; they will fly over
the ambushed enemy in twos and threes, and even
in large flocks, and give him plenty of shooting for
about a quarter of an hour. For this sport a quick
eye and good hearing are essential, as the first indication of the wild ducks' approach is usually the
whistling of their wings, especially on a still day.
The mouth of a river, where it runs into a lake, is an
ideal place for "flight-shooting," and every variety of
wildfowl can be shot in this way, as during stormy
weather, wigeon and teal will often come inland to
feed, the former of which can readily be distinguished
by their shrill whistle. The more stormy the night and
morning, the better chance one has, as the birds fly
lower, and are not so easily frightened away by a shot.

Nowadays, when duck are so much reared by hand, it is possible, as has been explained above, to keep them near the streams or ponds where they have been brought up. One rule, however, should be observed with regard to shooting wild duck if they are to be expected to remain, *i.e.* not to shoot them in or near these streams where they have been reared. Let these be sanctuary, as it were, for them, and then they will be found to return to these places again in the evening, as if being shot at were the most natural and harmless thing in the world. Supposing that there are two or three of these sanctuaries (which there should be if there be a large number of birds), let a man be stationed near each to frighten the birds away as they try to settle; then they will fly round and round, gradually rising higher in the air, and will give the guns plenty of shooting for two hours or so. The guns should stand in good high butts, circular in shape, made up from fir branches, or some such other natural cover, lined alongside a wood for preference, so that the birds may be shot as they top the trees. Of course, a great quantity of duck are required for this form of shooting, and there are few places in England at present where it is possible to enjoy the luxury of a duck drive; though, probably, in a few years it will become a much more common pastime. As was mentioned above, a horn is a very useful implement for calling wild duck in, and it is astonishing with what readiness they answer the call when they become accustomed to it.

Another method of killing wild fowl is to stalk them over a river bank and shoot them as they rise. They afford easy shots if successfully stalked, but half the pleasure lies in approaching them without giving the alarm, as they are very wary birds, and their sense of hearing on a still day is little short of marvellous. A useful thing to remember is to approach them, if possible, from the side from which the wind blows, as they rise against the wind and their breasts afford a good and vital mark. A young wild duck, bred in the river, has a great enemy in the pike. It is extraordinary how many birds this voracious fish can account for, and keepers can very well spend any spare time they may have in the summer in catching them. Even in innocent-looking ponds these fish may be found, and I have known the young duck disappear from a pond in a seemingly inexplicable manner, and yet the cause was not very far to seek, for eventually several large pike were taken out of it. The only way to catch these fish in a pond is with a rod and float.

Now, a word as to the best kind of dog to use for wild-duck shooting. An ordinary retriever, if she takes kindly to the water, is as good as could be desired, but this species of the canine tribe require most careful teaching. Nothing is more annoying than for a retriever to take the duck to the opposite bank of the river, drop it, and on being called, swim back without it; yet I have seen them do it often. A day spent in the early part of the season by the river bank, shooting an occasional flapper is excellent for teaching the young and inexperienced retriever; the water is warm, and the bird is not so likely to dive just as the dog reaches it. But on no account should a dog be made to take to the water by being thrown into it. Nothing gives them a keener or more lasting distaste for the business. He should also be prevented from getting into the habit of dropping his duck on reaching the bank for the purpose of shaking himself, as he may leave the bird in some inaccessible spot; he should, on the contrary, be trained to bring the bird up to his master's hand. The Newfoundland and water-spaniel are really the best dogs for this work, the former being a very strong swimmer. The latter requires to be taught to take no notice of water-rats, as these infest the river banks, and this species is very much inclined to hunt them. All water-dogs must be taught to range to hand, as their radius of vision is very small when they are in the water, and it is of material advantage to them if they can be guided and directed by the hand. It is very important, also, that all water-dogs should be very quiet, as the slightest bark or whine is fatal, and is sufficient to spoil a whole day's sport. The constant exposure of these dogs to cold and wet is liable to bring on rheumatic fever, especially if they are accustomed to sit most of the day before a roaring fire. The symptoms are: the dog will resent being touched, will snarl if you attempt to pat him, and will, as a rule, cower in a corner. The best cure is to give him a hot bath, dry him well before the fire, and then apply, by hard rubbing, a mixture of equal parts of spirit of turpentine, ammonia, and laudanum.

The directions which may assist the keeper in bringing up and shooting wild duck must, perforce, be of a general nature, as the method in each case will vary, depending largely on the conformation of the ground and the nature of the surroundings; but it should be observed that wild duck are very capable of looking after themselves, and that the keeper's chief difficulty lies in keeping the birds from straying, and his chief care in feeding them regularly when very young.

Note.—When the lie of the land is favourable, it is often possible to drive duck up a burn, from their feeding-ground, into an enclosure at a higher elevation. The guns being posted below, the birds are let out in twos and threes. The principle is very much the same as in the case of pheasant " showing." A. S. W.—P. J. M.

CHAPTER XV

NOTES ON WILDFOWLING IN SCOTLAND

By J. S. HENDERSON

IT is impossible to do justice to a subject so wide in an abridged treatise of this nature, and of necessity the writer must merely touch the fringe, but, in so doing, an endeavour will be made to bring forward those points which, strictly speaking, it is every gamekeeper's duty to be conversant with.

Flighting.

This form of sport, which is annually becoming more popular, is, in the writer's opinion, before all other forms of shoulder gun-shooting. Every keeper, upon whose beat it is possible to indulge in flighting, should make it his duty to be thoroughly acquainted with the feeding-grounds, and the lines of flight in different winds, and so be able to place the guns to the best advantage. One of the chief points to be observed in flighting is to remain perfectly still and keep well out of sight. The keepers should see that at the various stands satisfactory cover is available. The gun should always face down-wind, as it will be found that most duck beat their way up-wind, and in stormy weather fly very close to the ground. If no shelter is available, the gun should try to have his back to a peat stack, peat bank, or any dark object, and if that is impossible his next best course is to kneel on the ground and remain perfectly still. Duck, when flying to the feeding-ground, shy much more easily on seeing a dog or man moving about than they do at the sound of the shots. In flighting, one requires to keep very much on the alert with both ears and eyes. In uncertain twilight the birds are often heard before they are seen. The birds should never be allowed to pass the guns, but should be taken whenever they come up. This applies especially to morning, evening, and moonlight flighting, when the light is uncertain, and the birds are within shot almost always as soon, and sometimes sooner, than they are within sight. Some advocate heavy shot for flighting, but the writer is of opinion that Nos. 5 and 6 are the most useful for this form of sport at all times, except during the day, when No. 4 in the right and No. 3 in the left barrel will be found the most effective. The reason why the smaller shot is preferred for morning, evening, and moonlight flighting is that a far shot is rarely available in the uncertain light, as the birds cannot be seen at a long distance. The flighter should get to his ground early and be comfortably settled ere the flight begins. He should be careful to take the warmest of clothing and the strongest of boots. On fine nights flighting need hardly be attempted. The best sport can be got on stormy nights and in frost. On a fine night the birds will fly too high, and will very probably not start for their feeding-ground till considerably after sun-down, at which time it is impossible to see them except against a white cloud. The flighter should never be without a reliable dog, but he should not allow the dog to range for every bird that drops Runners and birds which have dropped into the water should be retrieved at once, as also birds dropped in soft mud, as the latter are frequently so deeply embedded, that if not picked up at once, they can rarely be found. Except in day flighting, when one can mark their birds down, it is wise always to listen for the result of a passing shot, as frequently a fast bird will drop with a considerable thud far behind the gun. A flighter should always be most careful to see that his dog is thoroughly dried on returning home, as the cold and the effect of the sea-water invariably, sooner or later, bring on rheumatism and deafness.

Times of Flighting—Evening.

In the evening for about half an hour just at

twilight, when the birds pass from their resting-ground at sea to their feeding-ground on some inland loch, burn, or estuary.

Moonlight Flighting.

It is a mistaken idea that a clear, cloudless sky is best adapted for this form of shooting. A good moon and lots of white, fleecy clouds are by far the best conditions for showing up the birds to advantage. In autumn, about harvest-time, excellent moonlight shooting may be got when the birds are passing to feed on crop, stubble, or potato ground. Barley and potato fields are the favourite attractions, and the best situation for the gun in a field of grain will be at any "laid" spot near the centre of the field.

Morning.

At dawn, for about the same space of time, the birds may be intercepted returning from their feeding-grounds to their resting-grounds for the day. This is rarely so satisfactory as evening flighting, as the birds do not conform to the same regular line of flight, and usually return to their resting-ground in large packs. Good sport, however, can sometimes be got by an alert "gun" posted by a creek or channel leading from the sea to the feeding-ground. The birds will nearly always follow this line of flight when returning at dawn to the sea.

Day Flighting.

Very good day flighting may sometimes be got in rough weather when the birds are driven from the open sea or lochs and are making for more sheltered quarters.

Feeding.

As so much good sport can be got without the trouble of artificial feeding, the custom is not often followed, but those who care to try it will find that barley and potato refuse make the most appetising meals for wild duck, although oats, or, indeed, grain of any sort, will serve the purpose. If feeding is resorted to, the ground should be "fed" for three or four nights before a shot is fired, so as to allow the birds to become accustomed to it. Care should be taken not to place the food in hollows where the duck, if they alight unseen, cannot be shot. The most likely spot for natural feeding is just where a burn empties into a loch, and artificial feeding in the near neighbourhood may often be conducive to good results.

The Best Season.

The best months for duck-flighting will usually be found to be November, December, and January, although the season varies a little in some districts. One of the chief interests and excitements in this class of sport is the variety of birds that may be killed before the "flighter" realises what he has "loosed off" at. Of course, such visitors (and they are frequent) as teal, wigeon, and plover herald their approach long ere one can give them the welcome " hail ! "

Shore Shooting.

There is little to be said on this subject from a gamekeeper's point of view, but from a sportsman's aspect, it is impossible to overestimate the advantages to be gained from this class of sport. One's knowledge for judging distance and pace can be brought to the highest standard by observing the results of the shots on the water, and varied indeed is the bag that may be got by a wary " shore shooter."

Bog Shooting.

The chief point to observe here is to mark down the birds carefully. The guns should never loiter about hunting for dead birds, but should move steadily on from the moment they enter the bog, as duck, so soon as they become suspicious, will take to the wing if they observe the line standing or hunting about, whereas they will nearly always sit close enough, to give a reasonably near shot, if the guns keep steadily on. Some bogs afford better and surer sport by being driven. To execute a successful drive, the wind is the supreme factor to be reckoned with.

Decoy Duck-Shooting.

Exceedingly good sport may be obtained, especially

on a very stormy day, by placing a few decoy ducks within good range of a gun stationed near the bank of a sheltered bay or eddy. The decoy can also be used with success when ducks are flighting to crop or roots.

Shooting Afloat.

When shooting from a small boat, especially with an 8-bore, the keeper must be most careful to keep the head of the boat well up to the waves. The recoil of an 8-bore is sufficient to rock the boat and topple the gun into the water, unless the boat's head is kept well up. In approaching from the sea towards duck feeding ashore, always manœuvre towards them along the shore, and never by direct frontal attack.

Punting.

This subject is a study in itself, and only a few practical points may be noted. The rest must be gleaned from experience. First beware of strong tides and southerly winds. A discreet punter will never leave the poling-ground with an uncertain wind, especially if it be from the south. When approaching a flock of duck, always give due heed to the sentinels that will be seen dotted here and there apart from the flock. Upon their conduct the punter should base his scheme of operations. An outlook should also be kept for black-backed gulls, as they are a frequent source of disturbance, and often mar what would have been ideal chances. Never attempt punting in rough weather, but watch and take advantage of the first lull after a storm. A punter should make a point of making as fast as he can for the scene of the shot to secure the wounded. This is especially essential if one be after ducks of the diving species, as they, though wounded, may give much trouble and often escape altogether. It will be found, however, that a wounded duck has considerable reluctance to go under water at first, and, if reached without loss of time, he can be finished off with a 12-bore ere he makes up his mind to dive.

The vermin which are most disastrous to wildfowl and their eggs in Scotland are the grey crow and the black-backed gull. The larger species of hawks do a certain amount of damage, but they are becoming so few and far between, and wildfowl are so plentiful, that the sportsman is only too glad to accord to them ungrudgingly their toll of birds. Every effort should, however, be made to destroy the two arch-enemies which I have just mentioned. On some of the rocks in the Outer Hebrides where wildfowl nest in large numbers, one will readily see that it is impossible to magnify the damage and depredation caused by such vermin as the grey crow and black-backed gull. The shells of countless eggs, not to speak of the bones of young wildfowl, can be seen on almost every rock or prominence in the nesting quarters of the wildfowl.

Wild-Goose Shooting.

To attempt this class of sport with any degree of success, one must first procure a double 8-bore gun, although at times, with great luck, a considerable bag is made with a 12-bore and heavy shot. There are three recognised means whereby the sportsman may get to the windward of the wily goose— *Stalking*, *Driving*, and *Flighting*. I have stated these processes in their order of merit, as I think that everyone who has had experience of wild-goose shooting will admit that stalking is by far the most interesting, although at the same time the most difficult, means of attack. Further, a successful stalk usually means a considerable slaughter. The wild-goose, when feeding or at rest, always has his position guarded by alert sentries, and to stalk him with success one must approach him up-wind and take advantage of every available piece of cover, having first carefully surveyed the ground with a telescope. The grey lag goose is undoubtedly the most difficult to approach, and he usually adds to his security by taking up his position in the centre of a flat, where it is next to impossible to approach him under cover. Sometimes, however, he will allow a horse and cart to get within easy shooting distance of him, provided a circular manœuvre is adopted, and not a direct approach. Bernacle geese are much easier to stalk, and they will usually be found on a piece of good green pasture.

Driving.—There are various methods adopted with

more or less success. One is by the usual process of taking cover. Another is by digging pits, both in the probable line of flight, which one should be able to gauge with considerable accuracy. Thereafter the geese should be driven towards the guns in as quiet a manner as possible without causing undue alarm. A method of driving usually successful is, where the geese are found on a small island, for the guns to take "post" in some narrow creek or channel, which the geese are known usually to take on leaving the feeding-ground. In such a course they will nearly always be got flying low and well within shot.

Flighting.—This is always an uncertain form of sport, and requires the exercise of much patience. A great deal of the matter bearing upon duck-flighting is applicable to geese-flighting, but the latter are best found, at least the grey lag and bernacle, flighting to corn and potato-fields. By an examination of the ground, the keeper will find ample indication as to where the guns should be placed, and if sufficient patience is exercised, success is practically certain to a more or less degree. The flighting hours correspond with those of duck.

Note.—As wildfowling is a sport practised only by a privileged few, it was thought inadvisable that it should be dealt with at any length. The reader is accordingly advised to seek further information from *The Encyclopædia of Sport*, from the volumes on *Shooting* in the Badminton Library, and from the works of Mr. J. G. Millais, Mr. H. C. Folkard, Mr. Abel Chapman, Mr. L. Upcott Gill, Mr. Horace Cox, and Colonel Hawker. Those who are interested in the question of shooting with swivel and other forms of guns will find full information in the works of many of these writers.

CHAPTER XVI

MISCELLANEOUS SPORT

Plover.

THERE is very little to be said with regard to the keeper's duties as they affect plover. He may be called upon to direct the guns how to proceed. There are no very definite laws to be laid down. Of course they should no more be approached in an open field than partridges should be, for plover are even more wary than the brown bird. They should be approached by the circular method described in the chapter on the Partridge. The best chances, however, are obtained by attempting to drive them down wind, the drivers approaching the birds in a circle, slowly and noiselessly.

The following is recommended by the *Fowler in Ireland*: "Another method of getting within range of plover congregated in a field is to tie a dog to a short stick and peg it down into the ground, leaving the animal a tether of five or six yards. Secure him a couple of hundred yards away from the 'stand' to windward, and every bird's eye will be turned in his direction as he moves or struggles. You may then steal up to them on their other flank against the wind, and will always get within fair, often easy, shot."

Pigeons.

Pigeon-shooting from traps hardly comes within the scope of a keeper's duties, but a few remarks may be made as to the killing of wild wood-pigeons. A few head may be obtained by simply beating a wood. When this is done, great care must be taken that the guns are placed a considerable time before the beaters enter the wood, as on the first crackle of a broken stick the pigeons will begin to leave the covert. The keeper should take care to note the customary flight of the birds, and place the guns accordingly. Pigeons generally fly from covert to covert, and as a rule take the shortest line to get out of a wood. The question of wind, of course, is important. In leaving covert pigeons seldom fly against the wind, but almost invariably do so when returning to it. But to obtain any large bag of pigeons in a short space of time, decoys must be used. These may either be stuffed pigeons or birds just shot. In the former cases, the decoys should have copper wire passing from within the bodies of the birds down the legs, with, say, some sixteen inches projecting from each foot. In the latter cases, the present writers have long found the following method efficacious :—Pieces of wire netting are cut so as to fix the fresh-killed birds with their wings clasped to the sides, and their heads erect, on to branches of trees. But, whatever the form of decoy, it must always be placed with its head facing the wind, and the gun or guns should stand some fifty yards away, facing it. " It will be found useful," says Lord Walsingham, "to be prepared beforehand with several short sticks, pointed at both ends, and when ten or twelve birds are down, to gather them quickly and set them up on open spaces beneath the trees as assistant decoys. With wings closed to their sides, resting on their breast bones, they can be fixed with heads erect or craning forward as if in search of food, by passing the upper end of the stick through the lower portion of the beak, the opposite end being stuck into the ground beneath the crop of the bird."

Great care should be taken by the keeper in selecting the cover for the " guns," and he should also warn the latter as to the necessity of their clothing being as near as possible akin to the colour of the cover in which they are standing.

Capercailzie

In placing the guns for capercailzie-driving, knowledge of the usual flight of the birds is of value. In

our experience capercailzie generally come out of
covert and then take a wide sweep round and close to
it and then fly in again.   They seldom fly out into the
open.   Guns should be placed quite near the covert.
In preserving the stock, care must be taken, as in all
other cases, to eliminate vermin.

Woodcock.

The keeper will have difficulty in knowing whether
he has woodcock in his coverts or not, and having
discovered them, he cannot tell how long they will
remain.   He can, however, be certain of the fact that
woodcock, as a rule, during the time they remain on
the ground, are loath to leave any favourite shelter
they have chosen, and will even fly back to the place
they have been flushed from in a beat.   Accordingly,
it is often wise to go over the same ground a second
time.   Markers outside the coverts will be able to give
important information as to whether cock have left
a covert or not, although it is often very difficult to
accurately mark the place where a bird has alighted.
Woodcock that have been marked down should be
followed up at once, as they have a habit of rapidly
changing their quarters when they know that guns
are about.   They often fly into the hedges or under
the dykes at the outside of the covert.   It is very
desirable that these should be well beaten.   The
covert ought to be beaten thoroughly, and if the

beat is especially for cock, the holly bushes and laurels should be well shaken. The best days to shoot woodcock are after clear moonlight nights, or days on which the sun is not too bright. Then the keeper may be certain that the woodcock, who is entirely (except under very pressing circumstances) a night feeder, has fed well and that he will lie well, being inclined to be sleepy and lazy. Cock, of course, vary their habitat according to the weather. After a frost they will be found where water can best be obtained. Accordingly the ditches and drains in the covert should be carefully explored.

The first days after a severe frost are the best for single or two or three guns. All likely places should be worked first, then the ground the birds have flown to, and the guns should finally return to the beat they first worked, but not sooner than two or three hours after they first shot over it.

When the birds are lying well—that is, after a bright night in which they have fed amply,—it is better to walk them up ; if they are lying badly, that is, after a night in which they have not fed well, it is better to have the birds beaten to the guns. In such weather, an outside gun walking with the beaters, or a little in advance of them, is of great importance, and he should be warned to keep a sharp lookout in passing any openings in the covert.

In looking for cock in the open, it must be remembered that they generally feed on the lee side of a hill, and may be found where they feed.   It is better to remember this rule than to trouble one's memory by north, south, east, or west.   When there is no wind, they choose the brightest or sunniest side.

Roe-Shooting.

In shooting roe-deer by driving, the main point to be remembered by the keepers is the tendency for the roe to break back through the line of beaters, and therefore he should advise, if necessary, that some of the guns should walk with the beaters.   The other guns should be kept absolutely out of sight.

Hares.

In considering how to maintain a good stock of brown hares, it is necessary for the keeper to remember that they require a lot of cover.

In driving hares, the drive should be down wind, there should be plenty of flanks, and the beaters should advance slowly and quietly.

For the improvement of stock, a few bucks and does should be turned down yearly.   They are easily obtainable from certain game farms at a moderate price.   It is better, however, to secure them from a more intimate source.   Owing to the size of the hare, which makes it an easy mark for the gun, the

stock needs constantly renewing, or it will soon
disappear altogether. A strict limit should be fixed
every season on the number of hares to be shot.

Poaching Hares.

Hare-poaching is generally carried out by driving
the hares towards a gate, on the outside of which
a net is fastened. On this account the bottom bars
of gates should be so close together that a hare
cannot bolt through.

Snipe.

The observant keeper should have a very definite
idea as to the haunts of the snipe on the ground
under his charge, and he should remember the
important fact that snipe are very conservative in
their habits, and that once they have selected a habitat
there will they always be found. From the many
facts known as to the habits, habitats, and shooting
of snipe, we select the following as worthy of the
memory of the keeper:—

(1) Snipe are markedly affected by the moon.
Choose a day for shooting after a clear night.
Then they will have fed well, and will lie
well to the guns. For, like woodcock, snipe
feed chiefly at nighttime, but after dark
nights snipe feed during the day, and are
very much on the alert.
20

(2) The best time to shoot snipe is during the thaw after a frost. During this time they get a plentiful supply of worms, which always come very near to the surface of the earth after frost.

(3) Snipe lie best in muggy weather, with a gentle breeze and a barometer which shows a tendency to fall, and after a moonlight night.

(4) Snipe lie worst in bright, fresh weather, with a high breeze, and after a dark cloudy night.

(5) In the generality of cases, in finding the birds, the guns should walk *down wind*—

    (*a*) In a thaw—when the birds will be lying well;

    (*b*) When the birds are lying badly during a strong wind.

On the other hand, the guns should walk *up wind*—

    (*a*) During a sharp frost, when the birds will be lying badly;

    (*b*) When there is but a light breeze (but not during a thaw) after a dark night;

    (*c*) In approaching a bird for the second time after flushing.

(6) The best hours to shoot snipe are those immediately following daybreak, and the hours just before dark.

(7) Snipe - shooting should not commence on August 1st, as commonly practised. The

end of September is the earliest time they
are likely to be found in good condition.

(8) Better shooting is obtained in big grass fields
soaked with water, or in bogs that have only
shallow pools, than in large flooded bogs and
extensive marshes. In the latter case a single
shot may cause a whole flock to rise " in wisps,"
and thus offer poor sport. In these cases it
is perhaps better to drive the birds. If suitable arrangements can be made, a rope may
be drawn across the bog or " moss." In those
cases where mallard and teal are also present,
capital sport can be obtained with good guns.

(9) It is wise to remember that, after being shot at,
snipe may fly or be blown long distances and
then fall dead.

(10) The best dogs for snipe - shooting are Irish
water spaniels and red Irish setters, the
latter being used for shooting over bogs or
large marshes, and the former for smaller
and drained marshes.

CHAPTER XVII

The Gamekeeper as a Fishing Gillie

By P. D. Malloch

With the space at my disposal it will be impossible for me to exhaust the subject or do little more than mention the principal duties of the fishing gillie.

River Salmon-Fishing from the Bank.—The first duty of the gillie is to see that the river is properly protected from poachers. Should there be no net shots on the beat, the places which could be netted ought to be protected; this can usually be done, and at little expense, by putting large boulders, anchors, or stakes in the river. When pools are thus protected, sweep netting, as a rule, will be prevented, and trammel netting also, in part. The latter method of netting is, however, difficult to put a stop to.

A careful lookout should be kept for any signs of trammel netting. If it be suspected that this method of poaching is being carried on from a boat, the gillie should observe if any scales of fish have been left in the boat or on the bank.

A sharp lookout should be kept in the morning to see that the pools are not fished before the owner comes down to the water. There is nothing more annoying to the angler than to find, from marks on the sand or grass, that the pools have already been fished by a poacher an hour or two before.

If the gillie is unable to keep watch in the morning, he should stretch a few threads across the paths where the poachers are likely to pass; he will at once be able to detect if anyone has been on the paths since he was last there. Should he find the threads broken he can set a watch for the intruders.

The gillie should have a knowledge of the time when the fish begin to run up, where and when they begin to rest at different seasons; the effects of snow water, frost, and fresh water on their running; and the time the river will take in coming into ply after a flood, so that he can advise the angler when his water is ready to be fished.

The temperature of the water should be taken daily. Much can be learned by doing this. When a daily record of the temperature of the water is kept, the gillie will have some idea what size of fly to recommend, and whether bait fishing should be resorted to or not.

A gillie who has an interest in his work will take every opportunity of watching the river, the fish, and the direction of the wind. He should also have a knowledge of all the pools and streams—their depth, the lie of the fish, and the state of the river which suits the fish best.   This knowledge is most important, and by the possession of it, much of the angler's time can be saved.   To acquire this knowledge requires years of careful observation on the part of the gillie, although much valuable information may be got from older fishermen who know the beats.

The gillie should discover the effect of the sun upon the pools, the direction of the wind that catches certain of them, and the best side from which the pool should be fished.

When the river is low and out of ply all the beat should be carefully inspected, and all dangerous roots and sticks, on which a fish might foul, should be removed.

The croys, if any, should be repaired, the paths along the banks put in order, and any parts of the banks of pools looked to after a flood.   As a rule, far too little attention is given to these questions, with the result that many fine pools become worthless. The clever gillie does not need to be told this ; he is always thinking how he can improve his fishing by erecting a croy at one point and another one on the opposite side, so as to contract a wide part into a narrow part, and thus form new pools and improve others, or by rolling a stone into a pool to make a rest for the fish.   This week (20th October) I killed three salmon behind a stone which a keeper rolled into a pool on the river Earn two years ago, where no fish had rested before.

Now I shall suppose that the gillie or keeper has instructions to telegraph to his employer, or angler for the time being, as the case may be, whether he should come or not on the opening day. His employer has never fished the water, or seen the keeper before. The river is in order, and plenty of fish are showing, and the keeper wires for his employer to come down.

If arrangements have not been made as to the terms on which the gillie is engaged, the angler ought to make it his first duty on arriving at his beat to rectify the omission. The wages should be fixed at so much per week, to be paid fortnightly or monthly, as may be arranged. When lunch is not provided, a money payment is usually given instead. The arrangements come to should be perfectly clear and definite, so as to save any possible annoyance to either party afterwards.

Before going to the river the gillie should see the tackle, rods, reels, lines, flies, casts, and baits which have been provided for the fishing; he will then be able to advise as to the best length of rod, the most suitable reel and line, cast, line, and fly in the stock, and what will be sufficient to take out for the day. He should not fail to see that there is a gaff, a suitable landing-net, a bag to carry the fish, and a basket or bag for the luncheon. *It is the gillie's duty to see that nothing is left behind.* He should run all the items over in his mind before starting for the river. Perhaps by repeating the following well-known rhyme he might assist the memory:—

> "Rods, reels, baskets,
> Hooks, worms, flaskets."[1]

With regard to the last-mentioned article, the gillie would do well to see that it contained no more spirits than he could safely carry home. The gillie or keeper who takes a drop more than he should do lowers himself more in the estimation of his employer than by anything else I know of.

Having got to the river, the first thing to do is to put up the rod, and then see that the reel fits tight, and that the line is put through all the rings without it being twisted round the rod. The gut cast should be carefully soaked, and then fitted neatly to the main line before the fly is attached. The cast and fly should then be tested, and the rod handed to the angler, who may then begin fishing.

---

[1] To modernise this old rhyme and make it so complete that it will include gaff, baton, landing-nets, fly-books and cases, waterproofs and luncheon, we suggest the following as being fairly comprehensive:—

> "Rods, reels, and hooks,
> Nets, bait, and baskets,
> Gaff, baton, books,
> Coats, lunch, and flaskets."
>
> A. S. W.

The following remarks might be overheard at this time, if one were within earshot of a well-trained gillie :—"Cast a short line to begin with, but when you get down to that ripple, let out a few more yards ; that is where they usually come. From that part, fish carefully down for another twenty yards ; we will then go on to the next pool."

The angler begins to cast, and during the first half-dozen casts there are anxious moments for the gillie. He knows by that time whether his employer is an experienced angler or not. He sees his employer is casting straight across, and politely requests him to "Cast a little straighter down, sir."

After a few more casts, something pulls down the rod and the line begins to run out. After a run or two, the fish shows itself to be a kelt. "Do not be particular with him, sir," you remark.

The fish is brought bankwards as quickly as possible. Instead of the gaff, the net is put under it and pulled ashore. The hook is carefully extracted, and the fish returned to the river with as much care as possible. On no account should the gaff be used. The fly is examined to see that the tinsel has not been torn by the kelt's long teeth.

Another start is made at the same place ; there is another pull, and the reel sings out again. A livelier fish this time, and he jumps into the air. "A spring fish, sir; be more careful." After a little time the fish nears the shore. The gillie remains quiet, gaff, instead of net, in hand this time. Several times the fish comes within a few feet of the gaff, and as often rushes out into the stream again. The next time it comes within reach of the gillie, who puts the gaff quietly over the fish's back and pulls. The moment he does this he stands erect, with the end of the gaff-handle pointing upwards, and the fish hanging on the gaff hook. He then walks quietly to a safe place, seizes the fish by the tail, takes out the gaff, lays the fish on the ground, and gives it three or four sharp knocks with his little baton; extracts the fly, weighs the fish, carefully washes it, and puts it away in the bag provided for the purpose. A note of the weight is then recorded in his book. The whole of this procedure should not take more than three minutes, at the end of which time the angler is again ready to begin.

He fishes down the pool, sees nothing more; walks on to the next pool, and is directed in the same way as at the last. This pool is fished down without a rise, and the gillie begins to think the fly is either too large or too small, or is not of the right kind; and advises that a more sombre-coloured fly two sizes smaller should be put on and the pool fished over again. This is done with the result that other two spring fish are added to the bag. The angler by this time sees that the gillie understands his work, and is accordingly willing to place every confidence in him. The two become friends, and the fishing turns out a success, being a source of pleasure to the angler, and of profit to the gillie.

When the fishing is over the rod is taken down, everything is carefully packed up and taken home. The gillie unwinds the wet portion of the line on to a line-drier, so that it may be thoroughly dried and ready for use the next day. The flies which have been used should be dried before being put away. The waders should be turned inside out and hung up to dry. The wading-boots and worsted stockings should also be thoroughly dried. Sometimes before looking after these details the fish have to be carefully packed, labelled, and sent away.

Before leaving, the time is arranged for starting next day. Day after day passes in the same pleasant way until the season is over.

What a contrast to the gillie who does not understand his work! He goes out in the morning with his flasket filled to the top. When he gets to the riverside he finds he has forgotten the reel, and has to walk or run back a couple of miles to secure it, leaving the angler on the river bank wasting the best hour of the day. The gillie knows that a certain pool is a good one, but does not know the exact spot where the fish rise. He tells the angler to begin at the top and fish to the bottom. Instead of fishing only fifteen yards, he fishes three times that distance when there is no real chance of hooking a fish.

When a fish is hooked, this inexperienced gillie tells the angler in a rough sort of way to hold up his rod, or to hold it, as the case may be, down. By the time the fish does come to land, he rushes up and down the side of the river frightening it, and takes double the time he ought to to bring it to the gaff. When a chance of gaffing is offered him, he is sure to miss it.

This stamp of gillie, to put it mildly, causes much annoyance and displeasure to the angler.

River Salmon - Fishing from a Boat. — In river salmon-fishing from a boat the gillie's duty is to see that before the anglers come out in the morning the boat is brought up to its proper place, the water baled out, and everything made clean and tidy, so that when the anglers appear no time is lost before starting. There should always be suitable landing-places for the boat whatever the state of the river. Where the boat has to be pulled up on to the riverside, the bushes should be cut every year and the footpaths kept in order.

The boat should be taken quietly to the side of the stream, sufficiently near for the angler to command it. The quieter the boat is worked the better the sport will be ; a boat always disturbs the water, although many gillies think the contrary. I have

many times proved this. After a good angler has
fished over the water in a boat, I have often quietly
waded in and killed many fish ; so, Mr. Gillie, never
go splashing over the water, and on no account cross
over a good pool if it can be avoided. The boat
should be held as steady as possible. After every
cast it should be let down a yard, and no part of a
good stream should be missed.

If the stream is so broad that the angler cannot
command it from one side, both sides can be fished,
but if too wide to be fished from both sides the boat
should be worked quietly first out and then in.
When a rise is got the boat should be pulled up a
yard so that the fish may get another chance of
taking the fly : this is easier said than done, as it is
difficult to keep a boat in the same place in a stream.
A sharp lookout should be kept for some bush, tree,
or stone that may be on the bank, and which may
serve as a guide to keep the boat in the exact spot
required. When a fish is hooked never be in too
great a hurry to get to the shore. As a rule the fish
will follow the boat. The angler will find that the
best way to get the fish out of the stream is to hold
his rod steady and not to wind in the reel. Should a
fish make a run, the boat should be stopped until it
settles down, then the gillie should pull towards the
shore, selecting a spot where the water is deepest as
the best place to land a fish. If possible, try to get the

fish up into the fished water, so that it will not disturb the unfished water. When the shore is reached, do not bump against it. If you do so, there is a danger of your upsetting the angler. When sufficient line has been taken in and the fish is under command, the seat should be taken away and the angler allowed to land. He should be told to keep well away from the bank, as he will thereby run less risk of losing the fish. The fish can be either worked towards the stern of the boat and gaffed then, or worked towards the land and gaffed from the shore. The gaff, by the bye, should be kept as sharp as a needle.

An expert will usually take the first chance of gaffing the fish, as it comes within reach many times before it is played out. Some gaff the fish under, others over the back, while others again gaff the fish in whatever way opportunity presents. When gaffing over the back, the gaff should be reached out, laid quietly over the back fin, and pulled. The moment the fish is gaffed the handle should be held perpendicular and the fish lifted into the boat. Before removing the gaff the fish should get three or four sharp knocks on the head with the baton. The gaff can then be removed, the hook extracted, the fish weighed, and a note taken of the weight, then washed and laid in the bow of the boat. Any blood in the latter should be carefully wiped up. All this should not take more than three minutes. A fish should never be gaffed near the head, as there is the risk of gaffing the line instead of the fish.

In gaffing, the gillie should try to get within reach of a fish as quickly as possible, but should never be in a hurry in striking. When the right moment arrives he must do it quietly and deliberately, not by raking at the fish three or four times in quick succession. If he does so he will be sure to make a mistake. The number of fish which are lost at the gaffing is enormous. I usually tell a man who has never used a gaff before to put it over the fish's back and pull, and he usually does it all right. The great thing is to keep perfectly cool.

Fish which are caught with minnow or prawn should always be gaffed. If landing-nets are used, the hooks usually stick in the meshes and the weight of the fish breaks them. The fish should always be killed before being laid down in the boat, or the hooks may stick in the bottom of the boat and get broken. Grilse of small size are difficult to gaff; they are much easier netted. Salmon up to 40 lb. can be netted, but over this weight it is safer to use the gaff.

In netting, the net should be quietly put under the fish, lifted up, and then pulled towards the shore. This is infinitely better than lifting it clear of the water and bringing the whole weight of the fish on the net.   The great thing to remember is to get the head of the fish away from the side of the net before lifting.   If this is not done the hooks are apt to catch in the net, the head does not get down, the tail part falls over the ring, the fish is outside, the hooks are attached to the net, there are one or two wriggles, and the fish is gone.   A gillie should never attempt to net or gaff a fish while wearing white sleeves, nor run up and down after a fish; he should rather wait quietly in one place and reach out the gaff when the fish passes him.   Many a time when alone I have dirtied the water by stirring up the mud at the side with my feet; when the fish has been guided into the muddy water it cannot see anyone, and the gillie is therefore quite safe in walking in and gaffing it.

Another opportunity of gaffing a fish may be obtained when the fish's head is out of the water, for in that position it cannot see.   If both the gaff and net have been accidentally left behind, the best way of landing a fish is by first tiring it out and getting it to turn on its side.   It can then be pulled up into shallow water.   A very large fish can be pulled up in this fashion.   Every time it moves a little pressure is put on, and in this way it can be brought on to the gravel and gradually landed high and dry.   The gillie may then go forward and catch it by the tail, and push it farther up or lift it on to the bank.

Harling a River from a Boat.—This method of
fishing is only resorted to on large rivers where
the pools cannot be conveniently fished from either
bank. It is done by placing two or three rods in
the stern of the boat, one at each side and another
in the centre. A fly is attached to each rod, a
minnow sometimes being substituted for one of the
flies. From twenty to forty yards of line are let out
from each reel. Two gillies row the boat from one
side to the other, dropping down a yard or two at
a time.

To be successful, the gillie must have a knowledge
of the river in its different heights. He must also
be able to tell the angler the proper length of line
to put out, the bait line always being a yard or two
shorter than those with flies, and the proper kind
and size of flies to use. The gillie must also know
the proper angle at which to keep the boat, so that
the lines and flies may be kept in correct position.
In turning, the boat should be brought slowly round
so as to give the flies plenty of time to turn.
Observant gillies who take an interest in their work
always excel in this style of fishing.

Trolling or Salmon Minnow-Fishing from a Boat.
—In this method of fishing the gillie's duty is to
find out which parts of the loch the fish frequent;
the different depths of the loch, so as to avoid
fouling in the bottom or coming against hidden

21

rocks; the kinds of bait to use (and to see that they spin properly); the proper length of line to put out; the correct weight of lead to put on the trace; and the direction of wind which affects certain parts of the loch. He must also know how to take the bait over a fish which has been seen to rise, without taking the boat over the place and disturbing the fish. Care should be taken to row sufficiently fast, so as to make the bait spin. When a fish is hooked, the boat should not be pulled all over the loch. Many gillies are never content unless they follow that bad practice, and they sometimes kill a fish a mile away from where it was hooked, thereby wasting valuable time and disturbing the water for the chance of other fish.

Trout-Fishing from a Boat in a Loch.—In Scotland more gillies and keepers are employed at this style of fishing than any other. The angler depends on them for his sport and pleasure. As a rule, the sport is proportionate to the knowledge of the gillie. The gillie's duty is to obtain a perfect knowledge of every part of the loch, its deeps, shallows, and bays, and the places where trout frequent at different seasons. He should know at all times where he is, the depth of water he is fishing, the nature of the bottom—whether gravel, rocks, mud etc.,—the places and time of day the flies hatch out, the direction of winds that suit the different places, the effects of cold and heat, sunshine and shade, the different kinds of flies,—whether strong or fine tackle should be used,—how to keep the boat to the wave in drifting, whether the bow or stern should point to a certain direction, and whether the boat is drifting too fast or too slow.

If there be only one angler in the boat, the gillie should be able to advise which end he should fish from, and whether it would be better to row the boat instead of allowing it to drift. All these points should be carefully studied and mastered before the gillie can be said to be an experienced one. When a trout is hooked, the net should be quietly put under it and then lifted out, the fish being caught with one hand, and the hook extracted with the other. The fish should then be knocked on the head, as nothing is more disgusting than to have a trout half dead wriggling about in the basket.

There is a great art in taking out a hook ; those who know how to do it can extract it very quickly without bending the iron or breaking the barb or destroying the fly. The cast and hooks will often get entangled, but the experienced gillie, with one or two shakes, will be able usually to set them free. These are some of the principal points the experienced angler depends on for filling his basket.

A clever gillie is always sought after. He is usually an agreeable and pleasant companion. I know of such a gillie. One I have in my mind I have known for upwards of thirty years. I considered he was the means of adding 10 lb. daily to my basket. He is far and away the cleverest gillie I have ever had. The way in which he lands a trout, extracts the hook, and unravels the cast is simply marvellous, the time he takes being little longer than it takes to make a cast. The way he will row to the centre of a loch and turn round the boat within thirty yards of a sunken island requires to be seen to be believed. This gillie is worth double the usual wage, and I am quite sure he gets it.

The worst enemy the gillie has to contend with is drink. It is very unkind of an angler to give his gillie more than is good for him. I daresay I employ more gillies than any man in Scotland. I always impress upon them never to make complaints or grumble to the anglers they are attending upon who come for sport and pleasure. The more they are assisted in the habits of temperance the better it is for all concerned.

Note on the Improvement of Loch-Fishings.

It is in every way desirable for the improvement of loch-fishings to attend to the following points :—

(1) The presence of spawning-grounds in the form of small burns entering loch.

(2) Removal of superfluous and harmful weeds, especially the American weed.

(3) Proper supply of food—

  (*a*) Suitable weeds and plants.

  (*b*) Mollusca, crustacea, and other forms of animal life.

  (*c*) Insect life, flies, etc., which cannot be obtained without the presence of forestry and shrubbery; where none exist, they should be planted on the prevalent windward side.

The absence of trees on many lochs accounts for poorness of the trout.

(4) Elimination of pike and cannibal trout.

(5) Restocking by rainbow, Loch Leven, and other forms of trout, which can be obtained from pisciculturists, of whom there are many, and who should be consulted as to suitable trout for particular lochs.

  The best time for restocking is winter-time, as fish cannot be " carried " in warm weather.

A. S. W.—P. J. M.

CHAPTER XVIII

SOME BROAD FACTS IN SCOTTISH ANGLING LAW

By HENRY LAMOND[1]

1. *Salmon.*

Legal Definition.—By statute the word "salmon" includes "salmon, grilse, sea trout, bull trout, smolts, parr, and other migratory fish of the salmon kind," and in this comprehensive sense the word is here used.

Public and Private Rights.—There is no public right of salmon-fishing in Scotland, either in salt water round the shores or in fresh water. Where the right is not in the hands of a private proprietor it is vested in the Crown. Hence any person fishing for salmon, whether by net or by rod and line, without a title, or without express written permission from one who has a title, is, in the eye of the law, a poacher, and liable to be prosecuted.

Close Time. — This varies in different localities. The appended table (see p. 322) gives a useful

[1] Modified from an article in *Glasgow Herald* by kind permission of the proprietors.

compendium of the close times for the whole of
Scotland. There is besides a weekly net close time,
"from the hour of six of the clock on Saturday
night to the hour of six of the clock on Monday
morning," and a weekly rod close time on Sunday.

Poaching and Illegal Practices and Tackle.—It is
illegal (1) to fish for salmon without a title or permission from one who has; (2) to trespass on any
ground or water with intent to kill salmon; (3) for
any person, not having a legal right, or permission
from one who has, wilfully to take salmon from
any water, including the sea within one mile of
low-water mark; (4) to put into a salmon river any
poisonous or deleterious matter injurious to the
fishings, failing proof that the best practicable means,
within a reasonable cost, have been used to dispose
of or render harmless such matter; (5) for three or
more persons, acting in concert, to be found at any
time between one hour after sunset and one hour
before sunrise on any ground adjacent to a river
or the sea with illegal intent to take salmon; (6)
to export prohibited salmon; (7) to fish for salmon
by net or rod within the annual close times for net
or rod fishing respectively, or by net within the
weekly close time, or by rod and line on Sunday;
to use a net having a mesh less than seven inches
round when wet; to intercept salmon leaping at
a fall; to prevent salmon passing through a fish

pass; to contravene any by-law of the Salmon
Fishing Commissioners; (8) to use any light or
fire of any kind, or any spear, leister, gaff, or
other like instrument, or otter, for catching salmon,
or any instrument for dragging for salmon, or to
have suspicious possession of such instruments; (9)
to fish with any fish roe, or to buy, sell, or expose
for sale, or possess any salmon roe, failing satisfactory
reason for its possession; (10) to take or destroy or
to buy, sell, expose for sale, or possess any salmon
smolt or fry [parr] or intercept them when running,
or injure them, or to wilfully injure or disturb salmon
spawn, or disturb any spawning-bed, or any bank or
shallow in which spawn may be, or during the annual
close time to obstruct the passage of salmon to the
spawning-beds; (11) to take or to buy, sell, expose
for sale, or possess unclean or unseasonable salmon
[kelts]; (12) to buy, sell, or expose for sale, or possess
salmon at a time when no fishing is legally open.

2. Trout.

Legal Definition.—By statute the legal definition of
this fish is "the common trout, *Salmo fario*," but the
definition has been held to include "Loch Leven"
trout, *Salmo levenensis*, in a Sheriff Court case.

Public and Private Rights.— There is no public
right of trout-fishing, except in navigable rivers so
far up only as the tide ebbs and flows. The right

belongs exclusively to proprietors of lands adjoining the fishing, and neither the custom of fishing for any length of time, nor lawful access to the water by boat, bridge, ford, right-of-way, or otherwise will give the public a right to fish for trout.

Close Time.—This extends from the 15th day of October to the 28th day of February, both inclusive.

Poaching and Illegal Practices and Tackle.—There is no law as to the taking of immature trout. It is illegal (1) to fish for, have possession of, or expose for sale common trout during close time ; (2) for any person (except for a sole proprietor of the fishing, or joint-proprietors with mutual consent) to net for trout, or for any person to trespass on any ground or water with intent to net trout or other fresh-water fish ; (3) to fish for trout or other fresh-water fish by double-rod fishing or cross-line fishing, or set lines, or otter fishing, or burning the water, or by striking the fish with any instrument, or by pointing, or by putting lime or any other substance destructive to fish in the water with intent to destroy the same, or to trespass on any ground or water with intent as above ; and (4) to use dynamite or other explosive to catch or destroy fish.

3. *Coarse Fish.*

There are no special legal restrictions in Scotland as to the capture of coarse fish, and it is doubtful whether the prohibitions as to their capture by net or otherwise, as in the case of common trout, apply to them ; but to kill them by means of explosives would appear to be illegal. There is no close time for such fish in Scotland. As in the case of common trout, the right to fish for them belongs to the proprietors adjoining the waters, except where the tide ebbs and flows in a navigable river.

Other Close Times.

1. *England and Wales—*

    (1) *Salmon, etc.*

        (*a*) Net, September 1st to February 1st.

        (*b*) Rod, October 1st to February 1st.

These times may be varied by the Board of Conservation, with the consent of the central authority.

In addition to an annual close time, there is also a weekly close time for salmon-netting from noon on Saturday to 6 a.m. on Monday. The Fishery Boards have power to extend this.

    (2) (*a*) *Trout*, October 1st to February 2nd.

        (*b*) *Thames trout*, September 11th to March 31st.

The Fishery Boards may vary the time.

    (3) (*a*) Coarse fish, March 13th to June 15th.

        (*b*) Norfolk and Suffolk coarse fish, March 1st to June 30th.

The law as to coarse fish does not apply to—

(*a*) Landowners fishing their own water.

(*b*) Persons to whom they have given leave to fish.

(*c*) To the catching of eels, except by rod and line.

Fishery Boards have power to except either the whole or the part of the district from the close time, or any particular kind or kinds of fish.

Ireland—

(1) Salmon, varies, as in Scotland (under control of Inspector of Fisheries).

(2) Sea trout, November 1st to February 1st.

(3) Coarse fish, varies between March 15th and June 15th.

Salmon Fisheries (Scotland) Acts, 1828 *to* 1868.

Meshes of Nets.—Notice to fishermen, fishmongers, and the trade generally. Under the above Acts it is provided that—

No net shall be used for the capture of salmon or sea trout the meshes whereof shall be under one inch and three quarters in extension from knot to knot measured on each side of the square, or seven inches measured round each mesh when wet, and the placing two or more nets behind or near each other in such manner as to practically diminish the mesh of the nets used, shall be deemed to be an act in contravention of this bye-law.

It has come to the knowledge of the Fishmongers' Company that quantities of salmon and sea trout are illegally fished for and taken (more especially on the west coast of Scotland) with nets of too small a mesh. Dealers and fishmongers are hereby warned not to purchase or deal in sea trout, which have been taken by any net having meshes smaller than permitted by the bye-law, as they are liable to seizure.

Any suspected contravention should be immediately reported to the undersigned.

J. WRENCH TOWSE,
Clerk of the Worshipful Company of Fishmongers.

Office in Scotland, 24 CHARLOTTE SQUARE, EDINBURGH.
Chief Office, FISHMONGERS' HALL, LONDON.
March 1904.

Salmon Fisheries (Scotland) Acts, 1828 *to* 1868.

Illegal Netting.—Warning to owners, masters, and crews of yachts, and others.   Under the provisions of the above Acts it is illegal for any person to—

Fish for or aid in fishing for salmon or sea trout during the weekly or annual close time with a net.

Fish for, aid in fishing for, or take salmon or sea trout with a net the meshes whereof shall be under one inch and three quarters in extension from knot to knot measured on each side of the square, or seven inches measured round each mesh when wet.

Fish for, aid in fishing for, or to buy, sell, expose for sale, or have in possession any unclean or unseasonable salmon or sea trout.

Note.—It is lawful for any person without any warrant or other authority than the Salmon Fisheries (Scotland) Act, 1868, *brevi mau*, to seize and detain any person found committing any of the above offences and to deliver such person to a constable.

Three or more persons acting in concert with intent illegally to take salmon or sea trout at night shall be guilty of a criminal offence.

No person may fish for salmon or sea trout without having legal right to do so, or permission from the owner of the salmon fishery.

Heavy penalties are provided in the Acts against offenders, which include the forfeiture of boats, nets, etc.

The Fishmongers' Company hereby give public notice that offenders will be rigorously prosecuted, and request that information as to offenders may be sent in confidence to the undersigned.—By order,

J. WRENCH TOWSE,
Clerk of the Worshipful Company of Fishmongers.

Office in Scotland, 24 CHARLOTTE SQUARE, EDINBURGH.
Chief Office, FISHMONGERS' HALL, LONDON.
April 1904

TABLE showing Annual Close Time for Netting applicable to Scottish Salmon Rivers, with extension of time for Rod-fishing.—Abstracted from Salmon Fisheries (Scotland) Act, 1868, Schedule C, and Tweed Act of 1859. (*Note.*—Dates are inclusive.)

NAMES OF RIVERS.	ANNUAL CLOSE TIME.	EXTENSION FOR ROD-FISHING.
Halladale, Strathy, Naver, Borgie, Helmsdale.	August 27 to February 10	January 11 to February 10. / August 27 ,, September 30.
Thurso.	,, 27 ,, ,, 10	January 11 ,, February 10. / August 27 ,, September 14.
Hope and Polla (Sutherland).	,, 27 ,, ,, 10	January 11 ,, February 10. / August 27 ,, September 10.
Tay	,, 27 ,, ,, 10	January 15 ,, February 10. / August 27 ,, October 15.
Drummachloy or Glenmore (Bute).	September 1 ,, ,, 15	September 1 ,, October 15.
Add, Echaig, North Esk, South Esk, Fyne, Shira, Aray, and Ruel	,, 1 ,, ,, 15	September 1 ,, October 31.
Bervie, Carradale, East Harris Waters, West Harris Waters, Fleet (Sutherland), Fleet (Kirkcudbright), Girvan, Howmore, Inner (Jura), Iorsa (Arran), Irvine, Laggan and Sorn (Islay), Luce, North Uist Waters, Orkney Waters, Ugie, Ythan	,, 10 ,, ,, 24	September 10 ,, October 31.
Annan, Nith, Stinchar	,, 10 ,, ,, 24	September 10 ,, November 15. / February 1 ,, February 24.
Shetland Waters	,, 10 ,, ,, 24	Sept. 10 ,, November 15.
Urr	,, 10 ,, ,, 24	September 10 ,, November 30.
Tweed	,, 14 ,, ,, 15	February 1 ,, February 14. / September 14 ,, November 30.
All other Waters (the great majority)	August 27 ,, ,, 10	August 27 ,, October 31.

CHAPTER XIX

DISEASES OF GAME

Grouse Disease.—There is not much that a keeper can do to directly attack disease in grouse, but as prevention is better than cure, he will take care that the directions given in Chapter IX. for the improvement of ground and stock are carefully carried out. We may in this place recall the principal causes that are known to be favourable to disease in grouse.

(1) The presence on the moor of "peppered" birds.

(2) Want of draining; much old and rank heather.

(3) The presence of decayed or decaying matter, such as the carcases of sheep, grouse, etc.

(4) Inefficient water supply in dry seasons.

(5) Absence of grit and lime.

(6) Interbreeding and over-stocking.

These conditions may not actually be the direct cause of disease, but they are recognised *predisposing* causes, and such are always taken into account in the study of disease.

When a dead bird is found, the keeper should endeavour at once to discover the cause of death. If

he is satisfied that it has been killed by wire fencing
or telegraph wires, the fact should serve to indicate
that there are remedies for such possible sources of
disaster. If no such cause is to be discovered, he
should cut the bird open and look for disease. All
grouse found dead on the moor should be burnt.

Pheasant Disease.—Overcrowding and interbreeding
are the main causes of disease in pheasants. When
disease breaks out, all affected birds should be killed,
and the rest of the stock moved to fresh ground, and
a careful examination made into the dietary and
hygienic surroundings of the birds. The bodies of
all pheasants killed by disease or killed on account
of disease should be burned. Disease is often caught
from the domestic fowls. The condition of the latter
should be carefully inquired into, and the same procedure taken with the affected fowls as with the
affected pheasants. It is wise, as soon as disease
shows itself, to give lime freely to all the birds.
Lime should constitute an essential part of the
food of pheasants and of the ground upon which
they live.

When worms appear, isolation of the affected birds
becomes imperative, and the removal of the unaffected
birds to healthier soil. The affected pheasants in
these cases may be sprinkled with a weak solution
of salicylic acid or salicylate of soda, and a little of
the solution should be added to the drinking water.

Mr. Shipley says : " In individual cases the worms may be removed by dipping a feather stripped of its barbules, except at the tip, into a mixture of one part of oil of turpentine and two of olive oil, or into oil of cloves, and then inserting it into the trachæa ; on its withdrawal it will probably bring with it the worms. The operation requires a little care, or asphyxiation may result. Garlic mixed into the food and rue mixed with the water have also proved successful."

Putting birds in boxes containing two parts, by weight, of powdered chalk to one of camphor is recommended by some authorities, while Mr. Tegetmeier recommends that the birds should be fumigated by volatilised carbolic acid. This can be done by putting the affected birds in a box in which a hot brick has been placed and pouring a solution of carbolic acid on the brick.

Gapes.—Lime dust sprinkled in the coops in the morning is useful in this disease. At a later stage garlic should be given with the food, once a day.

Cramp.—Change of soil is the treatment recommended here.

Ophthalmia and other Eye Affections.—The birds should be removed from their present rearing ground.

Diarrhœa.—A little starch mixed with food soon corrects this. Food should also be changed.

Scurfy Legs.—The coops should be thoroughly

22

cleaned and whitewashed, and the legs of the affected birds well soaked in hot water, the scales peeled off, and the legs then washed with some antiseptic soap. All affected fowls should be removed, and all affected pheasants isolated.

Partridges.—The remarks made above in regard to overcrowding, interbreeding, change of ground and food, cleanliness, and the burning of all dead birds, apply as equally to partridges as to pheasants. What has been said about supplying partridges with drinking fountains in very dry weather must be remembered in considering the question of gapes. Mr. Horace Hutchinson practically cured his estate at Newmarket of this disease by putting down numerous drinking fountains the moment dry weather set in after hatching time.

Rabbits.—The constant change of blood, attention to the feeding capacities of the ground, and the avoidance of turnips as a food are the best preventives of disease. If disease has spread to any large extent, the whole stock should be killed off. This applies also to partridges and to pheasants. The ground should also be thoroughly dressed with salt and lime.

CHAPTER XX

LOADERS AND GUN CLEANING

IT is only by practice that the loader can learn to come into sympathetic practice with the shooter. The harmony between the two must be complete, if success is to be looked for, a harmony so perfect as to make the practice of exchanging guns almost as automatic as a machine. But the first point for the loader to remember, and never to forget, is that the gun is an enemy to life, and that no weapon, whether it be 12-bore gun, fowling-piece, rifle, air-gun, or penny pistol, should ever be directed, either loaded or unloaded, with the barrels pointing at any living thing, except for the purpose of killing. The muzzle of a gun should always be *inclined* to the earth or to the sky, clear from everything whose life is of value. If these principles are borne into the intelligence, they will assist the loader in carrying out his duties with success. In loading he must remember to keep the point of the barrels clear of everyone, "to depress the muzzle while turning away from the shooter, and in shutting the gun always to raise the stock to the barrels, and not the barrels to the stock, so that if by any accident the charge explodes, it can only make a hole in the ground." The gun should never be closed, if loaded, while the loader is turned towards the shooter. Guns should never be loaded until the shooter takes his place at his stand, and should always be unloaded as soon as the drive is over.

It is highly desirable that a little rehearsal should take place between the shooter and the loader, if they are strangers to each other at the game. When the loader is the shooter's own servant, five or ten minutes' practice in the gunroom on "off" days should be indulged in, and also now and again during the summer. This will save a lot of bother, wasteful movements, and irritation when "the trouble" begins. The loader must always be keen and on the lookout, not at the birds, but at the man who is using the guns. He is not intended to spot the birds and call "left," "right," or "over"; he is only there to see that his shooter gets a loaded gun with the least degree of trouble. He must be on the alert to get out of the way, as the shooter varies his position so as to get a suitable angle to loose on his bird. The position varies most in partridge-driving, at which practice the capacity of the loader will be tried to the utmost. Coolness is a most valuable quality, and this is demanded most when rapidity of loading is an essential. All guns should be loaded as if they

were wanted quickly, even though the loader is
aware that there is no particular hurry. He errs
then only on the safe side, and the practice of quick
loading at all times will perfect his art in general.
To assist in the perfection of his practice, the loader
should rehearse the loading and unloading of guns—
at other times, of course, than shooting ones.

The position of the loader is varied by the preference of the shooter and the game to be shot. Some
shooters like their loaders immediately behind them,
some on the right and others on the left. On this
point Lord Suffolk and Mr. Craven write :—" When
rocketing pheasants are the sole objects, the loader
may stand right half-forward without in the least
interfering with his master, who, indeed, will be rather
helped than hindered ; but if hares and rabbits are
also coming out of covert, the man must be well half-
back. In grouse-driving, a position on the immediate
right is obviously to be recommended, for thus placed
the loader will only interfere with a shot which would
pepper the occupant of the adjoining butt on that
side. For partridge-driving over high fences or belts,
the rule is the same as with tall pheasants."

In changing guns the shooter throws up the barrel
and grasps the gun by the neck and turns slightly to
the loader, who takes it with his left hand and passes
the second loaded gun smartly forward with his right.
While holding the unused loaded gun, it should be

held just below the triggers with the right hand, and the right arm should be leant slightly across the chest so as to rest the barrels on the left arm. The barrels will then be pointing in the air to the left and behind.

Hints to Loaders.

(*a*) The loader should never touch the "safe" slide.

(*b*) In wet weather instead of holding the gun pointing obliquely over the left shoulder, or, as some loaders do, at an angle of forty-five degrees over the right, "it will be advisable to rest the butt against the top of the right thigh, triggers downwards, keeping the gun firmly grasped by the right hand and with the muzzle always pointing upwards."

(*c*) The loader in wet weather should protect the mechanism part of the gun as much as possible, and should wipe it from time to time with an oiled rag.

(*d*) Should any difficulty be experienced in working the lever, the gun should be carefully examined for dirt or any remains of cartridge paper.

(*e*) Damp cartridges should never be used.

(*f*) If mud or sand or other foreign substances get into the barrels, they should be well run through with the lead cylinder and the pocket cleaner.

(*g*) Always inspect the gun thoroughly after any accident of the nature of tripping or of dropping the gun. No gun that has the barrels badly indented should be used.

If a third gun be used, it should be held by a keeper or a second loader, who stands behind the shooter and first loader. It is this man who may keep his eyes on the birds, but never the loader.

CLEANING OF GUNS AND RIFLES.

In addition to the regular cleaning of the guns at the end of the day's sport, there is something to be said for cleaning them at intervals in the shooting. When there is much heavy firing, as in a big grouse or partridge drive, or a big covert shoot, it is in every way desirable that the barrels should be at least "run through" some time during the day. Clean barrels minimise any tendency to "rebound," or create it where it does not naturally exist. The procedure to be recommended in cleaning a gun is the following :—

(1) Take the gun to pieces, and place the barrels on a cloth.

(2) First clean the barrels with hot water, and run over and through with tow.

(3) Put finest paraffin or Rangoon oil on clean tow at the end of a rod, and run the barrels well through.

(4) Run through the barrels again with clean soft tow.

(5) Coat the inside and outside of the barrels with vaseline.

(6) Remove all grease from barrels and chambers before the gun be used.

In addition, the breach action should be carefully inspected and wiped over with vaseline. The ribs and the sides of the ejector part should be gone over with a soft mop dipped in the same. A similar practice is to be followed in the cleaning of a rifle. With the introduction of cordite and other new powders, it is often found necessary, especially in the cleaning of rifles, to use some special preparation like *Nitroclene*, or *Webley's* 303, or *Semper Idem*.

When a gun or rifle is put away and not inspected daily, the barrels should be covered with a mixture of paraffin and neatsfoot, and the inside of the barrels rubbed with the same mixture.

If there are signs of lead, this may be removed by corking the bore at one end and filling it with spirits of turpentine.

If a gun or rifle be very rusty, boiling water and then paraffin may be used, care being taken to remove the paraffin before the weapon is put away.

In addition to what has been said, the following points may be noted :—(a) No keeper or loader should interfere with springs, screws, etc. If the gun or rifle goes out of order, he should inform the owner as to the condition, and he will, unless he is himself an experienced mechanic, which is unlikely, send his weapon to the maker; (b) gun locks should never be cleaned with thick oil, as this is apt to collect dirt and become sticky, and so cause clogging; (c) no paraffin should be left wet on a gun, as it evaporates rapidly and causes rust. Refined paraffin should be used. Instead of paraffin, chronometer oil or refined neatsfoot has been recommended. Care must be taken never to lay a gun flat on the ground; it should always lean against something solid and firm—muzzle upwards.

Every gunroom should have a card, hung or pasted up, giving directions for the cleaning and the keeping of guns and rifles. These cards should be supplied by the gunmaker, and should have the following points in large print :—

(1) All guns to be thoroughly wiped immediately the shooting is over. (If the shooting is some distance away from the gunroom they should be wiped in the open.)

(2) All guns and rifles to be thoroughly cleaned

and freed from rust and lead as soon as possible after they are brought to the gun-room.

(3) Wet guns should not be put in a warm place, as this is apt to cause swelling and steaming and rusting of locks.

(4) All injuries or inefficient working of any part of guns or rifles to be reported at once to the owners of the same.

(5) Great care should be taken that when a gun or rifle is in the possession of keeper or loader it is not injured by falling or knocking against anything that will damage it in any way.

(6) If by any carelessness—for instance, by loading with a cartridge that has fallen on the ground—sand or grit gets into the breech or lock, special care must be taken in cleaning, in order not to scratch the mechanism.

Ammunition.

Note.—Cartridges are private property, as much as a man's horse, dog, gun, or money.

CHAPTER XXI

MISCELLANEOUS DUTIES

As supplementary to the many questions that we have discussed throughout this book, we append a few notes on questions of miscellaneous yet very important interest, which lie within the routine work of the keeper.

(1) The very first duty of a keeper on entering a new situation is to ascertain his boundaries and walk round his marches. When he is able to obtain the assistance of the outgoing keeper or of an under-keeper, this is simple enough, but there are often instances where he is unable to do this, and there are occasions when a keeper cannot at the time of his arrival obtain the advice of his master, who may not appear at the shooting till August or September. When the property is very extensive he will, of course, consult any plan or map of the ground that may exist, and should not hesitate to make inquiries from the farmers and shepherds. It often happens on very large moorland shootings that the new keeper has some diffi-

culty with the outlying beats, and may inadvertently trespass on ground not under his charge. He may under these circumstances discover his mistake by observing the marks on the sheep, and may note the difference between the ones he knows belong to his own ground, and those which are on the ground on to which he has inadvertently trespassed. The difference in the marks may help to put him right.

(2) Some time before the shooting season the keeper should make a systematic inquiry into the following questions :—

(a) Any necessary assistance in the way of under-keepers, gillies, beaters, and drivers.

(b) The hiring or buying of hill and other ponies and horses, panniers, game bags, cartridge bags, game carts, coop carts, etc. etc.

(c) Dogs, the number required, and if to be hired or bought ; their condition and capacity for work. Chains and leashes, condition of kennels, food and bedding, etc.

(d) Ferrets, number required ; their condition and capacity for work ; presence and condition of living accommodation, food, etc.

(e) Tools.—The proper supply of spades, flags and sticks for beaters and drivers, flankers and stops ; the accessories of the gunroom —oils, tow, etc.; the keeper's personal tools, e.g., corkscrew, cartridge-extractor, knife, matchbox, watch, flask, whistle, and whip.

(*f*) Baskets, boxes and labels for game.

(*g*) Arrangements for selling game.

(*h*) The keeper's gun and ammunition; condition of fishing rods, fly-book, hackle case, waders, gaffs, landing-nets, fishing-baskets and bags.

(*i*) Licences.

(*j*) Drugs for horses, dogs, and ferrets.

(*k*) Cleaning and disinfecting material for stables (where there are no coachman or stable hands), kennels, ferret boxes and runs.

(*l*) Boats—oars. Number and condition of repair —boat chains, balers, etc.

(3) The keeper and his underlings must always be on the alert to assist in the following courteous actions —(*a*) Giving all assistance in their power at luncheon time, for instance by supplying game bags or other forms of seats for the shooters, by putting soda-water bottles into running streams for the purpose of cooling, by opening wine, beer, or whisky bottles, by laying out the contents of the luncheon basket, and by carefully stowing away the débris of the luncheon before the guns start shooting again; (*b*) holding guns while the sportsmen get over or through dykes, gates, or hedges; (*c*) procuring waterproofs or any change of clothing which may have been brought on

to the shooting-ground; (*d*) carrying the gun of any sportsman who may desire to be temporarily relieved of it; (*e*) opening gates or otherwise assisting the guns to pass through or over obstacles; (*f*) indicating the proximity to good springs and burns; (*g*) making inquiries from time to time as to any desire on the sportsmen's part for more cartridges; (*h*) assisting the guns to make themselves as comfortable as possible in the butts; and (*i*) the hundred other little attentions that will suggest themselves to the courteous servant.

(4) The keeper must look to his health. This is not only a duty to himself, but also to his master; must wear flannels next his skin, and have clothing and boots that will give him suitable protection from the vagaries of climate. He must see that he does not fall back upon the idiotic notion that, by putting whisky in, he can keep cold out, and make this habit an excuse for not changing his wet clothes. The latter must be serviceable, tidy, and quiet, and not of a pattern and colour that will scare game a mile away. Hydrofuge, or some such substance, is useful.

(5) The keeper, when off active shooting duty should go about with a dog, and one which he gives a reputation for ferocity (even if it be as mild as a toy spaniel). He will thus be a terror to mischievous small boys and other minor depredators.

Of other miscellaneous duties the following will come under his observation :—

Larders.—It seems hardly necessary to say that there should be on every shooting lodge two larders, one for meat and the other for game. Larders should be large, clean, and airy. On no account should the flooring be too near the ground. An ideal larder would have the flooring four feet from the ground, and so placed as to ensure a free current of air passing beneath it. This ideal larder is built of stone or brick, tiled inside, and contains large windows, "paned" with perforated zinc, which open to the east, west, and north, the fourth side only being built solid and windowless for the sake of coolness. Height is an important point in the consideration of space, and on no account should a ventilator on the roof be omitted.

There should be shutters on the outside of the perforated zinc windows, which should be closed in stormy weather, to prevent dust, etc., from being blown into the larder. The shelves inside should be of slate, and, of course, there should be plenty of hooks on which to hang the game by the head, and in regular rotation as to the date of killing. Omission of the latter point is bound to lead to confusion in the mind of the cook. The larder, of course, must be kept thoroughly clean. The best site for a larder is a high mound, shaded, if possible, from the hot sun, and in a position to have the advantage of the prevailing wind and the benefit of any airs that blow. Spots under trees should be avoided, as the drip off the leaves is not favourable to that freedom from damp which is necessary for keeping game.

Disposal of Game.—When game is to be disposed of to dealers, arrangements should be made, before the shooting season, with respectable firms and a contract price fixed, if possible, for the whole season, as many dealers are apt to return any price they like, varying it according to the character of the sportsman. If the latter happens to be an indifferent, easy-going person, the price is likely to be a small one, but if he is an exacting man, the sportsman will find he is able to gather better quotations. The keeper should ask for estimates from several dealers before accepting any particular offer.

In packing game for the dealer, the following rules should be observed : — (1) All game should be thoroughly cool before being packed ; (2) Fur and feather should not be packed in the same basket ; (3) Feathers should be carefully brushed and straightened, the head being placed along with a piece of heather under one of the wings ; (4) The heaviest birds should be placed at the bottom ; (5) All badly shot birds should be kept for home use ; (6) Baskets should, if possible, be despatched by train or steamer on the evening of the day on which the game is killed. Many keepers are apt to postpone the despatch of game till the following day, and this often accounts for the bad returns sportsmen receive from the dealers. (7) A note of the quantity of game despatched should be given to the sportsman, and should also be sent to the game dealer.

Game Book.—The keeper's game book should be kept correctly, regularly, and methodically. Details of the day's sport should be filled in every evening, and on no account should they be left over till the following day. The facts entered should include the number of guns, the details of the bag, the number of hours the guns were shooting, the state of the weather, the part of the ground shot over, and any particular and interesting circumstances relating to the day's sport that may have appealed to the keeper. It is as well also that notes be kept referring to the points of interest connected with the breeding season, also as to the stock of birds left on the ground after the shooting season is over.

CHAPTER XXII

BAKSHEESH

IT is neither easy nor pleasant to speak frankly on the matter of tips, and as it is a question that essentially concerns the master and his guests, it might seem an irrelevant subject for a keeper's book. And yet we feel that it will not do any particular harm for the keeper to listen to us "thinking aloud," and whilst we address a few observations to all whom it may concern. What was originally a recognition of good and special service has now, in every branch of life, come to be regarded as a matter of form, apart altogether from the fairness or justice of the question. In the cases of certain well-known restaurants where waiters are not paid, and are even compelled in many instances to pay for the privileges of their positions, a tip is in reality no longer a tip—it is a wage ; and although the payment of it is not obligatory in law, yet it is one the justice of which appeals more or less to all concerned. But we do not wish to insult our friends by placing their servants in the same category as the unpaid waiter, and yet the conduct of many of these servants seems to be so regulated by the size of their tips that there is an occasional suspicion that the establishment in which they serve is run on the restaurant line. The practice of indiscriminate tipping has crept into every department of estate and household life, until the stable, the covert, the moor, the kitchen, and the pantry have all become free-flowing drains from the pocket of the guest. And it is not only the guest that suffers. The abhorrent practice of secret commissions and the high-handed way in which many servants demand them, have compelled even tradespeople to submit to this form of tyranny from pure sense of self-protection, with the result that the swindling is reflected back upon the master. In a large number of cases the tradesman is chosen, not from the quality and comparative cheapness of his goods, but from the liberality of his tipping capacities. This line of procedure harms the master in two ways: he does not get the best value for his money, and he has the price of his goods raised so as to recoup the tradesman for the money he has doled out to the master's servants in bribes. Let us take an example relevant to the particular class of servant we are at present dealing with. Every competent keeper should, of course, be able to prepare his own pheasant food ; if he is not, he does not possess one of the primary qualifications

for his post. Yet it will be observed how eager
many keepers are to run up large accounts with
pheasant food manufacturers—either from laziness
or more often that they may receive the commission
offered by certain firms to induce keepers to buy
their commodities. The present writers were told
recently by a dealer in keepers' requisites that,
when he began business, he tried to deal honestly
by the employers by not giving commissions to
the servant, but so unusual did he find the practice,
and so great was the dissatisfaction of the keeper,
that he found that his chance of doing business was
in danger, and he had, much against his will and
against his sense of right, to pay the usual " blackmail " to the keeper, the amount of which was, of
course, added to the price of the commodity supplied. Stable requisites from saddlers are increased
25 per cent. to cover the blackmail of coachmen
and grooms ; and a corn merchant recently informed
us that the demands for commission are so great
that they have become a severe tax upon his
profits, " for," said he, with feeling, "there is a
limit of price at which even the most careless
master will stop." Admitting those indisputable
facts, all employers, on engaging their servants,
while agreeing to pay them good, even liberal,
wages, should make it clear that they will allow
no secret commissions, and should indicate these

facts to all manufacturers and merchants with whom they are dealing, and intimate that any suggested change in their business relations must be decided by them and not by their servants. In the majority of cases the dealer would be only too pleased to do business on these lines. With servants running riot in this way, it is no wonder so many people cannot live on their own places, but have to let them and go abroad, and so escape from the thraldom of unscrupulous servants.

So universal is the practice of secret commissions in all departments of business that a bill has been introduced into the House of Lords by Lord James of Hereford to make it a punishable offence.

From this form of "baksheesh" we pass to the question of tipping as it affects shooting guest and keeper. Now it is quite unnecessary for us to admit that there are a large number of shootings at which the traditions of moderate tipping are so maintained that no one except the meanest or the most cantankerous misanthrope objects to the common usage of recognising the services of the keeper by a small present of money. While we condemn blackmail, secret commissions, or baksheesh *in toto*, our object is not to advocate the abolition of tipping, but merely to press home the point that it should be kept in moderation, and with this all sensible keepers will agree. But if we count these shootings by the tens, we can enumerate the other sort by the twenties, and so excessive are the expectations of some keepers in these latter cases, that it is only the man of unlimited or very great means who can accept invitations to shoot. The man of moderate means, in fact, has to fall back upon moderate shootings, and the only deduction we can draw from this fact is that a guest has in reality to pay for his sport. We all know the story of the "Sovs. and Half-Sovs." "Put the sovereigns at the wood end, Bill, and the half-sovs. can walk with the beaters and stop back." But nowadays "sovs. and half-sovs." pale before the two guineas and the five-pound notes which are expected by some keepers, not for rendering any particular individual services, but simply because they are *ipso facto* keepers, and expect to be paid by the guests for the birds which they have had sent over the guns. So marked is the disagreeable attitude of some keepers to men of moderate means, that we are not surprised to hear of the increasing difficulty experienced by some sportsmen of getting guns. And it is a curious fact that, in our small experience at least, some of the very best shots are comparatively poor men, and not scions of an irresponsible plutocracy. Nothing is more galling to a good sportsman than to challenge him with an unsportsmanlike action, and yet the mere fact that he encourages the pernicious habit of reckless over-tipping proves him to be careless of the interests of his brother guns. Such being the case, he is not a good sportsman.

We have constantly heard the argument put thus : " Surely the keeper of a good shoot should be tipped higher than that of a moderate one." Not of necessity. The keeper of the moderate shoot may show his birds better than that of the good shoot, if such a fact is to be taken into consideration. The same argument would apply in the case of a butler who gave us Château Lafite, and another who was only able to supply us with Médoc. " But," our friends reply, " in the case of the big covert shoot, look at the enormous labour involved." Are the guests, then, to be payers of wages? We reply, Certainly not. We give tips, not as part of a man's salary, but in recognition of special services rendered to us, or from desire to recognise the marked efficiency of the keeper : and in the latter case we give from our free will, and not in accordance with any stereotyped tyranny — a tyranny which found its most obnoxious and altogether unbearable expression in the case of a keeper who was seen to hold the proffered tip in his hand, to regard it with a look which combined curiosity with disdain, and then to hand it back with the remark that it was not up to his standard.

The following stories are vouched for as true,

though hardly credible. A sportsman was called away
to town after the first day's cover shoot, and, having
another shoot a few miles off, asked the keeper to
send on his gun and cartridges by train to be waiting
him there, tipping him a sovereign for the day's
sport.   Arriving at the shoot a few days later, he was
surprised not to find his gun, etc., and telegraphed
for them, and got back a reply from the keeper, "I
will send on your gun when you give me my proper
and usual tip, two sovereigns."   Sending this letter
to the keeper's master, he got the reply, "I can't
interfere.   Besides, it's the middle of my shooting
season and I can't afford to quarrel or part with
my keeper—better pay."   Another.—Smoke-room.
Host informs his guests, "My keeper's tip is a fiver."
They all decided to tip low.   None were asked back.
The only conclusion one can draw from these stories
is that the master looked to his guests to pay his
servants.

In studying the matter of tips it were as well to
get to the foundation of the habit.   Etymologically
the word means something small, and originally it
meant something secret or *sub rosâ*; now it has grown
to mean something big and something very much
advertised and above the table.   We began to tip
porters when we found that they had to deal with
very heavy luggage or when they ran for our cabs, or
were in any way particularly smart ; now we tip them

as a matter of course. A tip was, and ought to be now, a recognition of special service. We tip the valet because he looks after our clothes, and we tip the gamekeeper, not for having a fine stock of hand-reared pheasants, but because he cleans our guns, or holds them as we get over fences, or helps us at the luncheon hour. If every man remembered this fact, tipping would come back again to that level of moderation which seems not only desirable but necessary.

As we have said, it is no pleasant task to write on this subject. A charge of meanness is abhorrent to every Briton, and more so to the sportsmen of the race, and in the long run it is better to give too much than too little. But let not our argument be interpreted as a subtle apology for meanness. There are hundreds of first-class keepers who deserve every farthing they get, and there are no tips that are given with greater delight than the tips to the keepers who have shown birds flying high and strong, who have worked their beaters or their dogs to the satisfaction of everybody, and to the advantage of the bag, who combine in all they do, skill with courtesy and energy with patience, who present our guns every morning as clean as the day they left the gunmaker, and who, though we are but moderate shots, and possess moderate purses, have given us good stands by the covert side. Especially do we rejoice to recognise the keeper who gives us a good day over dogs, who is keen that we should go on, who works his ground for all that it is worth, and who is interested in the way we shoot, and anxious that he, his underlings, and his dogs should do us more than justice. Such a keeper does not look upon us as the mere carrier of a tip. He performs his duties out of respect to his master's wishes, out of love of the sport itself, and principally from that noble self-respect which is the foundation of all capable labour. Where such a keeper is in charge, there will not be heard the common complaint that a man cannot go for a week-end's shooting without five pounds in his pocket, two of which are to go into the pocket of the keeper, one to be given to a loader, and the other two to be distributed amongst the rest of the men-servants in the establishment.

It is not possible to suggest any absolute scale of tips that might be regarded as a reasonable average. Of course if a man be very poor his tip must be very small, and in certain cases it should not be given at all. For a week's stay at a house where there is, say, three days' shooting over dogs, an average and fair tip from each guest would be a pound from a man who was fairly well off, and ten shillings from the man of moderate means, a few shillings being given to the man or boy who carries the cartridge bag. For a single day's grouse shooting, five to ten shillings is a good and moderate fee; ten shillings is a very generous one. For a day's covert shooting the same applies, although we have generally found that the common tip, especially in England, at the first shoots, is a pound a day. It may be laid down as a safe and general law that no tip, unless in those very exceptional cases where a man has made a prolonged visit to a shooting, should exceed a sovereign, and that no man of moderate means should be ashamed of giving half that amount.

Without detracting from the force of the argument already laid down, we quote the following scale, which seems to us not too unreasonable. It is followed in several counties.

The scheme is based roughly on the principle of 5/- per 100 birds from each gun. The principle carried into practice would work out thus—

Examples :—

Sport.	Birds.	Tip.
Various.	100 and under.	5/-
Partridges.	40 brace.	5/-
Cover.	150 pheasants.	7/6 to 10/-
Grouse.	100 brace.	10/-
Mixed shoot.	200 head.	10/-
Rabbit-shooting		5/- a day.
Deerstalking . . .		One or two days, £1
„ „ . .		A week or ten days, £2
Fishing gillie		5/- a day.
Loader		5/- a day.
Cartridge-bag boy		2/- a day.

When these practices[1] are followed, only the head-keeper is tipped.   Under-keepers await their promotion before they are recognised.

Finally, let it be remembered by the keeper who has listened to us "thinking aloud" that, even admitting the fact that tipping is recognised as a legitimate practice, he has no right to *expect* anything.

[1] In some large houses it is the custom to place a money-box, marked "Keepers' Fund," in the hall,—a very excellent plan.— *Lord Walsingham.*

INDEX

Printed by MORRISON & GIBB LIMITED, *Edinburgh.*

www.ingramcontent.com/pod-product-compliance
Lightning Source LLC
Chambersburg PA
CBHW020333270326
41926CB00007B/159